Shakespeare and Psychoanalytic Theory

ARDEN SHAKESPEARE AND THEORY

Series Editor: Evelyn Gajowski

AVAILABLE TITLES

Shakespeare and Economic Theory David Hawkes
Shakespeare and Psychoanalytic Theory Carolyn E. Brown

FORTHCOMING TITLES

Shakespeare and Cultural Materialist Theory Christopher Marlow
Shakespeare and Ecocritical Theory Gabriel Egan
Shakespeare and Ecofeminist Theory Rebecca Laroche and Jennifer Munroe
Shakespeare and Feminist Theory Marianne Novy
Shakespeare and Film Theory Scott Hollifield
Shakespeare and New Historicist Theory Neema Parvini
Shakespeare and Posthumanist Theory Karen Raber
Shakespeare and Queer Theory Melissa Sanchez

Shakespeare and Psychoanalytic Theory

Carolyn E. Brown

Bloomsbury Arden Shakespeare
An imprint of Bloomsbury Publishing Plc

B L O O M S B U R Y
LONDON • NEW DELHI • NEW YORK • SYDNEY

Bloomsbury Arden Shakespeare

An imprint of Bloomsbury Publishing Plc

Imprint previously known as Arden Shakespeare

50 Bedford Square	1385 Broadway
London	New York
WC1B 3DP	NY 10018
UK	USA

www.bloomsbury.com

BLOOMSBURY, THE ARDEN SHAKESPEARE and the Diana logo are trademarks of Bloomsbury Publishing Plc

First published 2015

© Carolyn E. Brown, 2015

Carolyn Brown has asserted her right under the Copyright, Designs and Patents Act, 1988, to be identified as Author of this work.

All rights reserved. No part of this publication may be reproduced or transmitted in any form or by any means, electronic or mechanical, including photocopying, recording, or any information storage or retrieval system, without prior permission in writing from the publishers.

No responsibility for loss caused to any individual or organization acting on or refraining from action as a result of the material in this publication can be accepted by Bloomsbury or the author.

British Library Cataloguing in Publication Data

A catalogue record for this book is available from the British Library.

ISBN: HB: 978-1-4725-0324-4
       PB: 978-1-4725-0323-7
       ePDF: 978-1-4742-1613-5
       ePub: 978-1-4742-1612-8

Library of Congress Cataloging-in-Publication Data

Brown, Carolyn (Carolyn Elizabeth)
Shakespeare and psychoanalytic theory / Carolyn E. Brown.
pages cm
Includes bibliographical references and index.
ISBN 978-1-4725-0324-4 (hardback)-- ISBN 978-1-4725-0323-7 (paperback)
1. Shakespeare, William, 1564-1616--Knowledge--Psychology. 2. Psychoanalysis and literature. 3. Psychoanalysis--History. 4. Psychology in literature. I. Title.
PR3065.B76 2015
822.3'3--dc23
2014049822

Series: Shakespeare and Theory, 1234567X, volume 2

Typeset by Fakenham Prepress Solutions, Fakenham, Norfolk, NR21 8NN
Printed and bound in India

CONTENTS

Series Editor's Preface vii
Acknowledgements xi

Introduction 1

1 The Inception of Psychoanalytic Theory and Shakespearean Psychoanalytic Criticism 11

2 Shakespearean Psychoanalytic Critics through the 1970s 23

3 Shakespearean Psychoanalytic Critics in the 1980s 41

4 Shakespearean Psychoanalytic Critics in the 1990s 71

5 Shakespearean Psychoanalytic Critics in the Twenty-first Century 91

6 The Feminine Oedipal Complex in *All's Well That Ends Well* 107

7 A Psychoanalytic Reading of Homoeroticism in *Romeo and Juliet* 133

Epilogue 165
Notes 169
Bibliography 197
Index 213

SERIES EDITOR'S PREFACE

'Asking questions about literary texts – that's literary criticism. Asking "Which questions shall we ask about literary texts?" – that's literary theory.' So goes my explanation of the current state of English studies, and Shakespeare studies, in my neverending attempt to demystify, and simplify, theory for students in my classrooms. Another way to put it is that theory is a systematic account of the nature of literature, the act of writing, and the act of reading.

One of the primary responsibilities of any academic discipline – whether in the natural sciences, the social sciences, or the humanities – is to examine its methodologies and tools of analysis. Particularly at a time of great theoretical ferment, such as that which has characterized English studies, and Shakespeare studies, in recent years, it is incumbent upon scholars in a given discipline to provide such reflection and analysis. We all construct meanings in Shakespeare's texts and culture. Shouldering responsibility for our active role in constructing meanings in literary texts, moreover, constitutes a theoretical stance. To the extent that we examine our own critical premises and operations, that theoretical stance requires reflection on our part. It requires honesty, as well. It is thereby a fundamentally radical act. All critical analysis puts into practice a particular set of theoretical premises. Theory occurs from a particular standpoint. There is no critical practice that is somehow devoid of theory. There is no critical practice that is not implicated in theory. A common-sense, transparent encounter with any text is thereby impossible. Indeed, to the extent that theory requires us to question anew that with which we thought we were familiar, that which we thought we understood, theory constitutes a critique of common sense.

Since the advent of postmodernism, the discipline of English studies has undergone a seismic shift. And the discipline of Shakespeare studies has been at the epicentre of this shift. Indeed, it has been Shakespeare scholars who have played a major role in several of the theoretical and critical developments (e.g., new historicism, cultural materialism, presentism) that have shaped the discipline of English studies in recent years. Yet a comprehensive scholarly analysis of these crucial developments has yet to be done, and is long overdue. As the first series to foreground analysis of contemporary theoretical developments in the discipline of Shakespeare studies, *Arden Shakespeare and Theory* aims to fill a yawning gap.

To the delight of some and the chagrin of others, theory has dominated Shakespeare studies since 1980 or so. *Arden Shakespeare and Theory* focuses on the state of the art at the outset of the twenty-first century. For the first time, it provides a comprehensive analysis of the theoretical developments that are emerging at the present moment, as well as those that are dominant or residual in Shakespeare studies.

Each volume in the series aims to offer the reader the following components: to provide a clear definition of a particular theory; to explain its key concepts; to trace its major developments, theorists, and critics; to perform a reading of a Shakespeare text; to elucidate a specific theory's intersection with or relationship to other theories; to situate it in the context of contemporary political, social and economic developments; to analyse its significance in Shakespeare studies; and to suggest resources for further investigation. Authors of individual volumes thereby attempt to strike a balance, bringing their unique expertise, experience and perspectives to bear upon particular theories while simultaneously fulfilling the common purpose of the series. Individual volumes in the series are devoted to elucidating particular theoretical perspectives, such as cultural materialism, ecocriticism, ecofeminism, economic theory, feminism, film theory, new historicism, posthumanism, psychoanalysis and queer theory.

Arden Shakespeare and Theory aims to enable scholars, teachers and students alike to define their own theoretical strategies and refine their own critical practices. And students have as much at stake in these theoretical and critical enterprises – in the reading and the writing practices that characterize our discipline – as do scholars and teachers. Janus-like, the series looks forward as well as backward, serving as an inspiration and a guide for new work in Shakespeare studies at the outset of the twenty-first century, on the one hand, and providing a retrospective analysis of the intellectual labour that has been accomplished in recent years, on the other.

To return to the beginning: what is at stake in our reading of literary texts? Once we come to understand the various ways in which theory resonates with not only Shakespeare's texts, and literary texts, but the so-called 'real' world – the world outside the world of the mind, the world outside the world of academia – then we come to understand that theory is capable of powerfully enriching not only our reading of Shakespeare's texts, and literary texts, but our lives.

Evelyn Gajowski
University of Nevada, Las Vegas

ACKNOWLEDGEMENTS

I have written this study with the invaluable assistance of a number of people, whom I would like to acknowledge and to whom I want to express my gratitude for their guidance and support. First is Professor Evelyn Gajowski, whose profound knowledge of Shakespearean and early modern scholarship led her to perceive a need for this series on theory, and who had the vision to conceive it and the dedication to make it materialize. As the series editor, she gave me crucial direction and advice but also the freedom to explore new avenues of thought, never imposing restrictions on my typically unorthodox readings. I can never thank her enough for her friendship, generosity, and vital contribution to this book.

I would also like to thank Professors David Hillman and Carol Thomas Neely, whose essential advice at the early stages proved instrumental in making this into a more cohesive, informative study than it would have been without their assistance. I appreciate the advice of Margaret Bartley, publisher of the Arden Shakespeare, and Emily Hockley, assistant editor of Bloomsbury Publishing, both of whom reviewed the book through the stages of composition and alerted my attention to logical and argumentative lapses so that the final product could be more cohesive and persuasive. I am also grateful to Professor Richard A. Levin, who many years ago opened my mind to the marvelous complexity of Shakespeare and who taught me how to probe the deeper layers of his texts, to detect the psychological depth of his characters and begin to come to terms with their latent motivations. I had no idea of the extent of Shakespeare's understanding of the human mind until I had the privilege of taking his class and the good fortune to have him direct my dissertation. Shakespeare will forever be colored for me by what I learned under Professor Levin's tutelage.

I have been fortunate to teach at the University of San Francisco and would like to express my gratitude to the administration and the English department for giving me the opportunity to teach Shakespeare, hone my understanding of his art with each class that I taught, and develop my scholarship. My students through the years have always inspired me and helped me in countless ways to begin to uncover some of the mysteries of characters' psyches. One student in particular, Ashleigh Smallwood, my research assistant, deserves my thanks for the many hours she spent providing me with scholarly resources and for her indefatigable pursuit in tracking down obscure information. Kimberly Garrett, our English department's program assistant, also has my gratitude for the assistance she provided in getting essential documents to me when I was away from campus and for always being a source of inspiration.

INTRODUCTION

Psychoanalysts have long recognized the psychological orientation of literature and have explored it to inform and bolster their theories. Sigmund Freud credits 'creative writers' with first detecting and representing the unconscious and being in advance of psychological theory in their knowledge of the mind, 'for they draw upon sources which we have not yet opened up for science': their 'description of the human mind is indeed the domain which is most [their] own; [they have] from time immemorial been the precursor[s] of science, and so too of scientific psychology ... . Thus the creative writer cannot evade the psychiatrist nor the psychiatrist the creative writer.'[1] It makes sense, then, that Shakespeare, arguably the greatest writer of all time, would be gifted with an intimate understanding of human emotions. His writings were instrumental in the development of psychoanalytic theory, with Freud building some of his most essential concepts, such as the Oedipus complex, on an understanding of him. Psychoanalysts have 'studied Shakespeare's works to deepen their understanding of psychic conflict and to hone their interpretative skills'.[2] Shakespeare's reputation as one of the greatest literary psychologists, if not the greatest depicter of human psychology, is unassailable, a distinction that began long before Freud's recognition of it. Consequently, psychoanalytic theory has been applied to his works more than to those of any other writer, an application that has made psychoanalysis one of the largest fields of Shakespearean criticism.

This renown began early, with the following consisting of just a few of the early thinkers who note the psychological depth of his characters and his insight into the complexities of the human mind. John Dryden commends him on his ability to capture 'the images of [human] nature': 'he needed not the spectacles of books to read nature; he looked inwards, and found her there'.[3] Samuel Johnson labels him 'the poet of nature; the poet that holds up to his readers a faithful mirror of manners and of life' and '[he] must have looked upon mankind with perspicacity, in the highest degree curious and attentive'.[4] Samuel Taylor Coleridge attests to his 'minute knowledge of human nature,' what he calls the 'science in mental philosophy'.[5] Coleridge coined the term 'psycho-analytical' and advocated new developments in psychology should be applied to understanding Hamlet, in particular. Alexander Pope professes 'every single character in *Shakespear* is as much an Individual, as those in Life itself'.[6] Goethe labels him 'a great psychologist' from whose works we learn 'the secrets of human nature'.[7] A more modern appreciator of Shakespearean psychoanalysis is Harold Bloom, who believes he 'invented the human' and names him the founder of the psychological basis of human character, the distinguishing feature of the modern self, and Freud his successor: 'Shakespeare is the original psychologist, and Freud the belated rhetorician.'[8]

But psychoanalytic theories and their application to Shakespeare have not been without their setbacks. Freud's reputation has been compromised, with critics accusing him of the following: basing his fundamental concepts on 'erroneous and now outmoded assumptions from nineteenth-century biology';[9] misrepresenting and modifying patients' histories and accounts of life experiences; exaggerating the effectiveness of his treatment of patients; overemphasizing in his theories the importance of fathers' roles and minimizing those of mothers; and arriving hastily at conclusions without considering evidence that challenged his diagnoses.[10] Frederick C. Crews wrote a scathing condemnation of Freud's practices and alleged 'psychoanalysis was founded not on observation but on deductions from erroneous dogma, and as a result the entire system can make no claim on our credence'.[11] Psychoanalytic theory in application to Shakespeare has its detractors as well. Some of the censures that have been lodged include the following: 'monocausal reductivism';[12] ahistorical approaches that do not consider the differences between modern and early modern psychological constructs; overemphasis on a masculine, Eurocentric point-of-view; the imposing of a psychological strait-jacket on material that cannot accommodate it; the privileging of latent over demonstrable meaning; and the viewing of characters as living human beings and the text as a psychobiography of the author. Feminists in particular have objected to the phallocentric orientation of Freudian theory. In 1986 Stephen Greenblatt started a controversy when he wrote an essay entitled 'Psychoanalysis and Renaissance Culture' that retracted some of his earlier premises in *Renaissance Self-Fashioning* and argued that applying psychoanalysis to the early modern period is anachronistic because the transformation from a property to a psychology centred conception of identity was only in its early stages.[13]

But these criticisms have not attenuated the pervasiveness and effectiveness of psychoanalytic approaches to Shakespeare's works. The length of two bibliographies in two psychoanalytic anthologies of essays on Shakespeare indicates the expansiveness and continuity of the field: one covering the years 1964–78 includes 461 entries, the other covering 1979–89 includes 403.[14] In response to Greenblatt, some scholars have historicized their application of psychoanalytic theory to early modern literature and Shakespeare and, thus, bolstered the validity of such readings. Psychoanalytic theory, moreover, has managed to produce compelling readings of literary texts, especially of Shakespeare's works, by tackling his problematical characters and helping to offer solutions to puzzles that have vexed readers for centuries. It has helped us to realize, for example, that such an intriguing yet baffling character as Iago cannot simply be characterized as displaying 'motiveless malignity',[15] but, rather, can be regarded as harbouring repressed feelings for Othello and symbolically serving as a psychic double to Othello. It has shown that Freud's seminal constructs can be adapted to an understanding of the symbolic significance of his characters, with plays being read as allegories of the birth of the early modern self that results from a battle between the ego and superego. The sonnets have been shown to produce what we today would call interiority. Freud's dream theory also has proven to be congenial to an analysis of Shakespeare's plays, allowing critics to focus on fantasy and the plays as reflections of protagonists' dreams. Of course the most striking example of the theory's usefulness is the explanation it has provided for Hamlet's inability to kill the murderer of his father, an oedipal reading that highlights the interior complexity of Shakespeare's characters, who 'refer to an unseen space within'.[16]

As a discourse based on unacknowledged desires and impulses, Freud's theory has proven to be essential in revealing Shakespeare's awareness of the repressed or unconscious, the unexpressed and concealed dimension of the inner world, and has provided 'greater access than any other analytical method to the Shakespearean aura' by finding hidden in the plays 'the deepest intimacies of the Shakespearean psyche'.[17] What has become clear is the helpfulness of psychoanalytic theory in uncovering what characters themselves cannot admit into their consciousness. Thus, Hamlet provides various conscious reasons for why he is unable to take revenge on Claudius – the ghost may be an uncredible voice; he needs more conclusive evidence of his uncle's guilt; he does not want to kill him during prayer and inadvertently send his soul to heaven – all of which turn out to be unconvincing and unsatisfactory explanations. Freudian analysis illustrates that Shakespeare's characters deceive not just others but primarily themselves, that what complicates our task as readers is we can seldom believe what characters say about themselves or others. Hamlet cannot be honest with us because he is not honest with himself; he does not understand any more than we do why he fails in his mission to avenge his father. But Freudian theory has helped scholars explain what Shakespeare does not allow his main character to understand about himself: he harbours repressed resentment towards his father for sharing an intimate relationship with his mother, one he secretly wishes to enjoy himself, and, consequently, secretly wishes for his father's demise so that he can replace him in his mother's affections. Understanding key defence mechanisms such as reaction formation, projection, transference, displacement, splitting and identification proves enlightening in looking into characters' hidden motivations and desires. We come to realize Shakespeare, like Freud, is willing to probe the most forbidden impulses, not shying away from the most taboo subjects in plays of all genres. One of the reasons psychoanalysis so often treats Shakespeare's characters as real people, for which it is castigated, is they have so much psychological authenticity that they seem like living beings, just like us. This makes us want to know about their lives before the plays begin, prompting some critics to hypothesize about childhood experiences not supplied in the text. It also makes us want to know about the author whose characters have so much impact on us, leading some to infer Shakespeare's own psychological make-up from an analysis of that of his characters – techniques that lead to critical disapproval.

Psychoanalytic theory is a vast and complex field dominated by some brilliant theorists, such as Freud, Jung and Lacan. In fact, it is daunting because of its prominence; marked influence; specialized terminology, sometimes pejoratively referred to as psychobabble; and the large number of theorists and critics who apply the discipline to Shakespeare. This book endeavours to demystify psychoanalytic theory and its application to Shakespeare by providing clear definitions of sometimes confusing terminology, concise explanations of critics' application of this theory to Shakespeare's texts, and precise analysis of the key developments in both psychoanalytic theory and readings of Shakespeare. It clarifies the psychoanalytic theorists who have had the most impact on studies of Shakespeare and describes the inception and evolution of different schools of psychoanalysis. It chronologically surveys the major critics who have applied psychoanalysis to their readings of Shakespeare, specifying the theories they are enlisting; explaining the interaction of their approaches; and highlighting new meanings that have resulted from such readings. Because psychoanalytic scholarship is such a prominent and pervasive field, this book can cover only the more expansive and most influential of these studies; typically the works discussed are book-length, with only the most innovative article-length works receiving mention, unless they appear in an anthology devoted exclusively to psychoanalytic analyses.

The study begins with the inception of psychoanalytic theory and Shakespeare's integral involvement in it. It explains the fundamental elements of Freud's theories and his reliance on his interpretation of some of Shakespeare's plays, especially his major tragedies, to formulate and elucidate his ideas, such as the Oedipus complex, which he sees overtly displayed in Sophocles' *Oedipus Rex* and as repressed matter in *Hamlet*. Two other theorists and literary critics – Ernest Jones and Otto Rank – are explored for their development of Freud's key concepts, with particular attention to Jones's expansion of Freud's comments about the Oedipus complex and unconscious desires in *Hamlet* into a book-length study. The second chapter surveys and assesses theorists and psychoanalytic critics, many of whom are psychoanalysts themselves, through the 1970s, establishing the pronounced influence of Freud on early criticism of Shakespeare. The discussion of Carl Jung clarifies how he builds on and diverges from Freudian theory to develop his own concept of the collective unconscious and the 'Self', which assimilates the unconscious parts of the psyche (the shadow, anima/animus and id). It examines how Jungians universalize the import of literature, employ Jungian mythoi in their analyses and mythologize the oedipal schema, turning father and mother, for example, into archetypes and viewing them as allegorical representations of human tendencies rather than as real beings as Freudians often do. The chapter looks also at Lacan, who revised Freud's paradigms to formulate a triadic structure of the Imaginary, Symbolic and Real, and placed a stronger emphasis on the mother, with whom the infant forms an early bond, which is challenged once the child enters into language, the patriarchal nexus of signification, represented by the name of the father. His concentration on the importance of the mother accords with that of object relations theorists. Because he analyses *Hamlet* and bases some of his most important ideas on this analysis, I discuss his reading, clarifying the differences and similarities to a Freudian interpretation and the attention paid to subsidiary characters, such as Ophelia and Laertes, the ideal ego in the mirror stage. I also chart the genesis of the application of object relations theory to Shakespeare's works, with particular attention to D. W. Winnicott and Melanie Klein.

The next chapter, on psychoanalytic criticism through the 1980s, records its heyday, when it gains prominence and greater credibility, as literary scholars in larger numbers begin to employ it; book-length studies devoted exclusively to psychoanalytic readings of Shakespeare become more common; and criticism moves beyond the strict Freudian reading and psychobiography. It establishes that Jungian readings continue, but the theories of Erik Erikson, one of the originators of ego psychology, and Klein, Margaret Mahler and Winnicott, all at the forefront of object relations studies, appear more often in the criticism. The application of Erikson's stages of psychosocial development to Shakespeare's characters' maturation creates some controversy, with some contending twentieth-century conceptions of adolescence do not accord with those of early modern times. Klein's theory in particular proves to be compatible with feminist studies because it de-emphasizes in ego development the infant's relation with the father and, instead, focuses on the greater importance given to the earlier primal bond with the mother, one that begins with birth, and on primal objects, including body parts of parents, such as the mother's breasts. It also rejects Freud's physiological grounding of human motivation in favour of an objects oriented formation. The initial application of her theory to Shakespeare foreshadows later criticism that turns away from regarding characters as embodiments of real patients and, instead, concentrates on a more comprehensive reading of a play. The discussion of Winnicott concentrates on his concepts of transitional objects and the relationship between reader and text as taking place in potential space, an idea that enhances reader-response criticism. The analyses that explore the application of Lacanian theory highlight a turning away from character study to a closer reading of the text and language. This chapter records the symbiotic relationship that emerges between feminism and psychoanalysis, as object relations theory encourages a reassessment of the mother's role in male and female development that is congenial with feminism and provides a basis for feminist readings of texts that stress the passage of the subject from the pre-oedipal and oedipal stages into consciousness of gender. Some of the topics that are explored include the following: the impact of the maternal on the male psyche; the projection of male infantile fantasies onto women; and male characters' needs to identify with the father and separate from the mother. The survey of this period clarifies the growing diversity of psychoanalytic approaches.

Chapter 4 surveys the decade of the 1990s, the beginning of which sees the culmination of some of the most prominent Shakespearean psychoanalytic critics' scholarship. It surveys the continued eminence of feminist psychoanalytic approaches, most of which enlist object relations theory and gender studies to address masculine anxiety towards female power and the maternal body as a site of deformation. It establishes the growing expansiveness, sophistication and credibility of psychoanalytic approaches to Shakespeare, as scholars enlist not just one theory, but several simultaneously, or apply their own theoretical constructs to the literature. It shows as well the growing influence of Lacanian readings. Chapter 5 examines some of the most influential psychoanalytic studies of the early twenty-first century, many of which are not devoted exclusively to Shakespeare but, rather, broaden their scope to include other writers, as they explore threads of similarity between primarily early modern writers. Feminist studies continue, as a debate emerges between those who read the mother as devouring and annihilating and those who view her as nurturing and supportive and claim the former scapegoat her by placing sons' faults solely on mothers' shoulders. The chapter establishes the growing prominence of studies that combine psychoanalysis and historicism, an approach that most likely responds to the criticism Greenblatt and others lodged at psychoanalytic theory for being an ahistorical method that dehistoricizes and depoliticizes literature. The historicizing of psychoanalytic concepts in particular has mostly served to strengthen the psychoanalytic discipline, showing the compatibility of psychoanalytic readings to early modern literature. This survey of psychoanalytic theory and criticism from the beginnings to the early twenty-first century clarifies the ways scholars impact each other's interpretations, the similarities and differences in their approaches, the new insights that have resulted from such readings, and the burgeoning of new trends. It records the evolution from a strictly Freudian approach in the early years to a more fully nuanced, multilayered discipline that often combines different theoretical concepts.

Chapters 6 and 7 are offered as examples of psychoanalytic theory's application to actual readings of Shakespeare's plays. The first illustrates a more conventional psychoanalytic interpretation, presenting a largely Freudian reading of the oedipal complex, but not from the typical male perspective. Scholars have analysed oedipal desires in *All's Well That Ends Well* primarily as they impact and are embodied in Bertram, and have slighted the feminine component of the oedipal dynamic. My reading establishes the basis for the psychic connection between a surrogate mother and daughter, the Countess and Helena, and concentrates on Helena's relationship with her dead father as it is reincarnated in her feelings for Bertram, who becomes a substitute for the deceased paternal figure. Chapter 7 looks at non-normative sexuality in *Romeo and Juliet*, building on queer readings of the play to explore the eroticized relationship of Romeo, Mercutio, Tybalt and Benvolio. Queer and psychoanalytic theories have not forged an harmonious union. Queer critics object to the heteronormativity of Freud's theories, especially his view of same-sex eroticism as an early phase of development that is superseded by heterosexual maturity; psychoanalytic feminists' pathologizing of non-heterosexual relations; and twentieth-century developmental psychology's ahistorical view of adolescence as the key site of sexual development and notion of two opposed sexes and sexual orientation. Rather than entering into this controversy, I approach the play from the perspective of defence mechanisms, arguing one crucial defence – reaction formation – provides a key to unravelling the dynamics between the male characters.

Since psychoanalysis constitutes one of the largest bodies of criticism of Shakespeare and consists of some of the most specialized terminology, it can be a daunting field to try to understand. This book does not set out to give an account of the expansiveness of the discipline nor highlight all of the readings that have been generated from its application. Instead it concentrates on the most influential studies and elucidates complicated readings by explaining psychological concepts in understandable terms. It attempts to make what can be an arcane, convoluted approach more accessible to readers so they can more fully appreciate the usefulness and merits of a theoretical discipline that has produced some of the most probing analyses of Shakespeare's texts.

1

The Inception of Psychoanalytic Theory and Shakespearean Psychoanalytic Criticism

Considered the progenitor of psychoanalytic theory, Sigmund Freud is a seminal figure in the origins of human subjectivity and psychological approaches to Shakespeare. Even as later clinicians either modify or repudiate his concepts, his influence still appears in the body or at least the margins of their theories. With the standard edition of his works consisting of 24 volumes, he wrote a massive amount of material, some of it technical and arcane to the non-specialist, on a variety of subjects – not just psychology but also anthropology, culture, politics and literature. As an iconic figure whose theories about the human mind are now so embedded in Western culture that his terminology is a part of our everyday vocabulary, he has received much scholarly and analytical attention, with numerous books being devoted to him as a man and to his theories. He is a controversial figure as well, with some lauding him as a psychoanalytic genius and others discrediting his theoretical integrity. Obviously, the following short discussion of him and his influence cannot begin to do him justice. What it sets out to do is elucidate those of his concepts that impact the way scholars and clinicians read Shakespeare through a psychological lens; highlight how he applies his own theories to a reading of Shakespeare; and establish Shakespeare's pivotal position to the formulation of psychoanalytic theory.

Freud divides the mind into three parts: the conscious (the mental functioning, including the memory, that we can contemplate and discuss from a rational viewpoint); the preconscious (memory that can come into consciousness when necessary); and the unconscious (thoughts, memories, desires and feelings – often inappropriate or undesirable – that are not a part of the conscious mind and influence us without our knowledge). Psychoanalytic literary theory, especially as it is applied to Shakespeare, is interested in the subjectivity of characters, trying to come to terms with motivations and representations of consciousness, but the most intriguing concern is the unconscious.[1] In *The Interpretation of Dreams* Freud claims the repressed unconscious is accessible if we know how to detect it; it can give us insights into hidden motivations; and it is the purpose of psychoanalysis to make conscious what is repressed. Some of Shakespeare's problematical characters explain their behaviour by articulating conscious motives, but their explanations are often contradictory and inadequate, compelling us to suspect latent motivations lurk behind their actions – an interior space to which psychoanalytic critics devote much of their attention. Thus, psychopathological drama, such as *Hamlet*, is most suitable to a psychological interpretation because the conflict is between consciousness and repressed impulses.

Freud further divides the personality into three elements. First, motivated by the 'pleasure principle' or instant gratification of desires, the id is the unconscious component that includes repressed matter, the instincts and primitive drives, including fantasies and guilt. Second, the ego is a development of the id that tries to control the id's impulses and make them fit within the constraints of the 'reality principle' by repressing unacceptable urges.[2] Third, the superego is the moral arbiter, formed from the influence of parental and societal figures of authority, that suppresses inappropriate desires and tries to channel the ego into acting idealistically rather than realistically. Therefore, the Freudian ego is influenced by both instinctual and societal factors, including one's infantile reliance on other people, especially one's parents, and prescriptive societal pressures that degrade the quality of one's life. Psychoanalysis focuses on the conflict between these three elements, especially the ego's difficulties in trying to keep the id in check and the tenuousness of repression.[3] Psychoanalytic critics become especially interested in Shakespeare's characters when repressed desires threaten to come to the surface and overpower the ego. If the conflicts are overwhelming, anxiety can develop, and Freud believes defence mechanisms help the ego to deal with the battles between the id, superego and the reality principle. While Anna Freud, one of Freud's daughters, describes ten defence mechanisms enlisted by the ego,[4] on which Shakespearean psychoanalytic literary critics typically rely, Freud relies primarily on his own formulations of defences or 'disguises', as he describes them in *The Interpretation of Dreams*.[5] He concentrates on two disguises primarily – condensation (the combination of elements that the logical mind would maintain as separate) and displacement (the transfer of feelings from the intended objects to replacements). He also refers to projection (attributing one's unacceptable impulses to another person); splitting or decomposition (two separate and opposite versions of reality existing simultaneously); and symbolization (something representing something else). All of these defences play large roles in psychological studies of Shakespeare's plays.

Freud's theory of psychosexual development, which explains the evolution of personality through five stages of childhood (oral, anal, phallic, latent and genital), also holds a prominent, albeit controversial, place in psychology and presents the pleasure-seeking id as concentrated on certain erogenous zones. This theory is based on the importance of childhood experiences to the formation of personality, to the indelible impression infancy has on adult behaviour. If a person does not successfully pass through a stage, a fixation can occur and one could become, for example, orally fixated in adult life. It is during the phallic stage that a crucial event happens, one for which Freud is most famously known – the Oedipus complex – a stage that the child must navigate successfully or be forever marred. At the phallic phase, the libido is focused on the genitals, and the male child begins to want to possess the mother all for himself. He views the father as a rival for her affections and wants to replace him. However, the child fears he will retaliate, a phobia which results in castration anxieties of both actual and symbolic emasculation. Girls can develop a similar complex of desiring the father and resenting the mother, a situation Freud calls the feminine oedipal attitude. To resolve the issue, boys must identify themselves with the father and form the superego, a kind of internalizing of the father as a source of moral supremacy to suppress unacceptable urges of the id. The son defers his feelings for his mother until his mature years when he can transfer his desire for her onto a substitute outside of the family. If the repression is successful, the superego will dominate the ego later in life as a form of conscience or perhaps unconscious guilt. Conversely, the girl has to cease resenting her mother whom she holds responsible for her castration and identify with her.[6] In later work, Freud acknowledges the situation is more problematical for females because of their pre-oedipal attachment to the mother and lack of castration fears. They either develop 'penis envy' or desire a baby as a substitute for the missing organ. While Freud mentions the female dilemma, the emphasis throughout his theories falls on the male, and, as a result, feminists in particular criticize his work as phallocentric.

According to Freud, individuation (developing an autonomous self separate from others) and gender differentiation result from the resolution of oedipal desires, but conformity to societal demands comes at a great cost to human contentment. His theory rests on the principle that neurosis can always be traced back to a sexual cause, that it is a repressed or negative state of sexual perversity. The repressed sexual desires of childhood, in particular the Oedipus complex, can surface in various ways – for example, in dreams, jokes, slips of the tongue and free association. These infantile fantasies and drives may undergo modification as humans mature, but they continue to exist in the unconscious and are universal. Ultimately, he theorizes that 'the beginnings of religion, morals, society and art converge in the Oedipus complex', a claim that assigns the complex enormous influence and indicates its seminal importance to his psychosexual theory.[7]

Freud often demonstrates his theories by applying them to literature, especially to the works of Shakespeare, to whom he refers more than any other author. He does this in part to give credibility to what was considered at the time to be a dubious theory. In fact, Shakespeare is involved in the genesis of psychoanalytic theory, for while contemplating the Oedipus complex, Freud thinks of *Hamlet* and writes to Wilhelm Fliess, a fellow psychoanalyst, that he suspects Hamlet is afflicted with the same dilemma as Oedipus – loving his mother too much and resenting his father's intimacy with her, a situation he admits he experienced as a youth. He develops this idea further in *The Interpretation of Dreams*, asserting Hamlet cannot avenge his father's murder because Claudius represents the realization of his unconscious childhood phantasies; rather than hating Claudius, with whom he identifies, he hates himself for being like his uncle.[8] He later labels Hamlet 'a world-famous neurotic'.[9] He draws parallels between the working of the creative imagination and dreams, daydreaming and phantasizing, and believes the creative process often originates in a neurotic disorder.[10] Shakespeare's unconscious connects with the unconscious of his protagonist, which, in turn, connects with that of the audience, who must share Hamlet's psychological dilemma but not be fully aware of it for the play to have its full impact. The writer must not name the repressed desire, lest it cause the audience to disassociate from the hero. Freud contends dramatists elicit infantile traumas and provide the audience and themselves with a cathartic experience to deal with neuroses.

As a result, literature resembles psychoanalysis by helping repressed unconscious feelings to surface into consciousness, and authors are like psychotherapists in their ability to understand unusual psychological states. Freud believes philosophers and poets, and especially Shakespeare, have an intuitive understanding of human emotions and discovered the complexity of the psyche before him, and he provides only a scientific process by which to understand it. But he attributes great capabilities to this process by stating a full understanding of the great works of literature would not be possible without applying psychoanalysis, and the mystery of *Hamlet*, in particular, was not explained until the play was subjected to psychoanalysis. He professes *Hamlet* is more obscure than *Oedipus Rex* because of the 'secular advance[ment] of repression', making it more suitable to psychoanalytic analysis than Sophocles' work, in which parricidal and incestuous fantasies are openly revealed. He asserts that critics' inability to decipher the real reasons for Hamlet's inaction 'showed how ready is the mass of mankind to hold fast to its infantile repressions'.[11]

Freud's most expansive analysis of Shakespeare is of the fairy-tale motif of the three caskets in *The Merchant of Venice*.[12] Whereas his approach of exploring character motivation is more realistic in his comments on *Hamlet*, this later analysis is more concerned with symbol, myth and dream, and anticipates psychoanalytic archetypal readings of Shakespeare, approaches that often enlist Jungian analytical psychology. Applying insights from dream interpretation in which dreams often involve symbolic substitution for something that is not allowed into consciousness, he sees the caskets as symbols of women. He then makes a connection to *King Lear* when the King must choose between three women, just as Bassanio must choose between three caskets. Seeing similarities between the 'pale' lead casket and Cordelia's silence, he clarifies that in dreams dumbness, or silence, is commonly associated with death. Thus, Lear's choice of Cordelia at the end represents his embracing of and recognition of the necessity of dying. Cordelia's serving as a symbol of love involves a reaction formation, with a distressing concept being replaced by a more positive opposite. He argues the theme of the three caskets reflects the relations a man has with a woman – the mother; the mate who doubles for the mother; and Mother Earth, who receives him upon death. When Lear enters with the dead Cordelia in his arms, we are seeing 'replacement by the opposite' in which Shakespeare suggests a symbolic representation of his protagonist being taken by Death. While this reading deviates from Freud's typically phallic-centred interpretations, it foreshadows readings of Shakespeare by later critics, largely object relations theorists, who will place far more emphasis on the mother in the psychic development of the son. His later comments on *King Lear* are more character-driven and oedipal: they specify that 'the secret meaning of the tragedy' rests in Lear's 'repressed incestuous claims on the daughter's [Cordelia's] love', and Goneril and Regan have moved beyond and successfully repressed their oedipal preoccupation with their father while Cordelia has not, a psychic dilemma that accounts for her inability to express her taboo desires.[13] Lear's madness, which does not appear in Shakespeare's sources, is both his and Shakespeare's attempt to reject these desires.

Freud's comments on other Shakespearean plays are cursory and sprinkled throughout his writings. With regard to *Macbeth* he focuses on the 'childlessness' of the couple, which may derive from Macbeth's lack of sexual potency; Lady Macbeth's need to wash her hands as a symbolic act of trying to cleanse herself of moral impurity; her channelling her sexual frustrations of being married to an impotent husband into 'ambitious' designs; the splitting of Macbeth and Lady Macbeth as 'two disunited parts of a single psychical individuality', 'copied from a single proto-type', neither of whom is complete without the other; and the Macbeths' oedipal guilt.[14] He also tries to give credibility to psychobiography, maintaining one can draw parallels between the intimate details of authors' lives and fictional events in their works as well as decipher their personality from a study of their writings. As a result, he believes *Hamlet* reflects Shakespeare's coming to terms with his father's and son's deaths.[15]

Freud's brief comments about the oedipal reading of *Hamlet* serve as a basic foundation for many of the subsequent psychological readings of the play that provide convincing explanations for some of the most problematical issues. Ernest Jones, one of his students, more fully develops his comments in a study now considered one of the greatest contributions to psychoanalytic criticism of Shakespeare. He first published his ideas in 1910 as an essay on the subject and subsequently developed them into a book-length study.[16] Jones argues his reading with persuasive conviction, first discrediting the explanation of other readers (e.g. Hartley Coleridge, Hermann Ulrici, Wilbraham Trench) for Hamlet's delay in avenging his father's murder and then countering with the reading that Hamlet is suffering from 'inner conflicts' relating to his oedipal feelings towards his mother, father and uncle. Jones accentuates the importance of repression, which keeps Hamlet's desires for his mother at bay and prevents him from killing the surrogate father in Claudius. They threaten to come into consciousness, however, once he learns Claudius has acted them out by killing his father, for whom he harbours infantile jealousies for bedding his mother – his inadequately suppressed secret desire. What bothers Hamlet the most is not the murder of his father but the lust of his mother. He has concealed his resentment towards his father by using the defence mechanism of reaction formation and, thus, adopting the opposite sentiment of extreme love and deference for him.

Jones adds to Freud's ideas by looking at the splitting or decomposing in the play, and explaining how Hamlet's ambivalent attitudes towards his father are embodied in the splitting of both father and son into different characters: the fathers being the ghost, Claudius and Polonius; and the sons, Hamlet and Laertes. Hamlet has chosen a woman antithetical to Gertrude in temperament to ward off his attraction to his mother, while at the same time unconsciously desiring to pique her jealousy at his choice of another woman. Jones applies Freud's oedipal theory and defences to the play, asserting Hamlet uses Ophelia as a substitute for his mother and projects his resentment and anger onto her rather than Gertrude, an explication that reveals why his scathing denunciations of Ophelia do not comport with her actions or words. Enlisting Freud's *Mourning and Melancholia*, Jones adds the original claim that Hamlet's melancholia causes him to take suicidal actions in the last scenes of the play because he cannot fulfil his duty of killing Claudius, an act that would be equivalent to his enactment of the forbidden fantasy. As a result, Hamlet has to wait until his mother is dead before he can kill his uncle, so that he is not fulfilling his oedipal desire.

While Jones convincingly applies a Freudian interpretation to the play, there are some limitations. First, he bases his analysis on Hamlet as a 'living person',[17] a critically questionable strategy that characterizes the work of many psychoanalytic critics. Second, because Freud builds much of his theory of psychosexual development on the experiences of childhood and Shakespeare often does not provide details about his characters' early lives, Jones has to build his insights on surmises of what Hamlet's early years must have been like:

> How if, in fact, Hamlet had in years gone by, as a child, bitterly resented having had to share his mother's affection even with his own father, had regarded him as a rival, and had secretly wished him out of the way so that he might enjoy undisputed and undisturbed the monopoly of that affection? If such thoughts had been present in his mind in childhood days they evidently would have been 'repressed,' and all traces of them obliterated, by filial piety and other educative influences.[18]

But he shows an understanding of central concepts of Freud's theories, such as repression, psychoneurosis, the Oedipus complex, reaction formation, vicarious pleasure and slips of the tongue. His ability to apply them and arrive at a cogent analysis provides impetus for those who come after him to pursue Freudian readings of Shakespeare.

The other great psychoanalyst of this early period is Otto Rank, who ultimately breaks with Freud because of differing attitudes towards the shock of birth and its effects on later life. For many years, though, he was a traditional Freudian and agreed with the Freud–Jones interpretation of *Hamlet*, exploring incest themes and publishing a book on the subject.[19] Like Freud, Rank's emphasis in his discussion of *Hamlet* falls primarily on the father and the son's desire to kill him, with the ghost representing the continuing hostility the mature son feels towards the father and also the father's constraining influence on the son even after his death. Consequently, there are three fathers in the play, each highlighting Hamlet's different feelings towards the paternal figure: the dead Hamlet represents the cherished father; Claudius, the hated father whom the son wants to kill; and Polonius, the father who keeps the beloved away from the son. The incest motif as it relates to Polonius is one of Rank's chief enhancements of the oedipal reading. One of his crucial insights involves viewing Hamlet as a *Phantasiemensch*, a person who fantasizes so vividly that he substitutes phantasy for action.[20] Looking at the play-within-the-play, Rank explains Hamlet's exhilaration after the enactment of 'The Murder of Gonzago' as a sign that he so identifies with the stage murderer, it is as if he has killed either Claudius or his father himself, and he, therefore, expresses elation at the fulfilment of the first stages of his oedipal wish. Rank's insights about peeping or spying also highlight the importance of visualizing for Hamlet: Polonius' watching behind the arras is a projection onto a paternal figure of a child's wish to watch the primal scene and assume the father's role in coitus with the mother. Unlike Jones, Rank does not view literary characters as real people; rather, he is more mythical in his approach, but he does engage in some psychobiography, suggesting the ghost scenes are projections of Shakespeare's own ambivalent feelings towards his father and his oedipal desires for his mother. He also believes Shakespeare expresses his paternal feelings through the father figures.

His comments on other Shakespearean plays, likewise, focus on the shaky, resentful relationship between fathers and sons, and the oedipal situation that he detects in numerous works. He sees fathers as figuring prominently in *Macbeth*, *Julius Caesar*, *Coriolanus* (Menenius as good father, and Aufidius as bad father), *King Lear* and *Titus Andronicus*. Just as the father is decomposed or split in *Hamlet*, the son is decomposed in *Julius Caesar*: Brutus constitutes the ambivalence of love and hatred towards the father; Cassius the 'self-punish[ing]' side of Brutus; and Antony the faithful side of Brutus.[21] In *Macbeth* the murder of both Macduff and Banquo, who meld into one figure, represents the destruction of loathed father figures. This focus on fathers and sons will become a primary concern of some of the most prominent later psychoanalytic critics.

Convincingly arguing their readings of literature and especially Shakespeare, Freud, Jones and Rank inspired others to apply a psychoanalytic lens to literature. As a result, 'the relationship between literature and psychoanalysis has matured into one of reciprocity', and 'Shakespeare has been the favourite preserve of psychoanalytic literary criticism',[22] as the following chapters will illustrate. While relatively limited in their perspectives and focus, these early studies illustrate the compatibility of Shakespeare and psychoanalysis. Subsequent psychoanalytic studies of Shakespeare explore a more expansive field of interest, looking at such topics as primal scene phantasies, mourning and melancholia, narcissism, jealousy, sadism/masochism, pre-oedipal conflicts and phallic aggression. Although other psychoanalysts will formulate their own theories and apply them to Shakespeare, Freud's influence will still be marked.

2
Shakespearean Psychoanalytic Critics through the 1970s

With Freud and his followers illustrating the applicability of psychological thought to 'the work of the world's greatest poet-psychologist',[1] more readers – not just clinicians but also academics – turned psychoanalytic attention to Shakespeare. While most of the approaches to Shakespeare through the 1970s apply Freudian theory from either a mythic or realistic perspective, a few are more groundbreaking, applying the theories, for example, of Carl Jung or Jacques Lacan, who developed their own psychological constructs while being deeply influenced by Freud. Some psychoanalytic critics branch out even further to lesser-known theorists, such as Klein and Winnicott, and anticipate their prominence in studies by subsequent critics and the viability of object relations theory to studies of Shakespeare.

Essays that appear in the first anthology devoted exclusively to psychoanalytic readings of Shakespeare, entitled *The Design Within: Psychoanalytic Approaches to Shakespeare*, edited by M. D. Faber, illustrate the early approaches and include some innovative essays by Ernst Kris, Ludwig Jekels, Hanns Sachs, Martin Wangh and Freud himself. Although published in 1970, the collection consists of 33 readings that first appeared between the 1940s and '60s, often in psychoanalytic journals. Twenty-two of the essays explore the tragedies, six the histories, and five the comedies, the distribution reflecting the overwhelming interest in the tragedies as Shakespeare's most penetrating exploration of neurotic, tragic psyches. Faber claims the essays substantiate Shakespeare's skills as both a dramatist and psychologist and support his own thesis that psychoanalytic criticism is the one method that unlocks the mysteries of characters' motivations. They explore diverse topics, such as paranoia, sadomasochism, incest, matricide, megalomania, anal and oral obsession and homosexuality. The anthology makes clear that, in the first half of the twentieth century, psychoanalytic criticism was becoming a reputable approach to Shakespeare and a change in interpretation was under way. This study will assess only a few of the anthology's most outstanding analyses that best represent the approaches of this early period, most of which are deeply indebted to the ideas of Freud and Rank.

Hanns Sachs's essay on *Measure for Measure* does what many psychoanalytic studies do: it tackles the problematical, often disturbing behaviour of a character and refutes the standard condemnatory reading by offering a psychological explanation.[2] Sachs focuses on Angelo and counters the surface reading of him as a hypocrite, presenting him, rather, as a character wrestling with unconscious drives, the most dominant of which is his attraction to cruelty. He has deceived himself by sublimating his forbidden desire and living a life of stricture and severe self-restraint. His 'reign of terror' allows him to exercise his cruel tendencies under the acceptable front of being an officer of the law. When he meets Isabella, the sublimation fails him, and his sadism comes to the fore. In having the Duke propose marriage to Isabella, who has shown no indication of being in love with him, Shakespeare presents him as contemplating committing the same crime as Angelo, but in a sublimated way. Sachs claims Shakespeare is showing all humans harbour unconscious, repressed desires, with the judge being no better than the villain whom he judges: we 'are all linked together by the bond of common guilt; and it matters little whether we call it by its Christian name of Original Sin or by the psychoanalytic term: Oedipus complex'.[3]

Likewise, Martin Wangh concentrates, not on the primary protagonist, but on a secondary character – not on Othello, but the more problematic Iago, who professes various reasons for his puzzling actions, none of which seems convincing.[4] Wangh too enlists Freud's theories to delve into a character's unconscious, claiming Iago suffers from jealousy as severely as Othello and that it reaches the level of paranoia. He argues that Iago suffers from delusional jealousy, which Freud claims is 'what is left of a homosexuality that has run its course': Iago tries to deny his desires for Othello by projecting his feelings onto Desdemona according to Freud's formula of 'I do not love him, *she* loves him'.[5] He explicates Iago's lines when he claims to have shared a bed with Cassio while nursing a toothache (3.2.413–4) and sees them as indicative of a fantasy to gratify his unconscious desires of loving not Cassio but, rather, Othello. He looks at the dream symbolization of the tooth as a universal indicator of the penis. Iago's 'dream', as Wangh calls it, is a 'homosexual wish fulfillment',[6] by which he projects his jealousy onto Othello and provokes the Moor to destroy Desdemona, whom he perceives as his rival. Showing a character's actions are far from 'motiveless', as Coleridge claims about Iago (Coleridge, 1987, vol. 2, 315), Wangh illustrates how a psychoanalytic reading can probe the deepest recesses of the psyche and humanize a character.

At least two of the essays in the anthology are considered of noteworthy importance: Faber asserts that Kris's essay on Prince Hal is a 'pioneering contribution to the field', and Jekels's essay on *Macbeth*, indebted to Freud's and Rank's brief comments on the play, has 'influenced all subsequent treatments of the play'.[7] Both essays are Freudian and focus on the oedipal struggle between fathers and sons. Kris provides a psychological explanation for what non-psychoanalytic critics have called inconsistent behaviour in Hal, by claiming he is attempting to come to terms with a conflict similar to that of Hamlet. Like Claudius, Bolingbroke has killed a relative – a second cousin – to whom the prince had an attachment. As a result, Hal secretly resents his father and harbours parricidal impulses, but finds various means to repress them: he allows Hotspur, his alter-ego, to act out his hostility towards his father; he engages in passive-aggression, deliberating antagonizing his father by squandering time in the tavern rather than fulfilling his filial duties; he idealizes his father and, thus, denies his real anger; and he vents his hostility towards a father substitute in Falstaff. He tries to disassociate himself from his father's crime as a means to disavow his own unconscious desire to commit the same crime. The Oedipus complex is not fully developed, because mothers are largely absent from the play; consequently, Hal's struggle is acted out in an all-male society. Viewing Macbeth's rebellion against Duncan as that of a son against a father, Jekels, likewise, argues Shakespeare is playing to his audience's subconscious oedipal feelings, and Macbeth's attack on Banquo and Macduff embodies that of the father against his sons. Upon becoming a father, the son resents his own son because he fears he harbours the same parricidal impulses he has felt. Because this play features powerful women – Lady Macbeth and the three witches – Jekels views them in oedipal dimensions, as the 'image of the mother, symboliz[ing] the abyss separating father and son' and as 'demon' women.[8] Both the attention to father/son relationships and to women as sources of corruption will figure large in later psychoanalytic criticism, although primarily as two separate approaches.

Early psychoanalytic criticism is also indebted to Carl Jung, the creator of analytical psychology, who builds a theory around a second, deeper form of unconsciousness underlying the Freudian one of repressed desires and feelings – the 'collective unconscious'.[9] He claims it manifests itself in literature, mythology and dreams through myths and archetypes – recurring images, character types, story lines, symbols and settings – intrinsic to humans as memories of situations, happenings and relationships from the beginning of time, that have not happened to us personally but to our ancestors. He believes we are born not as a blank slate (*tabula rasa*) but with an ingrained archetypal program, with myths anchored in the deepest recess of our psyches. He asserts these 'primordial images' have become lodged in the collective unconscious since the beginning of humanity, and it is through them that humans experience archetypes and unearth the unconscious. The crucial concept of analytical psychology is individuation – the assimilation of opposites, including the conscious with the unconscious, the anima with the animus (feminine with masculine), and the preserving of autonomy, a process Jung considers crucial to human development. He is also a major contributor to dream analysis and symbolization.

Jekels illustrates the compatibility of Freudian and Jungian approaches by viewing *Macbeth*, for example, as a vegetation myth and Macbeth as a 'hibernal giant whose reign comes to an end when the May festival begins and the green wood [Birnam Wood] comes marching'.[10] But one of the earliest practitioners is Maud Bodkin who published a book on archetypes in literature that looked specifically at *Hamlet*, *King Lear* and *Othello*. She argues 'the most important contribution that has been made by the Freudian theory of dream interpretation to the understanding of the emotional symbolism of poetic themes' is the concept of splitting of type figures.[11] *Hamlet* embodies the split that a son feels towards his father in the images of the bad and good fathers (respectively Claudius and the ghost); the feelings of 'love', devotion and veneration, and the simultaneous, typically repressed impulses of resentment, 'jealousy, and self-assertion'.[12] *King Lear* captures the split that a parent feels towards a child in the images of the bad daughters (Goneril and Regan) and the good daughter (Cordelia); the feelings of hostility, fear and resentment, and the contrary ones of appreciation, gratefulness and love. Ancient stories, such as *Hamlet* and *King Lear*, naturally appeal to us because they help us to relieve our conflicting emotions. Relating our 'exultation' in Hamlet's death to 'the religious exultation felt by the primitive group that made sacrifice of the divine king or sacred animal', which signified a renewal of life, Bodkin claims the fall of the tragic hero has a purging or atoning effect on the audience and a connection to Christ of the Gospels.[13] The tragic hero becomes a sacrificial victim, an image that resides in the collective unconscious. She explains the archetypal pattern of tragic drama as a conflict between an undisciplined, self-assertive self and a submissive self, constrained by societal demands – a dilemma represented in the tragic hero, who embodies the self of 'imaginative aspiration' and whose death represents the submission to a greater power and the '"community consciousness"'.[14] She applies Jung's animus and anima dialectic to Othello and Desdemona respectively and argues they are the archetypal fantasy of man and woman in their union because they each find a part of the self in the other. She also views Iago as an archetype of the devil and provides a psychological description of him as representing forces that are already within humans, just as he is a projected image of the monster that is already inside Othello's repressed thoughts.

Others look for archetypal significance in Shakespeare's plays, such as Theodor Reik, a prominent psychoanalyst who was one of Freud's students. Moving away from a realistic approach to the psychological issues in *The Merchant of Venice*, he looks at the 'unconscious appeal of the play' and the evocation of certain religious figures in characters. He explains Shakespeare may have started out with the intention of exploring an encounter between a Gentile merchant and a Jewish money lender, but his collective unconscious compelled him to reach 'into the region where the great myths and religious legends of the people are born and bred' and transform Shylock into the God of the Old Testament, Jahweh, and Antonio into Jesus Christ.[15] The poet W. H. Auden also makes intriguing insights into the archetypal stature of some of Shakespeare's characters: he views Falstaff as both a perpetual child and a God figure, and Iago as a 'practical joker', similar to Jung's trickster or the Devil, who projects his self-hatred onto others. He compares Iago to a therapist, who has an uncanny ability to detect others' unconscious desires and fears and to bring them into consciousness, but, unlike a helpful therapist, he means 'to kill not to cure'. He is a projection of the hidden aspects of the major characters' psyches.[16]

In 1949 J. I. M. Stewart published a book-length study that employs both Freudian and Jungian theory and argues one has to search beneath characters' heroic surfaces to detect the 'hidden' being, of whom the characters are often themselves unaware.[17] Applying Freud's ideas about delusional jealousy, Stewart claims Leontes projects his homosexual desires for Polixenes onto his wife and accuses her of desiring Polixenes, as a way to both deny and vicariously express his attraction to his childhood friend – insights that have markedly influenced subsequent readings of *The Winter's Tale*. Influenced by Jung, Stewart proclaims people's motives are often obscure and subtle and reside in their 'primitive' minds, his version of Jung's collective unconscious. He looks at Macbeth's motives and declares, 'it is the crime and not the crown that compels' him,[18] as the criminal persona, which resides deep inside all of us, comes to the fore in Macbeth and embodies the attraction that bloodshed, horror and murder have for all humans. He probes Othello's character and finds in him a 'psychological type' of the suspicious character, who believes the ego ideal he projects, but readily responds to insinuations because he secretly harbours suspicions himself.[19] Stewart believes Shakespeare splits one psyche into two parts – Othello and Iago – that must be conflated to arrive at the true protagonist, with Othello representing the mind at war with itself, a psychic dilemma endemic to all humans. He views Falstaff in archetypal terms as a king substitute whose vicarious sacrifice is embedded in a 'whole mythology of the cycle of the year, and of sacrifices offered to secure a new fertility in the earth'.[20] As a surrogate king figure, Falstaff is sacrificed in order to reverse the misfortune brought upon the kingdom by the regicidal-parricidal Bolingbroke. Stewart asserts Shakespeare's characters can derive from archetypal drama and still be psychologically penetrating, and 'drama, like religious ritual, plays upon atavic impulses of the mind'.[21]

Concentrating on Shakespearean comedy and romance, Northrop Frye goes even further in outlining a theory of the arts based on archetypal criticism. He is undoubtedly influenced by Jung and enlists some of his key terminology to claim the meaning of Shakespeare's plays and characters must be understood in terms of the play's structure, lodged in an archetypal pattern derived from myth and ritual. His major premise is that literary works do not develop exclusively from an author's life but from a collective unconscious, the location of pre-literary stories that attempt to help us understand and come to terms with the complexities of the world. Writers unthinkingly enlist pre-existent genres with pre-established character types, plots and patterns of imagery embedded in myths and human rituals. He proposes four 'mythoi', or plot structures, that serve as the foundation for the four major genres, associated with the seasons of the year: comedy (spring); romance (summer); tragedy (autumn); and satire and irony (winter).[22] He also published an archetypal study of Shakespeare's comedies and romances that clarifies 'archaizing tendencies', primitive qualities that reflect a universal dramatic tradition with conventions derived from myths to which the audience responds instinctively.[23] Playing upon the death–rebirth myth embodied in the story of Persephone and Demeter that George Frazier in *The Golden Bough* sees as prominent in fertility myths, Frye claims comedy and tragedy, particularly Shakespearean, reflect this basic pattern.[24] The dream of the comedies comes to fruition in the romances where life emerges from death, specifically in *The Winter's Tale* where Shakespeare openly references the Persephone myth. Understandably, Frye's study is criticized for relying too heavily on myth and too little on the text itself; offering mechanical and monotonous critiques of literature; and ignoring the innovative qualities of Shakespeare's artistic vision. None the less, archetypal criticism held sway for two decades until it withered under the influence of other theoretical approaches.

Another psychiatrist and psychoanalyst whose ideas impacted both psychoanalytic theory and readings of Shakespeare in particular is Jacques Lacan, sometimes labelled the French Freud. He proposed his own theory of psychosexual development, deeply indebted to Freud but focused on semantics and the parallels between the unconscious and language.[25] His theory consists of three orders – the Imaginary, Symbolic and Real – and, like that of Freud, is based on the male model. According to Lacan, children are introduced into the Imaginary Order through the 'mirror stage', in which they have no concept of the self, but seeing themselves in the mirror, they mistake their image for the genuine whole self – an imaginary other. Children also identify with the mother, whom they see in the mirror as part of themselves and with whom they form an imaginary relation, associating their desires with those of the mother. Once the father enters the picture, though, the Law of the Father disallows this relationship with the mother but allows children to have desires all their own, a condition that introduces them into the Symbolic Order, subject to the law and language, but also free to form identities separate from those of mother and father. Lacan signifies the 'Phallus' as the desire of the Other that children must repudiate to gain access to the Symbolic Order. If the entrance to the Symbolic Order is blocked, children do not become their own subjects, and psychosis is the result. The birth of the subject coincides with the entrance into language and the loss of the object that causes desire.

Lacan delivered a series of seminars in Paris in the 1950s about his structuralist theories as they apply to a reading of *Hamlet*, later published in an essay.[26] His analysis is based on the contention that Hamlet never realizes his own desire but, rather, is subject to the desire of his mother, which accounts for his not curtailing the sexual union of Claudius and Gertrude. His inability to act results not from an oedipal desire for his mother, as Freud and Jones maintain, but from an obsession with his mother's desire, with an association with the (m)other and her desire. Lacan sees Gertrude as the Other of demand, sexually responsive to her son. Hamlet is stuck in the Imaginary Order and has not substituted the mother with another 'signifier', the *objet petit a* – in Hamlet's case, Ophelia, a name that Lacan presents as 'O Phallos'. He must take her as his object in order to become aware of his own desire. Lacan believes Hamlet is not able to take this step because he has not been able to adequately mourn, a necessary progression in removing desire from a lost object so the subject can desire another object. He has not had sufficient time to mourn his father's death and, as a result, becomes transfixed in his mother's desire, unable to mourn the loss of the Phallus. He desires Ophelia only after she dies, when she 'has become an impossible object',[27] and he does so because he continues to identify with another's desire – this time with Laertes. Still anchored in the Imaginary Order, he expresses a mirrored response to his 'double', but the imaginary identification releases his desires temporarily so that he can desire the *objet petit a*. However, he expresses Laertes' desire rather than his own. Even in the last act he accommodates himself to the desire of the 'Other' – to Claudius – 'wearing the king's colours' and rushing 'into the trap laid by the Other'.[28] He can only access his unconscious desire and its lost object, the Phallus, when he is dying. Leading to a psycho-analysis of textual and rhetorical processes with an emphasis on language, Lacan's theories and different reading of *Hamlet* impacted literary criticism and continue to influence the way the play and Shakespeare's other works are read. Unlike Freud's theories, Lacan's approach allows for a means to assess societal and linguistic influences on the psyche, which some scholars have found valuable, especially feminists who study the influence of culture in the form of the patriarchy on women's self-image and the construction of gender based on language and society.

Another influential early psychoanalyst, Norman Holland, published a major work entitled *Psychoanalysis and Shakespeare*, an expansive examination of all that had been written up to 1964 from a psychoanalytic perspective about Shakespeare the man and his works. He highlights the diversity of approaches and widespread attention Shakespeare has received for his psychologically rich characters. A large part of the study serves as a reference tool, summarizing and assessing the psychoanalytic readings of all of Shakespeare's works in alphabetical order. The large number of readings indicates the credibility psychoanalytic literary theory was quickly gaining and its useful applicability to Shakespeare. Understandably, *Hamlet* receives the most attention, with Holland clarifying the Freud–Jones interpretation as well as other psychological approaches, such as those that focus on themes of matricide. Another part of the book evaluates as well as defends the psychoanalytic approach to literature and more precisely Shakespeare, a section that indicates that while it was gaining acceptance, there was also some controversy. He includes in his study an essay on 'Three Ways of Psychoanalytic Criticism' that appears in an earlier publication and discredits two major approaches to literature that had come to dominate psychoanalytic scholarship – psychobiography and the treatment of characters as real people – a critique that probably added to their decline in succeeding years. He describes a better approach that Freud mentions in 'Creative Writers and Day-Dreaming', one that considers the literary piece 'not as a single unconscious wish, but as a totality of competing unconscious wishes', with the tragic hero being a projection of a wish to which the audience can relate.[29] Richard P. Wheeler rightly claims 'after Jones's *Hamlet and Oedipus*, [Holland's book] is the most notable post-Freudian psychoanalytic landmark of Shakespeare criticism'.[30]

Two psychoanalytic books on *Hamlet* appeared in the 1970s, one by K. R. Eissler and the other by Avi Erlich – two studies that indicate the play continued to provide fodder for psychological analysis.[31] Both attempt to differentiate their interpretation from the influential reading of Freud–Jones, but ultimately are indebted to Freud's theories. Rejecting Jones's belief he is suffering from a neurosis, Eissler 'normalizes' Hamlet by claiming that while the narcissistic stage in Hamlet's development has been marred by his mother's 'frailty' and the diminution of his father into a ghost and he suffers the loss of the idealized parental figures, he has not been permanently injured. Ultimately he is triumphant by the end and matures into an autonomous, responsible adult, freeing himself of 'all inappersonated remnants of paternal imagery'; taking 'possession of the mother' by dying with her; and being 'resurrected' ... 'in the form of Fortinbras'.[32] Ironically Eissler uses psychoanalysis to minimize the psychosis that afflicts Hamlet. As a 656-page tome, this work obviously is not devoted exclusively to a study of *Hamlet*; Eissler, like some of his predecessors, is still trying to react to the detractors of psychoanalytic criticism with a defence that proclaims the full meaning of Shakespeare's works can only be uncovered with psychology.

Erlich agrees with Freud's and Jones's oedipal reading, but argues Hamlet's problem is not so much that he sees himself in Claudius, as that he is overwhelmed by his mother's sensual nature and identifies with his absent father, who was too weak to defend him from her and Claudius. In fact, although Hamlet is searching for a strong father-surrogate, the play is filled with inadequate father figures, and Hamlet is primarily dealing with his psychological ambivalence towards his father. With much of this early psychoanalytic criticism being based on 'surmises', Erlich offers the conjecture that because Hamlet is suffering from a primal scene fantasy in which he has imagined his father experiencing castration during intercourse with the mother, he is afflicted with fears of castration himself. Mothers come into the analysis, for Erlich feels Gertrude is a destructive, phallic figure, who emasculates both father and son – a controversial charge of misogyny in Shakespeare's plays that later critics will more thoroughly develop. Like others before them, these two early psychoanalytic scholars treat characters as though they are real people and feel Shakespeare projects his own life experiences and unconscious desires onto them.

Two of the most prolific psychoanalytic critics of the 1970s are Stephen Reid and Murray M. Schwartz, both of whom are largely Freudian in their concentration on oedipal desires. Reid wrote eight articles appearing in the journals *American Imago* and *Psychoanalytic Review*, essays that could have easily been compiled into a book but, unfortunately, were not. His analysis of Goneril and Regan maintains they are suffering from 'thwarted love' for their father, whom they resent for turning from them to his wife and Cordelia, and whom they want to kill. They transfer this antipathy to Gloucester and fight each other for the love of his bastard son, Edmund, in an enactment of 'their earlier rivalry for their father's love'.[33] Similarly, Reid asserts that Desdemona's inability to defend herself against Othello's allegations of adultery and her acquiescence to her murder derive from a sense of guilt that goes back to her relationship with her father, whom she resents for preferring her mother to her and on whom she gets revenge by betraying him in a reciprocal fashion by preferring Othello to him.[34] Likewise, Othello resents his mother for rejecting him for his father; these repressed feelings become activated when he marries Desdemona, a maternal surrogate, on whom he vents his rage against his mother and deflects his guilt for betraying his father and loving his mother too much.[35] Reid also explores *Hamlet*, claiming Hamlet suffers melancholia upon learning his mother had an incestuous affair with Claudius before his father's death, a fact that unconsciously afflicts him as the loss of the oedipal mother.[36] Reid's analysis of *The Winter's Tale* argues that Leontes' delusional jealousy results from his 'boyhood homosexual attachment' to Polixenes and oedipal guilt, which he expresses towards his friend, a substitute for his father, and towards Hermione, a substitute for his mother, whom he punishes for his own unacceptable urges.[37] The major drawback to these approaches is that often Shakespeare does not provide much, if any, information about a character's familial unit. For example, we know virtually nothing about Othello's mother, other than the little he says about her when he describes the history of the handkerchief, and we never meet Lear's wife and must assume she is dead. So to claim Othello had an oedipal relationship with his mother, or Regan and Goneril had resentful relationships with their mother, has to be based on what Reid himself admits is 'speculation',[38] an admission that weakens his arguments' credibility since the text provides no supporting references.

While not oedipal, Reid's two articles on the pleasure principle in *Othello* and the sexual instinct in *Troilus and Cressida* and *Measure for Measure* are yet again intrinsically related to Freud's theories. He enlists ideas from *Beyond the Pleasure Principle* to argue a 'deeper, more archaic level of motivation' in Othello derives from self-injury dictated by the 'death drive', the movement towards self-destruction and extinction, as opposed to the 'pleasure principle', an embracing of reproduction, sex and survival. Othello has diverted his aggressive self-abuse towards war and specifically Desdemona, when he perceives his career as a soldier has come to an end.[39] Reid bases his reading of the problem plays *Troilus and Cressida* and *Measure for Measure* on ideas from 'The Most Prevalent Form of Degradation in Erotic Life', on Freud's assertion that '"something in the nature of the sexual instinct is unfavorable to the achievement of absolute gratification"'.[40]

Only in one essay does Reid venture outside the Freudian boundaries to apply Klein's theories to his critical approach to Shakespeare: he claims Timon's 'beneficence and misanthropy are rooted in what Melanie Klein calls the "paranoid-schizoid" position' and relates Timon's depression and persecutory anxiety to early childhood experiences with important objects, such as his mother's breasts.[41] One of the originators of object relations psychology, Klein divides infantile psychic development into two positions – paranoid-schizoid and depressive. The first occurs in the first six months of children's lives and involves their relation to other people, primarily the mother, and objects, typically to parts of objects and people, such as a mother's face or breasts. The paranoia derives from the children's fear of annihilation, a projection out of the death drive. Infantile egos rely on the defence mechanism of splitting to cope, dividing objects and themselves into good and bad entities and identifying with the good until they mature and can cope with the less benign aspects of life. In the next position, the children begin to realize the good objects also contain the bad qualities they try to avoid, a duality that leads to depression. To escape the depression, the children either regress to the former position or resort to a manic state of denial.[42] Reid contends Timon's situation indicates he does the former, which leads to his later problems in adulthood. While he notes Klein's theories did not 'have general currency among the psychoanalytic critics' when he was writing his article in 1969,[43] a slighting indicated by an absence of references to her in the index of Holland's massive study, she will have an influential impact on future psychoanalytic readings of Shakespeare, especially by feminists. Reid is one of the first critics to illustrate her theory's applicability to psychoanalytic criticism of Shakespeare.

Schwartz wrote three essays on *Cymbeline* and *The Winter's Tale*, which, like Reid's essays, are highly indebted to Freud, with oedipal anxieties continuing to dominate psychoanalytic explorations of Shakespeare's plays. Concentrating in *Cymbeline* on Posthumus' unresolved oedipal feelings and his angst about female sexuality, Schwartz views Cloten and Iachimo as projections of his psyche: Cloten represents phallic aggressiveness and Posthumus' attitudes towards sexuality as defilement; and Iachimo embodies his sexual fantasy and sublimated sexual desire.[44] The problem again comes down to maternal imagos, the nurturing mother in Imogen and the phallic, castrating mother in the Queen, and although Posthumus ultimately achieves a symbiotic relationship with the supportive mother, Schwartz feels the original anxieties still lurk beneath the play's surface.

His two essays on *The Winter's Tale* have been called 'the fullest and most nuanced psychoanalytic account of the play' and have influenced subsequent psychological readings, especially those that focus on mother–child relationships.[45] He asserts Leontes projects onto Polixenes and Hermione his own internalized images of parents, his friend becoming the father Leontes fears, and his wife being the diseased, malevolent mother. Viewing the image of the 'spider' in the play as a representation of the engulfing mother whom Leontes fears, he suggests Leontes tries to sacrifice Hermione, the 'catastrophic mother', to recreate the revered ideal of motherhood.[46] His second essay on the play expands the preceding discussion and proposes the play 'is governed by such a deeply rooted terror of and wish for maternal power'; he looks at Paulina as the embodiment of Leontes' maternal terrors and Perdita, conversely, as the idealized mother imago.[47] The play ends with the statue of Hermione that awes all with both her passivity and power, embodying the ambivalence towards women in the play. Leontes' wife ultimately consoles him with the nurturance he has mistakenly seen as poison and helps him to unite with the maternal imago.

While Schwartz's aforementioned essays are embedded in Freudian theory, he wrote one essay that is credited with pioneering the use of Winnicott's theories in approaches to Shakespeare.[48] He focuses in particular on Winnicott's key concept of 'potential space', a term that denotes a comfortable environment in which people can be spontaneously playful either alone or with others, just as babies are with their mothers. Winnicott believes play is instrumental to the formation of genuine selfhood, since it allows people to be spontaneous, natural and unencumbered with societal personas.[49] Schwartz views the 'transitional area of the theatre' as Shakespeare's play space, which shatters in the worlds of his tragedies largely because of what he calls the 'demonic, sexualized' female characters, who make the potential space between masculine and feminine aspects of the self and relations between characters untenable, embodied especially in Lady Macbeth in the 'violent interruption of a nurturant, communal interplay'.[50] But with Antony and Cleopatra he sees the re-emergence of the play space in the lovers, as

Antony accepts his feminine as well as masculine self, a play space that appears in the late romances as well, especially in Bohemia of *The Winter's Tale* where play is embodied in the pastoral festivities and in Hermione as a living statue – 'a potential space within a potential space'.[51]

Jung continues to wield influence in a study by Alex Aronson, who focuses on his universal archetypes, one of the most interesting being the 'Shadow', a primitive personality that is repressed from the 'persona', or conscious being (ego), a side people do not want to acknowledge because it conflicts with the image they project to the outside world.[52] Aronson argues Iago and Cassius, for instance, signify unconscious projections of the egos of their dramatic complements. Specifically, Cassius embodies the ambitious and ruthless nature of Brutus that resides in Brutus's unconscious; Iago represents the suspicious, jealous and sensual nature lying beneath Othello's romantic dedication to Desdemona. He looks at Shakespeare's technique of unveiling the unconscious nature of his characters by projecting it onto other characters and applies the animus/anima archetype to various pairs of characters, such as Claudio and Hero, Ferdinand and Miranda, and Lear and Cordelia.

Psychoanalytic approaches to Shakespeare in this period rely primarily on Freudian theory and offer amazingly insightful interpretations of characters and actions that stumped readers for many years. They illustrate the richness of Shakespeare's knowledge of the human mind and show that Freud will always provide a gateway into the depths of his characters. But in this period, as we have seen, a few scholars discover the theories of Winnicott and Klein and begin to apply them in a limited fashion to their readings, foreshadowing their popularity in following years. This chapter has charted the beginnings of a growing change in emphasis – from the influence of fathers on the psychic makeup of their children to that of mothers; from an interest in Shakespeare's portrayal of the psychic dilemmas of males to those of females. This prepares for some of the approaches of the next decade when feminists will establish a reciprocity with psychoanalysts and try to come to terms with Shakespeare's attitudes towards women. The next decade will illustrate the increasing sophistication, complexity and diversity of psychoanalytic readings of Shakespeare's works.

3

Shakespearean Psychoanalytic Critics in the 1980s

Psychoanalytic approaches to Shakespeare flourish in the 1980s, with less prominent theorists than Freud getting more notice than in earlier decades. Finding Lacan an invaluable resource, several major studies centre on the psychological import of Shakespeare's language. The real breakthrough, though, is in the area of object relations theory. Feminists who shun Freud for his primary focus on the male experience discover these theorists are more to their liking because they focus on early relations with family members and, in particular, place the mother at the centre of importance to a person's psychic maturation. But Freud still wields enormous influence, both directly and indirectly. In fact, some of the psychoanalytic scholarship of this period relies primarily on Freud and continues to concentrate on some of the standard topics, such as oedipal relations, especially between fathers and sons.

David Sundelson's *Shakespeare's Restorations of the Father* concentrates on two Freudian concerns: the importance of father figures (i.e. not just fathers *per se* but kings, surrogate fathers, authoritarian males) and male fears of women.

Viewing Shakespeare as almost fixated on father figures, he discusses the 'central Shakespearean pattern: not just the fall of fathers but their restoration; not only death and absence but revival and return'.[1] He emphasizes the importance of this pattern to the patriarchal culture of the history plays, a few of the comedies and *The Tempest*, and uses Freudian constructs and symbolization to offer a fairly conventional reading, arguing Shakespeare believes mothers must be sacrificing and fathers strong in order to establish stability and ward off the destructive influence of dangerous women. He views the weaknesses of the royal fathers Richard II and his successor Henry IV as resulting in a chaotic kingdom and a crumbling paternalistic structure in which all forms of rivalry – father versus son, brother versus brother, women versus men – abound because fathers cannot control their sons and assume their proper place of power. Conversely, the male hegemony and order are restored in the figure of Henry V, whom he views as a 'potent father and a triumphant son'.[2]

Sundelson sees this same pattern recurring when the patriarchy is destroyed in the tragedies only to be resurrected in the romances, and in the early comedies, such as *Love's Labour's Lost*, where paternal figures are missing and/or weak, only to rebound in the later comedies, such as *The Merchant of Venice*, where fathers and patriarchy assume a dominant but ultimately ambivalent stature in Antonio, Shylock and Portia's dead father. Again, he views a 'robust, protective father' as 'indispensable for Shakespeare's comic resolutions'.[3] Comparing Portia to Hamlet, he asserts she splits her ambivalent feelings towards her dead father and resolves her conflict with him by identifying with him and becoming herself the spouse/father that her father's will specifies. But this associates her with the 'engulfing mother' and 'androgyny', making her a 'horrifying' spectre, who embodies men's fear of loss, such as castration, and resulting in misogyny in such plays as *The Merchant of Venice* and *Measure for Measure*.[4] Sundelson ends by interpreting *The Tempest* as resolving these psychological problems in Prospero, 'the father *par excellence*', who combines both maternal and paternal qualities, protects his children from the threatening mother Sycorax, and arranges their rebirths.[5] He resolves the oedipal tensions by overcoming his 'paternal narcissism' and giving Miranda to Ferdinand, a representative of a strong future patriarchy.[6] Presenting Shakespeare as an apologist for a paternalistic belief system, Sundelson illustrates that a psychoanalytic approach can be useful in proving even the most orthodox reading. But his discussion of oppressive female characters raises more unorthodox topics and foreshadows the concern of later psychoanalytic feminist scholars.

Freud also figures large in *Shakespeare and the Experience of Love*, in which Arthur Kirsch applies two approaches usually regarded as incompatible – Christian and Freudian – to Shakespeare's plays. He sees the following parallels between the two: sexual guilt from the oedipal conflict is analogous to the Pauline concept of original sin; Freud's primal innocence and primary narcissism are akin to 'the quest for a return to Eden' in Christian theology; and the 'conception of the id, if not of the entire unconscious, suggests analogies with Christian ideas of eternity and of heaven and of hell'.[7] He alleges the search for love in Shakespeare causes distressing conflict, but it can also reach resolution in what St Paul describes as an ideal union of generosity and charity, or in what Freud calls mature mutual affection. The major impediment, he believes, is what Freud describes in the essay 'The Most Prevalent Form of Degradation in Erotic Life' as a polarization of affection and sensuality, when one venerates the beloved but regards the sexual act as disgusting and degrading, a concept Shakespeare could have found articulated in Montaigne's 'Upon some verses of Virgil'.[8]

Kirsch explores this dichotomy in five plays: *Othello*, *Much Ado About Nothing*, *Cymbeline*, *Measure for Measure* and *All's Well*. In an argument similar to that of Reid in the previous decade, he believes Othello sees Desdemona as a mother surrogate, whom he has idealized and exalted but whose sexual attraction to him causes him to see her as depraved. The situation of Beatrice and Benedick is much brighter, for Claudio and Hero act out the fantasies of polarized love that the complementary couple share and, thus, free them of that burden, allowing them to experience what Freud in *Civilization and Its Discontents* describes as the removal of 'the boundary between ego and object' and the achievement of a spiritual, psychic intimacy, embodied in the 'primal source of wit'.[9] Kirsch views Duke Vincentio in *Measure for Measure* as fulfilling the role of the psychoanalyst described in Freud's 'Psycho-Analysis' and bringing into characters' consciousness their repressed sexual desires. The Duke frees them of 'destructive libidinousness' and encourages a healthier view of sexuality – a strategy less successfully performed by the beneficent providence of Helena in *All's Well*.[10] In Kirsch's discussion of *Cymbeline*, he enlists Freud's *Interpretation of Dreams* to examine both Posthumus' dream and the play proper, looking at how Posthumus works through his unconscious, primitive feelings of sexual aggression 'as they would be in a dream, by displacement onto the figure of Cloten', whose death releases Posthumus of such feelings and promotes his spiritual rebirth, making him a suitable marriage partner for Imogen.[11] Culling ideas from a number of different writings by Freud, Kirsch illustrates the manifold ways in which Freud can assist a reading of Shakespeare, especially in uncovering characters' troubling repressed desires.

While Kirsch couples Christianity with psychoanalysis, the philosopher Stanley Cavell combines philosophy with psychology in *Disowning Knowledge in Six Plays of Shakespeare*. Although published in 1987, it contains some essays he wrote earlier: 'The Avoidance of Love: A Reading of *King Lear*' (1969); '*Othello* and the Stake of the Other' (1976); and 'Who Does the Wolf Love? *Coriolanus* and Interpretations of Politics' (1983). Although Cavell references the British psychoanalyst Klein, the more psychoanalytically driven essays are largely Freudian and look at the psychological/philosophical constitution of early modern manhood. Focusing on the dumb show and the play of Gonzago, his reading of

Hamlet is influenced by W. W. Greg's assertion they are 'a play Hamlet might have dreamed'.[12] He proposes the dumb show is an enactment of Hamlet's fantasy about a primal scene of parental intercourse and that Hamlet reverses one object into another by 'replacing the figure of Claudius with the figure of Gertrude (the reversal of a thing into its opposite)'.[13] Thus while we view Claudius triumphing over a sleeping king, Hamlet sees his mother as the powerful king kissing the crown; and while we see Claudius pouring poison into the king's ear, Hamlet sees his father inseminating his mother (passive transformed into active figure).[14] Enlisting both Freud and Klein's ideas about the importance of mourning, Cavell perceives Hamlet's problem as 'the refusal and the incapacity to mourn', an insight similar to that of Lacan.[15] His father's burdening him with avenging his death and telling him of his mother's 'sin' precludes Hamlet from lamenting the death and letting his father pass, so that he can assume his place in the world and establish his 'individuality or individuation or difference' from his parents, especially from his father.[16] This results in Hamlet's never participating in the world, which he sees as a theatre from which he is excluded.

Cavell's analysis of *King Lear* concentrates on the importance of eyes and vision, and contends a central motif is the avoidance of recognition, a desire to hide from oneself and from one another, induced by a sense of shame and a feeling of unworthiness to be loved.[17] Cornwall's depriving Gloucester of his eyes signifies his shame at his cruelty that 'cannot bear to be seen. It literalizes evil's ancient love of darkness'.[18] Similarly, showing 'how radically implicated good is in evil', Shakespeare has Edgar's refusal to reveal his identity to his blinded father link him to Cornwall and 'the sphere of open evil', a connection that indicates his shame for falling prey to Edmund's scheme and his inability to face up to his father's vulnerable, impotent state, which ends his childhood.[19] Lear's refusal to be seen derives from his shame of bringing misery on the wrong child and loving that child in an improper fashion, with Cavell intimating an incestuous longing.

He argues Othello's problem centres on his avoiding the recognition of the truth about his relationship with Desdemona – on an inability to acknowledge her as a sexual being, as separate and imperfect. If Othello rejects 'separateness', Coriolanus craves it, with his narcissism isolating him from human existence – a foreshadowing of the isolated and hidden condition of modern life. Cavell focuses on the missing father in the play and reads Coriolanus' obsession with warfare as a search for the father, a mission in which he competes with Christ. The allegorical component of the play consists of the founding of the city and the creation of the political, involving 'the overcoming of narcissism, incestuousness, and cannibalism'.[20] Cavell's views of *The Winter's Tale* centre on Leontes and his inverted oedipal conflict with his son, a situation that causes him to be jealous of his son's intimacy with his wife and to wish him dead, a fantasy that comes true. Consistent with Freudian readings, the concentration is on issues of maleness and the posing of questions about missing fathers and sons, rather than on absent or present mothers and daughters. However, Cavell's research embodies a growing trend in this decade of not relying exclusively on Freudian theory, but, rather, branching out to apply the ideas of other psychoanalytic theorists to an interpretation.

In the 1980s scholars continued to apply Jungian theory to Shakespeare's texts. In particular H. R. Coursen enlists it in his book entitled *The Compensatory Psyche: A Jungian Approach to Shakespeare* to explore the need for certain male characters in Shakespeare to acknowledge their anima and female characters their animus in order to reach 'individuation'.[21] He believes the tragedies of Hamlet, Othello and Lear all derive from their alienation from the potentially compensatory anima, and characters can be defined within Jung's eight 'personality types', based on two tendencies – extraversion and introversion – and four functions – thinking and feeling; and sensation and intuition. He views Prince Hal as the extraverted thinker; Gertrude the extraverted feeling type; Hamlet the introverted thinker; Othello the introverted sensation type; and Desdemona the extraverted intuitional type. Lady Macbeth, as extraverted thinker, and Macbeth, as introverted sensation type, are opposites, and it is her animus that overwhelms his anima. But as her repressed feelings come to the surface, his recede inside him, and at the end they are just as opposite psychically as at the beginning, except they have exchanged orientations. Coursen considers the one character who achieves individuation to be Prospero, who acknowledges his shadow, embodied in Caliban, and integrates his androgynous nature. One of the advantages of this kind of reading is it avoids the pitfalls of speculating about childhood traumas, but it tends to reduce Shakespeare's psychologically rich characters to allegorical constructs and the dramatic structure to predictable patterns.

This period also produced Shakespearean scholarship that moved away from reliance on standard psychoanalytic theorists. At the beginning of the 1980s an important anthology was published – *Representing Shakespeare: New Psychoanalytic Essays*, edited by Murray M. Schwartz and Coppélia Kahn – important because it officially establishes the academic acceptance and popularity of psychoanalytic approaches to Shakespeare. It contains a lengthy bibliography, which proves the burgeoning status of psychological and psychoanalytic Shakespearean scholarship. Thirteen critics contributed essays, some being parts of book-length projects, such as Kahn's *Man's Estate: Masculine Identity in Shakespeare*; Janet Adelman's *Suffocating Mothers: Fantasies of Maternal Origin in Shakespeare's Plays, 'Hamlet' to 'The Tempest'*; Richard P. Wheeler's *Shakespeare's Development and the Problem Comedies: Turn and Counter-Turn*; and Richard P. Wheeler and C. L. Barber's *The Whole Journey: Shakespeare's Power of Development*. These books indicate that psychoanalytic criticism had become a dominant force in Shakespearean studies by the 1980s. This criticism is different from many of the previous publications because it is written by literary scholars rather than psychoanalysts, who typically are more interested in psychological than literary theory. The 'new' aspect mentioned in the title of the anthology designates a turning away from primarily Freudian, ego psychological readings and simplistic symbolic analyses to a more diverse psychological perspective, one less reductive that relies on post-Freudians, such as Erik Erikson, Klein, R. D. Laing, Harry Stack Sullivan, Mahler and Winnicott.

The essay in the anthology by Norman Holland illustrates the evolution of psychoanalytic literary theory by analysing from three different perspectives Hermia's dream in 2.2.145–56 of *A Midsummer Night's Dream*, in which she sees Lysander smiling while he watches a crawling serpent about to eat her heart. Holland first clarifies how it would have been interpreted ten years earlier from a solely Freudian perspective, with the emphasis falling on the symbolic significance of the snake as phallic and the dream as embodying an adolescent girl's oedipal fears and anxieties about the sexuality of men, an approach he characterizes as illustrative of 'overly simple one-to-one symbolic equations so popular in the first exuberant years of applying psychoanalytic symbolism'.[22] He goes beyond that reading in applying Erikson's 'modal terms *intrusive* or *penetrating*' to offer a broader reading of the dream as indicative of a fear of an 'intrusive, penetrating, possessive lover', a situation that could relate back to an earlier familial relationship, perhaps with an overprotective mother, and one that reflects the overall thematic 'ambivalence in the comedy' about 'separations that are both loving and cruel'.[23] He characterizes such approaches as based on the assumption that dramatic characters can be regarded as real people. The third approach, which he considers the direction of psychoanalytic criticism in the 1980s, involves not applying psychological theorizing so literally and restrictively and instead introducing one's own experiences into an interpretation, and broadening the psychoanalytic import to a reader's psyche, topical cultural issues and universal human questions.

Much of the scholarship in the anthology follows Holland's third approach: it addresses broader issues, such as how the dynamics of the family impact human identity, and is more comprehensive in scope, looking, for example, at not just one play but the tragedies as a whole and the movement to the late romances. Typically the essays are devoid of arcane psychoanalytic terminology and theory, and do not speculate about the shadowy childhoods of Shakespeare's characters when the texts make no mention of them. Most operate on the assumption, however, that characters can be compared to human beings and theories that elucidate humans' behaviour can explain characters' actions. The 'new' scholars are less interested in phallic images and castration fears and more in social roles and identity formation. While Freud still wields influence, the major shift is from a Freudian oedipal to a pre-oedipal orientation, relying primarily on object relations theory and focusing on the importance of the early mother–infant bond; mother–son interactions rather than father–son relations; male anxieties about maternal figures and feminizing influences; the stages and difficulties of masculine identity; and the growing connection between psychoanalysis and feminism.

A primary concern of several of the essays is what C. L. Barber calls the 'central and problematical role of women in Shakespeare'[24] and Shakespeare's attitude towards them, as feminist scholars apply psychoanalytic theory to their analyses. Joel Fineman believes Shakespeare displays a 'defensive gynophobia', which he embodies in his male characters, who must distance themselves through misogyny from 'horrible, catastrophic women' lest they turn them into 'terrorized infants'.[25] Likewise, Adelman looks at how Volumnia has destroyed her son by depriving him of a nurturing upbringing and making him into a machine of war with no signs of vulnerability or softness.[26] On the other hand, David Leverenz argues Shakespeare is not 'gynophobic', but, rather, the world of the play in *Hamlet* is alienated from what females represent – sensitivity to one's heart and a private identity; the real tragedy is Hamlet's denying the woman in himself.[27] Shakespeare's women are powerful, and his men fear their ability to weaken or feminize them. The problem of assessing

Shakespeare's attitudes towards women and men's relations to them becomes a central concern of feminist psychoanalytic criticism of Shakespeare.

Meredith Anne Skura, both a literary critic and a psychoanalyst, contributed an essay on *Cymbeline* to the above-mentioned anthology and published *The Literary Use of the Psychoanalytic Process* the following year. Her essay focuses on the 'familial matrix that underlines all human experience' and contends Posthumus cannot establish an identity until he establishes a connection with his family, even if he has to recreate it in a dreamlike state because our lives are shaped by a 'symbolic force from the past'.[28] Her book is not about Shakespeare *per se* but, rather, the viability of psychoanalytic approaches to literature. Articulating one of the typical criticisms against psychoanalytic readings, Skura objects to regarding literary texts as 'case histories', in particular to subjecting fictional characters to a kind of clinical psychoanalysis that leads to probing the unconscious. Additionally, she complains that critics who look at fantasy and dream often still overemphasize childhood conflicts. She advises psychoanalytic critics to approach a text as good psychoanalysts would a patient in therapy, by rejecting reductiveness and embracing expansiveness, restraining the urge to mold a patient's symptoms into a textbook interpretation and being receptive to discovering the prognosis is other than it first appears. The culmination of her argument is a reading of *Measure for Measure* that highlights the application of the 'total psychoanalytic process' to a literary piece. Like an analyst, Skura 'works through' the different readings critics have offered of the play: she looks at the various themes and motifs, and notes the selfishness and detachment from human feeling in characters, the duplicity of Duke Vincentio in particular, and the associations of sex with death and violence, which result in sexual fantasies. Ultimately all of these complicated parts lead her to the unexpected conclusion that the theme of the play is fairly basic: it is about 'the difficulty of growing up', of being less narcissistic and more sociable, of shunning an isolated existence and engaging in a more 'fruitful exchange' ... 'of moving from the realm of fantasy to the social realm of language'.[29] Dispelling the belief that psychoanalytic criticism must be abstruse and far-fetched, she shows it can make literature more accessible and germane for the reader by uncovering topics pertinent to the psychological growth of all of us.

Skura also wrote a noteworthy psychoanalytic study of *The Tempest*, a reading that pits post-colonialism against psychoanalysis – two disciplines that have not been viewed as compatible.[30] She observes that both Prospero and Caliban are not so unique or different from some earlier characters and draws parallels between their relationship and that of Antonio and Shylock, Prince Hal and Falstaff, Duke Senior and Jacques, and Duke Vincentio and Lucio. As Prospero does with Caliban, each of the men of power lashes out in irrational anger at the 'Other', who serves a psychological function for the protagonist as an 'object' on whom he can project his unacceptable desires and appetites. Consequently, Skura does not view Prospero's treatment of Caliban in a specifically colonialist dimension and instead argues for a psychological significance. While similar to Shakespeare's other 'Calibans', the one in *The Tempest* is his first representation 'in its purest and simplest form [of] the original "grandiosity" or "megalomania" of a child'.[31] For her, Caliban is the 'willful child' in Prospero, whom he ultimately comes to accept in himself rather than negate in his quest to assert his adult sense of power. The play stages 'a final "crisis of selfhood"', whereby the 'old infantile narcissistic demand for endless fulfillment and the narcissistic rage and vengefulness against a world that denies such satisfactions' awaken at the prospect of ageing and death – the end of the self.[32] Skura believes Shakespeare's investment in universal psychological issues takes precedence over any political or colonialist motives and argues the paramount importance of psychology to an understanding of Shakespeare and to seeing literature as enhancing an understanding of the maturation of the psyche.

In *Shakespeare's Reparative Comedies: A Psychoanalytical View of the Middle Plays*, Joseph Westlund, like Kirsch, looks at idealization and degradation, and believes Shakespeare so clings to the ideal that it appears in almost all of his plays. He objects to criticism that 'overemphasize[s] the unresolved and the problematic' in the problem comedies and suggests that although these plays do not support idealization, their final message is positive.[33] He eschews Freud, whom he considers too negative in his emphasis on neurosis and debilitating guilt and, instead, tangentially draws upon Heinz Kohut's and Otto Kernberg's ideas about narcissism and focuses on Klein's theories that stress reparation, by which people 'make good what they feel they have spoiled or lost', as a way to overcome 'guilt and unresolved conflict'.[34] Westlund believes that Shakespeare's comedies provide a model of reparative action that reflects a benign world where characters can interact harmoniously with others. Labeling some characters as reparative, such as Viola, Duke Vincentio, Don Pedro and Helena, he observes they act as therapists, assisting others to overcome their anger, selfish isolation and self-involvement in order to gain self-knowledge. *As You Like It* is the exemplary play of reparation, because cruelty never becomes realized, goodness always outweighs the bad, and Rosalind's confidence and self-sufficiency 'mirror and confirm our own independence and self-esteem'.[35] While reparation and idealization are easy in *Twelfth Night* and *As You Like It*, later plays, such as *All's Well*, include more of the realities of life that prevent idealizations and make reparations more challenging, probably most so in *Measure for Measure* and *The Merchant of Venice*. Extending his attention to audience response, Westlund thinks the audience also tends to respond according to the psychological extremes Klein describes as degradation or idealization, and the idealization makes his plays into a kind of therapy for those who experience the treatment vicariously. That even he has to admit, however, that some of the comedies do not easily fit the 'benign pattern' indicates he may be trying to overlook the problematic and darker nature of these plays, which psychoanalytic theory is better at uncovering.

Richard P. Wheeler's *Shakespeare's Development and the Problem Comedies: Turn and Counter-Turn* is considered groundbreaking in that, while relying on Freud, it also cites object relations theorists, such as Erikson, Winnicott and Mahler, in whom Shakespearean psychoanalytic critics will develop more interest in coming years. Enlisting 'The Taboo of Virginity', in which Freud argues post-coital 'flaccidity' embodies men's castration fears, he detects in both *All's Well* and *Measure for Measure*, the primary focus of his study, as well as in *Hamlet*, *Othello* and *Macbeth*, a fear of women, especially potent female figures, whom the male characters perceive as 'imaginary specter[s]', able to make them feminine and powerless – a 'deep mistrust of impulses within the self that are provoked in men through relations to women'.[36] He also examines the oedipal phase of development, exploring the Freudian staple of incestuous desires in key characters, such as Bertram, the King of France, Isabella, Angelo and Duke Vincentio, and infantile resolutions of the oedipal situation, which result, for example, in Angelo's extreme identification with the authority of the father and Isabella's excessive chastity.

Relying on infantile development theories, Wheeler sees the problem plays in particular, like the tragedies, as centring on a lack of what Erikson calls 'basic trust', an integral quality to a stable personality that develops in a child in the earliest interactions with the mother.[37] In contrast, the festive comedies, especially *The Merchant of Venice* and *As You Like It*, in the figures of Portia and Rosalind, dramatize the fulfilment of trust in these faithful women, who provide assistance to others when needed and serve as a benign maternal presence. The romances move from loss, especially similar to that in infancy of the maternal figure, to restored trust in the return of the mother.

In the last section of his book, he broadens his perspective to examine more of the Shakespearean canon, looking at some of Shakespeare's plays from the perspective of 'conflicting impulses within the needs for trust and autonomy'.[38] In his discussions of *Hamlet*, *Othello*, *King Lear* and *Antony and Cleopatra*, he feels the eponymous characters' need to trust or establish a bond with another outweighs the efforts to assert power and autonomy, with the danger being they will experience self-estrangement by too deeply merging with another. Conversely, in the sections on *Troilus and Cressida*, *Macbeth*, *Timon of Athens* and *Coriolanus*, he feels the protagonists recoil from relations of absolute trust in order to search for autonomy, but ultimately experience only isolation and desolation. He labels the two groups as 'trust/merger' and 'autonomy/isolation' and bases these psychological patterns on family experiences of crises when a child must establish a self that is differentiated from the original symbiotic state of 'oneness' with the mother, as elucidated by Mahler, who sees humans' eternal struggle as one against fusion and isolation.[39] Wheeler's subtitle of 'Turn and Counter-Turn' refers to the wavering between trust and autonomy in the plays. He enlists Winnicott's theories on the importance of mothers' helping children to experience their separateness and independence from others, a process crucial to the formation of both trust and autonomy in an individual. He places *All's Well* in the trust/merger group and *Measure for Measure* in the autonomy/isolation group and finds that neither satisfactorily resolves the psychological tensions by the end. Some might find this categorization reductive, a criticism commonly lodged against psychoanalytic readings, but his turning to psychoanalytic theorists other than Freud leads to some new perspectives and adumbrates the approach of some later Shakespearean scholars.

Wheeler also helped *The Whole Journey: Shakespeare's Power of Development*, conceived by C. L. Barber, to come to fruition after Barber's death in 1980. Although co-authored by Wheeler, who transformed Barber's unfinished manuscript and notes into a completed study, the book largely represents Barber's ideas about the entire Shakespearean canon. His approach is primarily Freudian, concentrating on the expected topics of oedipal conflicts, fratricidal impulses and incest anxieties, and takes both a historical and a biographical perspective, a strange mixture of new and old approaches. It is historical in its assertion that the Reformation's deconstruction of Catholic ritual and the idolatry of the holy family led people to turn to the theatre for a substitute of what they had lost, a search for the sacred in the human family in a society that 'was modifying a ceremonial and ritualistic conception of human life to create a historical, psychological conception'.[40] He claims Catholic beliefs and rituals had helped people to work through early infantile conflicts, especially oedipal, but with the Reformation they futilely turned to tragedies to fulfil these needs. It is psychological/biographical in its argument that Shakespeare was working through his own personal dilemmas in his art, especially his father's financial destitution and betrayal of his mother, and his own rivalry with younger brothers – a technique common in the earliest psychoanalytic criticism and much maligned for its basis on conjecture, in which Barber indulges.

He sees Shakespeare as concerned with the dynamics of the family, but largely adopting in his early comedies and histories a defensive technique by avoiding oedipal concerns, especially problems with paternal figures, and instead focusing on the dependence on an overpowering mother who leads men to assume nurturing stances. *Hamlet* is the transitional play in which Shakespeare delves both dramatically and personally into the oedipal complex, in particular father and son conflicts. He asserts Shakespeare's gaining a social status higher than that of his father allows him to tackle the deferred topic at this point in his career. Because a religious solution is lacking to the problem the ghost poses to Hamlet, he assumes a messianic, sacrificial role himself and splits the father into the benign, deified dead father and the malevolent stepfather. In his search for manhood, Hamlet assumes a passive position with father figures and acts like a child, rather than an adult – an inadequate resolution of the oedipal conflict. To try to resolve his dilemma, Hamlet resorts to a theatrical instead of a religious technique, employing his play-acting as a means to vent his aggressiveness. Like Hamlet, Shakespeare himself uses 'his art for theatrical aggression'.[41]

The movement in Shakespeare's plays is between submission and assertion: the first half of his canon centres on the submissive response, embodied especially in the sonnets, which present the poet as living vicariously through the young man and adopting the role of a loving parent rather than establishing his own manly selfhood; and the second half, starting with *Hamlet*, centres on the heroes' frustrated attempts to assert masculine authority. The transition from tragedy to romance signals Shakespeare's attempt to 'restore a sense of the magical and sacred in human experience' and reconstitute a 'benign relationship to feminine presences' by discovering 'the Holy Mother in the wife'.[42] The romances dispel father–daughter incest, just as *Hamlet* and *Othello* resolve aggressive oedipal urges, and, as a result, Shakespeare serves as his own therapist by healing his psychic crises through the creative process. Regarding Prospero as an embodiment of the resolution of the conflicts presented in earlier works, Barber views him as being both a 'cherishing father' and an aggressive, assertive figure of masculinity, 'which in the early histories is subverted by the disabling presence of overpowering women'.[43] Barber's focus on early infantile conflicts and the difficulties of navigating the transition from earlier to later stages of development anticipates the pre-oedipal connections that will become more dominant in subsequent psychoanalytic studies.

Joel Fineman's *Shakespeare's Perjured Eye: The Invention of Poetic Subjectivity in the Sonnets* is one of the first Shakespearean studies to make use of Lacan's theories about the formation of subjectivity, which claim it develops in the movement from the Imaginary to the Symbolic Order, with 'the visual imaginary' being 'rupture[d]' by its 're-presentation' in language.[44] He perceives a difference in poetic stance between the sonnets to the young man (1–126) and the dark lady (127–54) and describes the first as embedded in a Petrarchan tradition that is based on visual praise called 'epideixis', a poetry of idyllic unity with the praised subject; and the second in 'linguistic language', 'the latter understood as a kind of self-consciously mimetic and paradoxical troping of the former', based on hostility and distance and called 'the paradox of praise', or mock encomium.⁴⁵ The subversion and parody in the dark lady sonnets happen when, for example, they offer praise that actually mocks the woman, or highlight her darkness rather than her beauty. When the poems imply the young man does not live up to an ideal, the collapse of the epideictic tradition is already present in them, although not to the same degree as in the poems to the dark lady. Fineman contends that, while Petrarch voices concern over the 'same kind of issues that later become the thematic center of Shakespeare's sonnets', Shakespeare exemplifies the inevitable inability of a poetic language to express a visionary and ultimately inexpressible ideal.⁴⁶ The poems 'articulate thematically the paradoxical duplicity of a language that is verbal, not visual' and, thus, 'substitute for a language of true vision a language of true-false word'.⁴⁷ They express for the first time 'a new first-person poetic posture,' represented in sonnets 135 and 136 when the poet puns on his name of 'Will', and give 'expression to the original verbal difference that the sameness of a visionary language is committed to leave out'.⁴⁸ This change allows the poet to 'speak in a persuasive way about ... his distance from himself', expressing the 'resonant hollowness of a fractured verbal self'.⁴⁹ The application of Lacan's ideas helps Fineman to offer a novel approach to the psychological significance of language, a topic less compatible with Freudian readings.

Harry Berger, Jr also turns to Lacan in a rhetorical approach to Shakespeare that concentrates on the latent hostilities between family members, especially fathers and sons, and unveils the more problematic motivations of seemingly noble characters. While his subject matter is standard for psychoanalytic studies, his approach is more novel. He is particularly intrigued by language games and the unconscious as a 'discourse network'. He lodges a criticism that has plagued psychoanalytic criticism almost from its inception, rejecting the assumption that characters can be treated as though they are like living humans who have a psychological history preceding the play's beginning about which the critic can surmise. He concentrates only on what readers learn about characters from the discursive level of the text. In his study of the *Henriad*, he looks closely at the language of Gaunt and Bolingbroke to show 'ritual speech is being used to hide, mystify, or justify other motives than those expressed, and that no one knows exactly what those motives may be – least of all, perhaps in some cases, those whose motives they are'.[50] Claiming a '"true inheritor" [is] a true competitor', he shows that lodged in Gaunt's formal language is resentment towards his son for replacing him and a desire to see him defeated for daring to challenge him.[51] Likewise, even as Richard II embraces Bolingbroke, his language contains a subtle mockery, which Bolingbroke detects and counters with some of his own, hidden in his eloquence. Berger looks at the 'latencies in the text' to uncover the '"inward wars"' ... 'that divide a father from his son and from himself', verbal combat that is concealed in the ritualized speech and can be uncovered by psychoanalysing the text.[52]

In an article on the Gloucester family, Berger does much the same with the language of both Gloucester and Edgar to detect the ambivalence they both feel for each other. Like Gaunt, Gloucester perceives Edgar as a potential competitor and wants to see him defeated, and Edgar resents his father, wants to usurp him and torments him when they meet, later in the play. There is a 'shared complicity of father and son', which Edgar avoids acknowledging by adopting the role of a 'redemptive or heroic figure'.[53] In '*King Lear*: The Lear family romance', he explores how Lear assumes the victim role and provokes his two elder daughters to abuse him, so he can avoid acknowledgement of his own sins, especially his cruelty to them, and how Cordelia does the same to him by provoking him to banish her, so she can break free of his hold on her and avoid her complicity by assuming the roles of victim and later of redeemer.

In 'What Did the King Know and When Did He Know It? Shakespearean Discourses and Psychoanalysis', Berger formulates a 'theory of discourses' largely derived from the aforementioned studies and certain features of Lacanian theory. He asserts we can get deeper into characters' motivations by studying their discursive mode rather than surmising about their infantile experiences. The discourses are the following: the sinner, motivated by a desire to be punished, judged or forgiven; the victim, whose refrain is 'more sinned against than sinning'; the saint, who professes pure motives out of a need to deny what is truly reprehensible; the donor, who engages in generous acts to make the recipient feel a bond of obligation; and the speaker of honour, who 'engage[s] in self-justifying language-games'.[54] He further clarifies the discourses are always 'situated in specific positional scenarios', such as the donor's discourse is related to the 'authority of the father or ruler'.[55] Illustrating his theory by applying it to an analysis of King Henry IV's long speech that opens *1 Henry IV*, he shows that the King's language veers between that of the victim and of the sinner, as he projects his own treacherous nature onto the Percy family, whom he has incited into rebelling so that he can use them as scapegoats to alleviate his bad conscience. He illustrates that he adopts the discourse of the unappreciated donor as well, deluding himself that he sacrificed his own chance at redemption by defeating Richard for the well-being of his country and, thus, avoiding the guilt for his own ambitious treachery. Berger's emphasis on 'speech acts' allows him to probe the deepest recesses of characters' psyches and explore such techniques as disownment, self-deception, displacement and self-exoneration – the intricacies of a self-reflexive discourse.[56]

Ruth Nevo's study is also largely interested in the unconscious – that of the writer, reader and character – based on 'Lacan's model of the transaction between reader and text'.[57] Lacan alleges 'the unconscious speaks' 'from within the speech of consciousness, which it undercuts or subverts', and the reader's unconscious must connect with that of the author and/or character and bring it into consciousness to arrive at a 'universal' interpretation of the dream, with the reader serving as both analyst and analysand.[58] Nevo relies on Lacan to realize her goal of discovering 'the "unsaid" that lies in the [w]holes of the discourse', which she uncovers through an 'oneiric' reading of the romances that approaches the literary text as though it were a sequence of dreams.[59] She reads most of the fathers – especially Pericles, Cymbeline and Prospero – as plagued by incestuous desires, incapacitated by a death wish, and split off into several characters, and concentrates on the fantasizing, which she sees as pervasive in *Cymbeline*. Sometimes introducing Shakespeare the man into her analysis, she regards Cymbeline, for example, as a 'proxy' figure for the author, who also struggles with incestuous desires for his daughter. Nevo views father–daughter incest as deriving from an oedipal boy's unresolved desire for pre-oedipal symbiosis with his mother, a feeling that makes him susceptible to fantasies of sexual union with his daughter, who in his mind substitutes for the mother. Claiming Leontes of *The Winter's Tale* regards Hermione as a mother figure, Nevo concentrates on his infantile anxiety about maternal separation and fear of engulfment and interprets the first half of the play as an embodiment of a childhood nightmare about the death of a sibling rival and a father-substitute – figured in the death of Mamillius. The split-off part of Leontes' personality is Antigonus, who, as a representative of his king's 'destructive, ambivalent will', must die as a 'scapegoat for [Leontes'] guilt', with Hermione being the agent of his rebirth.[60] Although the approach is complex, the resultant readings are not that different from those of other psychoanalytic critics who enlist a purely Freudian perspective, but it does illustrate critics' growing awareness of the usefulness of Lacan's theories to an understanding of the deeper nuances in Shakespeare's language.

Kay Stockholder in *Dream Works: Lovers and Families in Shakespeare's Plays* also focuses on the dream structure of the plays and arrives at readings similar to those of Nevo. She interprets the plays 'based on dream theory, which assumes the protagonist to be the dreamer of the work in which he or she appears', with other characters and the world of the play embodying projections of the dreamer's unconscious.[61] Although claiming any character can be regarded as the protagonist, she suggests 'the figure whose experience is most immediate and most strongly organizing' is the best candidate, although at times her choice seems subjective. In the comedies the choice is more challenging because 'often the most potent organizing principle' lies with a figure in the background, such as Duke Senior, Malvolio and Oberon.[62] Stockholder concentrates on 'the depth and intransigence of the dark forces embedded in the family', as well as male fears of strong women, which reach nightmarish proportions in their imagining 'women's cruel power to emasculate'.[63] Her analysis of *Othello* and *The Winter's Tale* looks at the homosexual attractions between the male protagonists. Her study is like that of Nevo: while the interpretative concept of her analyses is intriguing and innovative, the insights she derives from it are not that different from typical Freudian readings. In almost every play – and there are many – that she studies, she highlights incestuous desires, especially fathers' dark desires for their daughters and sons' feelings for their mothers. Consequently, her reading of *Hamlet* does not add much to the standard Freud–Jones interpretation. Although interpreting the 'dark image of woman arising from the corrupt male imagination' from a feminist perspective,[64] much of the study views Shakespeare as engaged with patriarchal constructs, and her choice of characters on whom to focus as dreamers is predominantly male, even in the comedies where the female characters are often more central to the play world.

Just as psychoanalytic criticism begins the decade of the 1980s with an anthology, so it ends with one – *Shakespeare's Personality*, edited by Norman N. Holland, Sidney J. Homan and Bernard J. Paris. The collection consists of 14 essays delivered by prominent psychoanalytic scholars – some of whom have already been discussed – at a conference at the

University of Florida in 1985. In the introduction Holland acknowledges the anthology arrives 'at a moment in literary criticism when its "subject" (in several senses) has disappeared'.[65] In one sense he is referring to psychobiography – inferring Shakespeare's personality from his plays and detecting aspects of his life reflected in them. Especially at the inception of psychoanalytic approaches to Shakespeare, critics engaged in this kind of exploration – to much disparagement – so it is surprising this volume appears when its major subject matter had fallen from favour years before. None the less, Shakespeare's character is one of the primary concerns of this anthology, with almost all critics concurring he harboured much aggression, deriving from his familial situation of having to experience 'his father's financial and social failure' and 'the birth of a young brother'.[66]

Wheeler adapted for the anthology a chapter from C. L. Barber's *The Whole Journey: Shakespeare's Power of Development*, which argues Shakespeare's father's loss of paternal authority because of financial duress deprived his son of the idealization of the father figure of early childhood, a situation that led him to create fictional characters who search for the ideal father he himself had lost.[67] His father's decline also complicated his need to express aggressively his own separate identity, so he channeled his aggression into his dramas. Sharing this insight, Kirby Farrell argues Shakespeare reacted against the patriarchy when he had Romeo and Juliet try to escape their fathers' control by finding meaning solely in each other. He developed a dramatic style of equivocation that permitted him to pay tribute to traditional institutions and values while simultaneously debunking them.[68] Sherman Hawkins believes Shakespeare displaced his aggression in his history plays and came to terms with his father's financial deterioration by portraying sons who vindicate their fathers through their own success.[69] Likewise, Holland argues some of his works focus on idealized relationships of fathers and sons, who serve as surrogates for the fathers, but also on the potential for the destruction of the father–son bond through aggression or erotic betrayal.[70] Paris agrees Shakespeare had a deep-seated need to release his aggression without feeling guilty about it and accomplished this through such characters as Prospero and Henry V, who engage in justified revenge.[71] Marianne Novy expands the thesis proffered by Conrad van Emde Boas years before that Shakespeare lodged his resentment at the birth of a younger brother not by explicitly writing about brothers competing for a mother's love but by obliquely referring to it in husbands' or lovers' anxieties about women's fidelity, reflecting an infant's fears of losing the mother's love.[72] The last two essays in the volume almost undercut the previous arguments: David Willbern claims we, like Shakespeare, project ourselves into the plays and know him only through our own reflection in his work; and Barbara Freedman applies Lacan's *méconnaissance*, or misrecognition, to assert we form a personality for Shakespeare by displacing and dislocating our desires into our conception of him.[73]

The other dominant theme of some of the essays is Shakespeare's attitude towards women. The anthology is a strange mixture of old and new: while psychobiography harkens back to the earliest psychoanalytic criticism, the feminist slant is reflective of a burgeoning new field in the 1980s. Holland claims Shakespeare presents his female characters as impediments to healthy relations between fathers and sons and advocates 'taming' to contain them, although he comes to trust them by giving women in later plays the power to provide 'for male-male agency'.[74] Declaring a misogynistic view of women as threatening runs throughout the plays, Carol Thomas Neely compares Shakespeare's fictional women to actual women in Stratford, as outlined by historians, to claim Shakespeare portrays females as weaker than they were in reality, yet more powerful, threatening and treacherous in an unrealistic sense.[75] Both Adelman and William Kerrigan feel Shakespeare has problems with sexuality, the former contending he tries to reconcile the sex act with the sacredness of marriage, and the latter arguing he expresses repugnance for female genitals.[76] Shirley Nelson Garner looks at five plays that centre on real or imagined female unfaithfulness to claim Shakespeare does not disparage women but, rather, his male characters discredit them by first idealizing them and then projecting their own sick fantasies onto them. She feels that, as his career progresses, he develops a more realistic and appreciative view of females.[77] The essays illustrate the difficulty of determining when Shakespeare is projecting his own feelings, fears and anxieties onto his characters, and when he is creating characters whose psychological make-up is quite different from his own. That some of his male characters regard women with suspicion and contempt does not necessarily mean that he shares the same views.

Feminists have long objected to what they perceive as the phallocentric orientation of Freudian psychology, with Madelon Sprengnether (née Gohlke) observing 'Freud's elaboration of the Oedipus complex ... does not serve the needs of contemporary feminism', which is not centred on the 'phallocentric formulation of femininity as absence' but, rather, on a 'gynocentric language of presence'.[78] Becoming more aware of the 'theories of object-relations, narcissism, schizophrenia, and separation-individuation' and their applicability to a mother and child's early bonding, feminists began to see that psychoanalysis could enhance their readings.[79] They became intrigued by the theorists' claims that images primarily of parents, especially mothers, and parts of them can be transformed into objects in the unconscious of a child and become internalized. Shakespearean feminist critics, such as Sprengnether (née Gohlke), Kahn, Adelman and Valerie Traub, began to apply object relations theories to their analyses.

Sprengnether's (née Gohlke's) essay '"I wooed thee with my sword": Shakespeare's Tragic Paradigms' appears in both a psychoanalytic anthology (the aforementioned Schwartz and Kahn, 1980, *Representing Shakespeare: New Psychoanalytic Essays*) and a feminist anthology (Lenz et al., 1983, *The Woman's Part: Feminist Criticism of Shakespeare*), attesting to the fusion of the two theoretical approaches. Her focus is not on studying Shakespeare's portrayal of and attitudes towards female characters but, rather, on his male characters' relations with and perception of their female counterparts and women in general. She asserts that while Shakespeare endorses the values associated with femininity, his male characters are angst-ridden, perceiving women as threatening, emasculating and adulterous, and, consequently, fear association with them will make them weak or feminine. They fear wives, lovers, daughters and mothers and view femininity as weakness, even though female characters themselves most likely are far from weak. In her essay in *Shakespeare's Personality*, she looks at how Shakespeare's use of boy actors to play women's parts allows him to consider gender issues, such as femininity as an unacknowledged component of maleness, without offending a male hegemonic society and subverting traditional gender constructs.[80]

One of the first extended psychoanalytic feminist readings is Kahn's *Man's Estate: Masculine Identity in Shakespeare*, an exploration of a series of 'psychosexual stages' that Shakespeare's men undergo in their formation of male identity. She bases her analyses on psychological, historical and cultural suppositions and explores a 'particular crisis' in each chapter, with 'successive chapters follow[ing] the ages of man' and progressing through Shakespeare's canon.[81] Disagreeing with scholars who believe Shakespeare shares the misogynistic beliefs of his age, she sees him as disparaging a patriarchy that bases its order and masculine identity on a 'destructively narrow and brittle foundation of identification with the father to the exclusion or repression of identification with the mother'.[82] Her study does not apply Freudian theory with its emphasis on castration anxiety but, rather, the theories of post-Freudian ego psychologists, primarily Erikson and his stages of maturation, with support from object relations theorists Mahler, Edith Jacobson and Winnicott; Peter Blos's studies on adolescence; and feminists Dorothy Dinnerstein and Nancy Chodorow, who study gender difference.

Ego psychologists emphasize the importance of the mother in a child's developing sense of identity and the differences between a girl's and boy's maturation: a girl's femininity develops in her relationship to her mother since they are of the same sex, while a boy's 'masculinity is threatened by the same union and the same identification'.[83] The boy's achievement of masculinity is more fraught with potential pitfalls, such as 'engulfment by the mother' and failure at the pre-oedipal stage of '"dis-identifying" from his mother and "counter-identifying" with his father': 'while the boy's sense of *self* begins in union with the feminine, his sense of *masculinity* arises against it'.[84] A man has to separate from his mother in early life to achieve individuation, only to re-establish a union with a woman in later life when he marries. Furthermore, while men maintained a pre-eminent status in the early modern patriarchy, with absolute power over the opposite sex, women exerted control over men by validating their manhood through their subservience and faithfulness as wives and daughters. These are some of the constructs Kahn applies to her reading of Shakespeare.

Kahn's first chapter on *Venus and Adonis* looks at 'an adolescent rite de passage in reverse', with Adonis rejecting a sexual relationship with Venus and an opportunity to achieve manhood, because he views her as a devouring maternal figure.[85] Unable to differentiate from the maternal matrix, he regresses into a state of childhood, sacrificing his identity and ultimately his life. The second chapter examines the two history-play tetralogies in which the male protagonists attempt psychological growth from boyhood to manhood through the father–son relationship and avoid and reject women. In the first tetralogy the sons are inducted into manhood through war and death rather than through merger with women, and compete with their fathers or resort to vengeance in the name of the father, actions based on patriarchal tenets that result in the destruction of the family and that Kahn believes Shakespeare is criticizing. In the second tetralogy the process is more successful, because sons form their identity through a reciprocity with their fathers with some room for 'free play, some space for departure from paternal priority and for experiences fundamentally opposed to it', a procedure that ultimately results in the son assuming the father's identity to maintain the family inheritance.[86] The third chapter on *Romeo and Juliet* looks at adolescence and the need to separate from parents by establishing an intimate relationship that supplants the bonds to the family. The conflict is between two different conceptions of manhood: one as public violence in the name of the father, on which the feud is based, and abuse of women to bolster men's faltering self-esteem; and the other as separation from the father and private union with a woman. Romeo tries to defy the violent patriarchal code of Verona that defines men and love as violent, and although he dies, he asserts his independence by rejecting the paternal concepts of identity.

The chapter on *The Taming of the Shrew* depicts the play as a 'farcical representation of the psychological realities of marriage in Elizabethan England' and a satirical depiction of 'the male urge to control woman', and argues the woman holds the power to confer manhood on the male, as Katherine outwardly submits to Petruchio and bolsters his public persona as a masterful husband.[87] The next chapter on *Othello*, *Hamlet* and *The Merry Wives of Windsor* considers the recurring motif of cuckoldry, equated with 'psychosexual castration' and an assault on masculine identity.[88] If women can validate a man's virility, they can also shatter it through cuckoldry. Kahn notices post-Freudians ignore Gertrude's cuckolding of her husband and posits Hamlet's shared shame with his father over his mother's sexual betrayal adds to his inability to kill Claudius. The chapter on *Macbeth* and *Coriolanus* once again highlights the fear and repudiation of everything associated with women – 'tenderness, pity, sympathy, vulnerability to feeling' – and the influence of the phallic culture on Lady Macbeth and Volumnia, who as both its victims and its instruments have become 'half men' themselves and encouraged the men in their lives to thrive on bloodshed and become 'unfinished men', who have not achieved a fully individuated, manly identity separate from them.[89]

The last chapter spotlights in five plays the passage from a dependent state in a family to independence and adulthood. Kahn interprets the image of a tempest and a shipwreck as representative of 'the violence, confusion, and even terror of passing from one stage of life to the next'.[90] *The Comedy of Errors* and *Twelfth Night* record the evolution of sexual identity from the 'narcissistic mirroring' of Antipholus S., Viola and Olivia, who begin their plays without having separated their identity from their brothers (twins in Antipholus S. and Viola's case), to differentiation from the family connection, and finally to adult independence in choosing appropriate mates.[91] The romances present the dilemma of trying both to seek an identity outside of the family and remain in it, with daughters serving as mothers to their fathers and helping them to achieve new identities as fathers. Shakespeare shows that when fathers pass their daughters on to other men, they accept the feminine by controlling it. Consequently, patrilineal inheritance, based on sons in earlier plays, relies on daughters in these later plays. But only Leontes becomes both husband and father and, as a consequence, wins 'the fullest acceptance of woman'.[92] While a trailblazer in psychoanalytic feminist approaches to Shakespeare, Kahn has been criticized for not anchoring her study in historical underpinnings that would consider the differences between early modern childhood and that described by twentieth-century psychoanalysts – a criticism often lodged against psychological approaches.

In a noteworthy essay on *King Lear*, Kahn continues to take a psychoanalytic feminist perspective, uncovering 'the hidden mother in the hero's inner world' and claiming Lear conceals 'his repressed identification with the mother', which results from the imprint of the maternal on the male psyche.[93] The play depicts Lear's deep emotional need for Cordelia to serve the role of his daughter-mother, as he approaches a decline into old age and yearns to re-establish a child's pre-oedipal symbiotic union with his primary caregiver. He regresses into a childlike state and rages against his daughters, whom he projects into the role of a rejecting mother. She suggests that only in his last plays, written in 'genres of wish-fulfillment', did Shakespeare 're-imagine a world ... in which masculine authority *can find* mothers in its daughters, in Marina, Perdita, and Miranda', and asserts maternal figures are very much present, even in those plays in which they do not tangibly appear.[94]

This chapter illustrates that Shakespearean psychoanalytic criticism burgeoned in the 1980s. But it experienced a set-back in 1986 when Stephen Greenblatt published an essay that posits the Renaissance view of identity differs from that of psychoanalytic theory, and, thus, any interpretations of Renaissance texts derived from that theory are 'marginal or belated' – anachronistic. While one can see in this period the early stages of the development of our concept of psyche, he believes it 'had by no means already occurred'. He claims psychoanalytic discourse 'functions *as if* the psychological categories it invokes were not only simultaneous with but even prior to and themselves causes of the very phenomena of which in actual fact they were the results'. He does not advocate the cessation of such readings, but directs psychoanalysis to 'historicize its own procedures'.[95] These insights are particularly alarming, because they are made by the author of the ground-breaking *Renaissance Self-Fashioning*, a book that gives support for the unconscious at least being implicit in the humanist concept of 'self-fashioning' or selfhood.

Understandably the essay has generated impassioned defences of psychoanalytic theory, some criticizing his approach of assessing the relevance of psychoanalysis and others following his advice by presenting historical evidence for the theory. One of the first to respond is Holland in his introduction to the previously discussed book *Shakespeare's Personality*. He observes that Greenblatt asserts identity in the Renaissance was based on one's 'place in a complex community of kinship, ownership, duties, privileges, and rights (by custom and by contract)', a fact he does not find inconsistent with modern psychoanalysis, which since 1930 has increasingly defined a self that is similar to that of the

Renaissance, one that is 'inextricably involved with its social surround'.[96] He claims Lacan, Karen Horney, object relations theorists and even ego psychologists regard the self as in constant interaction with a reality outside of itself, a world of culture and language, and asks the question, 'Does the fact that psychoanalysis is a result of the Renaissance rule out its being an explainer of the Renaissance?'[97]

4

Shakespearean Psychoanalytic Critics in the 1990s

In the 1990s scholars more regularly apply not just one psychoanalytic theory to their analysis but several, resulting in more complex, expansive approaches. Although Freud still has a marked presence, Lacan, Winnicott, Klein and Horney become more central to Shakespearean studies, and some theorists apply their own theories to offer a unique psychological analysis. Some scholars also combine different disciplines in their studies, for example, melding psychoanalysis with deconstructivism, cultural materialism and/or historicism. Several studies, though, highlight the continuing relevance and compatibility of Freud's theories to other psychoanalytic theories, claiming he provides a foundational basis for all of them. Feminist psychoanalytic criticism continues to have a large presence in the decade, with several important studies concentrating on male anxieties about female sexuality and overpowering mothers and women in general. Consequently, developmental and object relations theories assume a dominant position in these works, overshadowing Freud.

One of the most important feminist psychoanalytic books of this period is Janet Adelman's *Suffocating Mothers: Fantasies of Maternal Origin in Shakespeare's Plays, 'Hamlet' to 'The Tempest'*, a study, as the title suggests, of male characters' infantile maternal fantasies, including those of Shakespeare, in plays from *Hamlet* onwards and their adverse impact on men's sexual relationships with women and masculine identity. Fathers are either absent or weak, unable to protect sons from the contaminating, malevolent mother, embodied in every woman whether she be a man's wife, lover, daughter, mother or stepmother. Like Kahn, Adelman relies on object relations theories, especially those of Winnicott, to explore pre-oedipal anxieties, focusing on the male child's need to form his masculine selfhood by differentiating himself from the mother's femaleness. While there are a few powerful mothers in his earliest plays, their essential disappearance until *Hamlet* allows Shakespeare to explore sexual and familial dynamics and the construction of male identity without much complication. But the return of the mother in *Hamlet* signals the collapse of that relatively benign situation. The women who follow Gertrude are like her – 'more significant as screens for male fantasy than as independent characters making their own claim to dramatic reality'.[1] For Hamlet, Gertrude represents maternal contamination, spoiling him by his origin in her 'rank' body and consigning him to death by his conception. Her major crime is unruly sexuality, which he sees as exerting control over Claudius and inducing him to kill the King, an influence that in his mind accords her some responsibility for the killing. His fixation with his mother makes him more concerned with reforming her into 'the asexual mother of childhood' than in avenging his father's murder.[2]

Once Shakespeare introduces maternal sexuality into his plays, it dominates his tragedies, and the motherly body can never be denied but, rather, remains crucial to masculine subjectivity. The subsequent protagonists try to avoid the mother's malevolence either by merging with an idealized maternal figure – the strategy of Troilus, Othello and Antony – or excising all female presence and establishing autonomy – the approach of Macbeth, Coriolanus and Timon. No matter the tactic, the men cannot avoid the fears and suffer the same destiny. As the first set of men enters into sexual relations with women, they view them as whores, what Adelman terms the perception of women in the 'morning after fantasy', compelling them to make the women suffer for their sexual natures and 'excis[e]' ... 'their sexual bodies', such as Othello's 'revirgination' of Desdemona and Shakespeare's of Cordelia.[3] In the absence of this approach, the men have 'parthenogenetic fantasies of exemption from the "woman's part"', which they hope will fend off maternal corruption.[4] In *Troilus and Cressida* the female body is corrupted, but in *Othello* it is the male imagination that is diseased, a difference Adelman believes constitutes Shakespeare's attempt to dissociate himself from such fantasies. She interprets the storm in *King Lear* as symbolic of the contaminating maternal place of origin that surfaces not only in the lechery and cruelty of his two elder daughters but also in Lear, who directs his anger against himself for harbouring *'hysterica passio'*, or 'the mother', within his own masculine authority. Ultimately he dissolves into a child seeking the mother in Cordelia, whom Shakespeare has return as the ideal maternal figure and reward Lear for his suffering, but who must die for being the 'displaced and occluded mother'.[5]

In *Measure for Measure* and *All's Well*, Angelo and Bertram share the fantasy of despoiling a virgin and abandoning her thereafter because of her psychical transformation into a whore – another enactment of the morning after fantasy that reflects the incompatibility of legitimate sexuality and marriage, as articulated in Montaigne's 'Upon some verses of Virgil'. The close association of Helena with Bertram's mother renders them nearly indistinguishable, making her the embodiment of the maternal influence that overpowers the male child, who 'discovers that she is always the woman in his bed'.[6] The bed tricks rescue Bertram and Angelo from their fantasies, as they discover the soiling has taken place only in their minds. The ensuing marriages, however, are unsatisfactory to both the characters and the audience. *Antony and*

Cleopatra is an exception in that it imagines 'the possibility of a maternal space that is neither suffocating nor deforming', a benign concept that emerges in *The Winter's Tale* where 'Shakespeare figures the loss and recovery of the world in the mother's body'.[7] But in *Cymbeline* and *The Tempest* the former order is reinstated, with the domination of the father and the demonizing of the mother figure. Furthermore, Imogen must be revirginated at the end to help Posthumus escape contamination in his union with her. Adelman believes this inability to undo the cycle reflects Shakespeare's own ambivalence towards the maternal body, a feeling that haunts him to the very end of his career.

In *Desire and Anxiety: Circulations of Sexuality in Shakespearean Drama*, Valerie Traub illustrates the complementarity of psychoanalytic, feminist and historicist approaches in an analysis of Shakespeare's representations of sexuality in nine of his plays, with an emphasis on the following: the 'containment' of women's eroticism in *Hamlet, Othello* and *The Winter's Tale*; males' anxiety-ridden fantasies of the 'female reproductive body' in *1* and *2 Henry IV* and *Henry V*; the repulsion by sexual relations, which in its most extreme form associates desire with disease in *Troilus and Cressida*; and 'the pleasures and anxieties occasioned by homoerotic desire'.[8] Traub claims anxiety always accompanies sexuality, largely because of the social and political pressures imposed upon one's desires. Since Hamlet, Othello and Leontes feel vulnerable to the erotic power of the woman's body that can effeminize them, they develop a defensive strategy to deny it: they metaphorically and dramatically 'monumentalize' women by transforming them into 'jewels, statues, and corpses'.[9] In an argument that makes insights similar to those of Adelman, she observes that male anxiety about female sexuality causes men to view women as whores and trust them only when they are dead. She goes so far as to label this defence as 'the fetishization of the dead': she asserts the struggle between Hamlet and Laertes at Ophelia's tomb 'suggests an underlying necrophiliac fantasy' and labels Desdemona's demise an 'eroticized death', as Othello sexualizes his wife only once she no longer poses a threat to his masculine subjectivity.[10] In her discussion of *Troilus and Cressida*, Traub looks at how men's anxieties about women's sexuality cause them to view sexuality as a deadly disease and women as agents of a deadly, contagious infection, such as syphilis. The only sexuality in the play not viewed as syphilitic is male homoeroticism.

Like Adelman, Traub asserts 'the maternal [is] a locus of profound ambivalence' in Shakespeare's works and other early modern texts. She notes his plays, especially the *Henriad*, and psychoanalytic theory similarly view the female body as 'grotesque' and stage 'a conflict between "paternal authority and maternal priority"'.[11] She applies Lacanian theory to the *Henriad*, in particular the concept of the child's losing symbiosis with the mother and 'falling into a pre-existing order of culture that ... enforces an always-divided subjectivity or "lack-in-being"', a psychic castration signified by the phallus.[12] Unlike the Freudian reading of the *Henriad* argued by Kris, who views Falstaff as a surrogate father, she views him as the female grotesque body, a false phallus, a representation of the fantasized pre-oedipal maternal, from whom Hal must separate and differentiate himself in order to follow Lacan's Law of the Father and the established order of language and culture, one that segregates all things masculine and feminine. Hal achieves adult heterosexuality by rejecting Falstaff, the representative of the 'suffocating mother' and homoerotic desire, and engaging in 'sexualized violence and a violent sexuality'.[13] She finds fault with both psychoanalysis and Shakespeare for marginalizing the maternal, for not giving the mother a voice and identity of her own.

In the second part of the book she explores 'the erasure of erotic difference' – the separating of gender from sexuality – in particular reference to Shakespearean homoerotics.[14] She focuses primarily on female-to-female desire and female subjectivity, going against a phallocentric system that accords women agency only in regard to masculine needs. She believes in *As You Like It* Shakespeare presents a more receptive environment for 'homoerotic play', with Rosalind leading 'the play into a mode of desire neither heterosexual nor homoerotic, but both heterosexual *and* homoerotic', the beginning perhaps of 'what we know as modern homosexuality'.[15] Ultimately, she finds Freudian and Lacanian theories of homoeroticism inadequate and inapplicable to Shakespearean representations of same-sex desire.

Like Traub, Juliana Schiesari in *The Gendering of Melancholia: Feminism, Psychoanalysis, and the Symbolics of Loss in Renaissance Literature* looks at how women have been marginalized in a largely phallocentric discourse. While not devoting her book exclusively to Shakespeare, she addresses *Hamlet*, as well as psychoanalysts' conceptions of melancholia. Enlisting psychoanalysis, feminist theory and Renaissance historicism, she explores how thinkers throughout the ages have 'encod[ed] a gendered bias within the melancholic syndrome', presenting sorrowful males as in heightened states of awareness and creativity while characterizing mournful women as incoherent, demonic and unreliable representations of lamentation.[16] Likewise, men are described as suffering from melancholia, a condition generally regarded as a 'sign of spiritual greatness', while sad women are said to be mourning or, worse, depressed, a term she describes as 'banal and unprestigious'.[17] Schiesari applies a feminist reading to the influential essay 'Mourning and Melancholia' to illustrate that Freud regards the melancholic as creatively inspired and 'morally superior', resulting from a 'hyperconsciousness, of a stern and severe superego that judges itself' and others.[18] Since he claims in 'On Femininity' the superego of women is immature and in 'The Ego and the Id' a potent superego is dependent on bonding with the father, Schiesari sees Freud as 'implicitly reserv[ing] this particular characteristic for the male'.[19] After all, in 'Mourning and Melancholia', he refers to Hamlet as the most striking embodiment of the melancholic. She also finds gendering in Walter Benjamin's and Lacan's view of Hamlet's melancholia as a landmark moment signaling 'the advent of "modern" subjectivity', and clarifies that both Freudian and Lacanian models privilege the male subject, regarding the concept of loss (especially of the mother) more from a male perspective.[20] The discourse of melancholy exempts females, but at the same time usurps the 'lack' they represent as women.

Taking a closer look at *Hamlet,* Schiesari observes that melancholia, as embodied in Hamlet, expresses itself in an extreme misogyny and projection on 'women [of] the lack [the melancholic] would deny in himself', with Gertrude and Ophelia being the recipients of his 'profound denigration of women'.[21] Although Ophelia experiences loss and mourns, neither Shakespeare nor others view her as in a heightened state of melancholia. Lacan reads her as an object whose importance relates only to Hamlet's state of mind, punning on her name ('O Phallos') and reducing her into the 'lack' or loss of the phallus, of the link back to the father that denotes Hamlet's alienation from the world. Ultimately Schiesari claims 'mournful women [in all of these dialogues] are reduced to the banality and particularity of their existences and times, whereas melancholy men become exemplary of the "human condition"', with Shakespeare participating in this denigration of female mourners.[22]

The anthology entitled *The Undiscover'd Country: New Essays on Psychoanalysis and Shakespeare* contains several essays clearly written within the feminist school of psychoanalytic criticism. It includes studies by academics from different disciplines and psychotherapists employing 'Freudian, Jungian, Kleinian, Winnicottian and other psychological perspectives', with the emphasis being on object relations theorists and their explorations into pre-oedipal fantasies and the hidden and terrifying forces in literature.[23] Although the word 'new' leads the reader to expect groundbreaking insights, some essays reach conclusions made by earlier critics, even if they express the ideas in different terms, and some explore 'character criticism', an outdated technique criticized by such scholars as L. C. Knights and Holland. None the less, the anthology's essays reflect a broader understanding of psychoanalytic theorists beyond Freud and enlist several different theories within each essay.

The essay by anthropologist Philip K. Bock examines the 'multivocal avian symbols' in *The Phoenix and the Turtle* that embody the audience and Shakespeare's 'nostalgia for a lost unity' between mother and child, an early psychic developmental stage when children are still symbiotically bound to the mother, but on the verge of differentiating themselves into their own individual egos.[24] He further argues this poem and knowledge of early developmental theory can help us to understand Hamlet's dilemma: the prince feels ambivalent towards his mother, both wanting to re-experience his symbiotic union with her yet fearing her engulfment of him – an argument similar to that of Adelman. The essay by M. D. Faber takes up where Bock's essay ends, arguing 'the deepest urge of the Western tragic hero is to resolve the mystery of maternal ambivalence' and Hamlet, in particular, suffers from this 'reactivation of early object relations'.[25] Such a reading supports the Freud–Jones interpretation of the play, but places more emphasis on the oral aggressiveness of Hamlet's attack on both his mother and Claudius. Faber characterizes Gertrude as an overprotective, seductive mother, who sends her son mixed messages and encourages an unhealthy dependency in Hamlet, who displaces his desire for his mother with a longing for death. Lyn Stephens, a psychotherapist, offers a reading of *The Merchant of Venice* that applies ideas from various psychoanalytic theorists – Freud, Jung and Klein – and repeats some insights made by earlier critics, who see Shylock as a scapegoat and a 'carrier of many of the split-off and denied parts of the other characters (and of course, ourselves)'.[26] But the pre-oedipal, object relations orientation of her analysis leads her to make some intriguing insights about Antonio, who she feels embodies 'the mark of the feminine' and harbours 'unconscious maternal phantasies', because he is fearful of losing a son to another woman;[27] and about Portia, who is far from a maternal figure and who uses Shylock as a replacement for her father, on whom she wants revenge for his attempt from the grave to control her life.

Angela Sheppard focuses on audience response, enlisting Klein's theories about envy to propose a psychoanalytic explanation for why Troilus and critics view Cressida so contemptuously: our expectations of women are 'highly idealized', based on our view of the 'first and most important woman in our lives, our mother', and since we perceive all women as if they were mothers, it arouses our 'envy and/ or a sense of abandonment and rejection' when a woman shows herself to be self-sufficient.[28] Cressida is not perverse and criminal but, rather, a woman who follows her ego-ideal, which instructs her how to 'change the bad into something good (or even better!) or at least how it may contain the bad and prevent it from getting worse'.[29] She finds herself in an untenable situation and, instead of just accepting defeat, she decides on a way to survive. Sheppard relies on Freud's theory that because women do not completely sever their attachment to mothers, with whom they must identify in order to form their own selfhoods, they do not value autonomy as much. She believes this psychological explanation can account for why Cressida resorts to conciliatory strategies. Last, she labels Cressida 'the personification of disillusionment', the one who must herself face the hard facts of reality and, like a mother, disabuse her children of the illusion that mothers belong solely to them by introducing them to separateness and loss.[30]

The essay by B. J. Sokol, the editor, applies a Kleinian perspective, only to reiterate ideas expressed by others: Prospero engages in 'unconscious projection and psychic splitting of good from bad', with Ariel being the good, cerebral side he acknowledges and Caliban the bad, lustful side he denies in himself in order to repress his incestuous desires for Miranda.[31] That he ultimately acknowledges Caliban as his own bodes well for the healing of his psychic splitting, a process that allows him to accept his daughter's marriage and his own corporeal nature. Last, Sokol relates the images of feeding and the denial, or spoiling, of food and drink in the play to Klein's ideas about the 'archaic oral phase of development' and the necessity of 'oral terrors' to a 'fundamental sequence of growth' in order to argue Prospero provides a means for his enemies and himself to grow psychically.³²

Robert Rogers in *Self and Other: Object Relations in Psychoanalysis and Literature* devotes a chapter to Shakespeare's major tragedies to offer primarily a feminist reading and illustrate the usefulness of object relations, particularly the theories of Klein, to a deeper understanding of the cruxes of literary texts. He clarifies that Shakespeare's tragedies focus on separation or loss that causes intense depression or anxiety in the protagonist. Hamlet suffers from object loss that causes his selfhood to collapse – the obvious loss of a father; the loss of the 'internalized good mother'; and the 'psychologically comparable loss of Ophelia' because of her father's prohibitions.³³ Explicating Klein's theories about loss in adults, Rogers examines what she calls the 'depressive position', which includes object splitting, idealization and both damaging and reparative omnipotent fantasies – psychological conditions he argues Hamlet exhibits. Hamlet's delay in avenging his father's murder results from his not having sufficient time to work through his conflicted feelings of both hatred and love for the lost others, to restructure the 'representations of self and other that the mourning process requires'.³⁴ Rogers believes the 'transitional objects' that help Hamlet work through his conflicts are words: the 'Prince of Wordplayers' continually verbalizes his problems, 'play[ing] with words transferentially'.³⁵

Turning to *Othello* and viewing Desdemona as an embodiment of the pre-oedipal mother, he asserts that Othello is suffering from separation anxiety, just as young children do when they must be out of their mother's presence: 'Desdemona's imagined sexual departure [is treated] metaphorically as a departure in space', with the play 're-enact[ing] at the deepest levels of [Othello's] being some prior, painful separation from his mother as a child, an experience of separation that led him to become an anxiously clinging, jealous man'.³⁶ This reading harkens back to some of the earliest psychoanalytic criticism, such as that of Reid, that surmises about undisclosed childhood experiences. Likewise, *King Lear* explores abandonment issues: turning his affection from his children, Lear ironically experiences the same situation at the hands of his daughters, who become his parents as he regresses to a helpless infant. The syndrome pervades the play as other characters – Kent, Edgar, Cordelia, the Fool and Gloucester – are figured as children forsaken by primary attachment figures. Last, Rogers applies attachment theory to his analysis of Macbeth's dilemma, viewing Lady Macbeth as a maternal figure, whose threats of separation compel Macbeth to attach to her out of fear of losing her. Introjecting his ruthless mother, he loses his own selfhood; Lady Macbeth's aggressive personality forces a 'suffocating', symbiotic melding with her son rather than a 'potential space', where he can distinguish himself from her. Referring to Winnicott's 'false-self' personality, he claims Macbeth has so attached to his mother/wife that he becomes 'a lethal extension of her destructive personality'.[37] He credits Freud's essay 'Mourning and Melancholy' with influencing his object relations reading and acknowledges the seminal impact of Freud on subsequent theorists.

Like Rogers, Julia Reinhard Lupton and Kenneth Reinhard in *After Oedipus: Shakespeare in Psychoanalysis* view Freudian theory as the basis for all subsequent psychoanalytic theories and argue for its continuing relevance to psychological interpretations. They focus on *Hamlet*, *King Lear*, Freud and Lacan, and the interrelationship of feminism and psychoanalysis, expressing consternation that 'feminist discussions of psychoanalysis too often oppose the pre-Oedipal mother of object-relations theory and the castrating father of the Oedipus complex associated with certain versions of Freud and Lacan'.[38] They call this a false opposition, since in Freud's earliest discussions of *Hamlet* the idea of maternal loss reverberates as well as a 'structural imbrication' of oedipal and pre-oedipal theory.[39] The second half of the book concentrates on *King Lear* and relates Freud's 1913 essay 'The Theme of the Three Caskets', in which he reads the play by means of the casket motif in *The Merchant of Venice*, to Lacan's revision of Freud. Freud's view of the feminine as womb, wife and tomb is translated into Lacan's three orders: 'the first casket (womb) pictures the Imaginary and the second (wife) represents the Symbolic, the third casket, death, indicates the Real'.[40] Cordelia is read as upholding the law of the Symbolic by rejecting 'incest without castration', which her sisters represent, and, instead, advocating 'cultural renunciation and substitution'.[41] They claim the essay is seminal for later psychoanalytic criticism of the play: oedipal readings 'take place in the symbolic space of the middle casket, whereas pre-Oedipal ones, which emphasize the play's dream of maternal unity, are projected onto the fantasmatic screen of the first'.[42] Object relations readings are indebted to Freud's essay, with the first casket signifying symbiotic union of child and mother and the third casket denoting the collapse of the pre-oedipal stage by loss. The third casket represents woman as 'an enclosed void, a structure of occlusion whose contents are its dis-contents'.[43] Relying on Lacan, the authors assert the play is nihilistic and links woman with death, a reading indebted to Freud's essay on the play. Closely reading Freud's writings, they are able to show his influential impact on Lacanian and object relations readings of Shakespeare.

H. R. Coursen in *Shakespearean Performance as Interpretation* applies psychological, feminist and cultural materialist criticism to performance criticism. He believes that because Shakespeare appeals to 'what is latent, unconscious, and unique in each of us', spectators have different responses to productions.[44] He specifically looks at how Hermia's dream in *A Midsummer Night's Dream* can be central to understanding the psychic situation of both Hermia and Titania: the former 'resists a necessary progression [while] Titania makes a useful regression'.[45] Hermia's nightmare of a 'bestial' serpent is a reflection of Titania's actual experience: having repressed her 'natural instincts', the queen of the fairies is forced to explore 'the bestial undernature' in her union with Bottom, during which she regresses to make a 'reintegration with her psyche'.[46] Interpreting the serpent as a Freudian symbol of the male sexual organ, he reads the dream as a representation of Hermia's fear of leaving childhood and entering into adulthood and sexuality. He explains that if the serpent is viewed from a Jungian perspective, it can have a more positive significance of healing and regeneration, a necessary step that Hermia must take in order to come into full consciousness. He also looks at the psychological significance of Hamlet's disruption of his performance of 'The Murder of Gonzago', which he interrupts after Lucianus has killed Gonzago, but before the murderer makes the amorous conquest of Gonzago's wife. He theorizes Hamlet's unconscious breaks through his conscious plan and causes him to catch his own psyche, rather than that of Claudius, in a play that becomes his own dream. In a Jungian reading, Hamlet's problem is his denial of 'unconscious energies of androgyny, or the anima', resulting in deep self-hatred that he projects onto Gertrude and Ophelia.[47] Coursen ultimately asserts the psychological content of Shakespeare's plays can be adapted to performances and provides for more rewarding experiences for the audience than performances that shy away from it. He argues the enduring relevance of Freudian and Jungian psychology to subsequent psychoanalytic theories.

Barbara Freedman in *Staging the Gaze: Postmodernism, Psychoanalysis, and Shakespearean Comedy* applies primarily Lacanian, object relations and deconstructive theory to a reading of some of the comedies. Proposing a theory of theatricality indebted to Lacan's ideas about 'the gaze' and models of subjectivity, Freedman defines theatricality as centring on a consciousness of being seen, which is reflected back to the spectator, displaced in the very act of spectatorship.[48] It involves a 'fractured reciprocity whereby beholder and beheld [occupy] reverse positions in a way that renders a steady position of spectatorship impossible'.[49] Shakespeare's comedies 'reverse the look and entrap the audience' by misleading us to think we hold a 'position of mastery' and then mocking that position in making us realize we have made mistakes in recognition.[50] Visual appearance is figured as a 'site of errors', as illustrated by the identical twins in *The Comedy of Errors* and *Twelfth Night*, and 'visual disguise and illusion' in *The Taming of the Shrew* and *A Midsummer Night's Dream*.[51] Likewise, the comedies 'stage resistance to meaning'.[52] Freedman uses Lacan's term *méconnaissance*, or 'misrecognition', to describe our failures as audience and critics to find stability. Most likely responding to Greenblatt's prodding to historicize psychoanalysis, she observes that both Renaissance faculty psychologists and Freud and Lacan use optical metaphors when describing the mind, an argument meant to establish a connection between Renaissance and modern representations of the psyche.

She uses the term 'uncanny' to characterize the world of *The Comedy of Errors* and suggests we cannot understand all of the connections in the play, because it invites us to make sense of it yet insists on its own meaninglessness, 'assuming misrecognition as a principle of meaning'.[53] Both Freudian and Lacanian, her reading of *The Taming of the Shrew* asserts the play records the entry into the Symbolic Order and a repressive patriarchal culture that entraps people into sacrificing their real selves in order to adopt the social mask of society. The play enacts the Oedipus myth with a slight change: whereas the narrative of Oedipus 'identifies civilization with male payment for his own sexuality, [Shakespeare's play] identifies civilization with male control over disordered female sexuality".[54] Similarly, *A Midsummer Night's Dream* celebrates a patriarchal ideology, associating correct vision with the law and faulty vision with imagination. For example, Oberon claims the Indian boy was stolen from a king, while Titania offers another version that presents the mother of the boy as one of her followers who died and for whom she raises the boy in her absence. To present Titania as an 'erring spectator', Oberon squeezes the juice of the flower in her eyes and distorts her perspective, an act that validates his patriarchal ideology.[55] Men are equated with correct perspective while women are presented as irrational in judgment and erring in vision.

In her reading of *Twelfth Night*, Freedman enlists object relations theory, especially that of Winnicott, who claims humans have to accept loss and the separateness of objects, and children must gradually accept their separateness from the mother, developing a trust in the withdrawal and return of the maternal object. The mother must 'gradually disillusion the infant by carefully withdrawing immediate nurturance in accordance with the infant's growing capacity to tolerate frustration and to accept his separateness'.[56] She believes Shakespeare does something like this in *Twelfth Night*, leading us through illusion into creative play with life and then disillusioning us so we can accept our separateness, with the play becoming a transitional object to help us cope. The play records characters' attempts to come to terms with loss or disillusionment: for example, Malvolio's duping embodies the disappointments of childhood, especially maternal rejection, and the professional failures of adulthood; and although Viola's belief in her brother's survival embodies 'what object relations theorists term "trust in the reappearance of a good object"', she 'deals with loss through near-morbid over identification' with Sebastian.[57] Viola's statement of 'I am not what I am' indicates she accepts the loss of self upon coming into the Symbolic Order, while Orsino and Olivia try to replace their personal loss by achieving what Lacan calls *objet petit a*, an object of desire outside of themselves. Last, she asserts 'the guilt of the survivor syndrome permeates' the play, feelings that Shakespeare himself may have experienced for surviving the death of both a sibling and a child.[58]

Bernard J. Paris published two books on Shakespeare in the early 1990s that rely on the theories of Karen Horney, who had not received much attention from Shakespearean scholars before him. She rejects Freud's 'diachronic mode of analysis that explains the present in terms of the past' and leads to suppositions about characters' childhood experiences not delineated in the text.[59] Horney concentrates, instead, on adult defensive strategies, more suitable to a 'synchronic' approach towards character analysis, one that emphasizes what the author tells us about the present. In accordance with 'Third Force' psychology, she explains people inherently have an 'evolutionary constructive force', a 'real self' that compels them to realize their potentialities and fulfilment, but if this intrinsic nature is thwarted, as is the case for many of Shakespeare's characters, they resort to strategies to compensate for the thwarted true desires.[60] She delineates five defensive strategies – self-effacement, narcissism, perfectionism, arrogant-vindictiveness and resignation – each with its own set of values and appropriate code of behaviour.

In *Bargains with Fate: Psychological Crises and Conflicts in Shakespeare and His Plays*, Paris examines the tragedies, focusing on people's belief that if they follow the dictates of the defensive posture(s) they adopt, they will attain impossibly lofty goals in their 'bargains with fate'. A few examples from the many characters he studies will highlight his approach. Hamlet's dilemma is that his self-effacing posture prevents him from openly expressing his anger and aggressive instincts, a case of repression that compels him to vent his aggression either on himself or indirectly on others. When he violates his defence by killing Polonius, he seeks his own death as a way to make reparations for the disintegration of his idealized image. In the last half of the play he switches to an aggressive value system that allows him to reconstitute himself as an avenging angel. King Lear has both a narcissistic bargain with fate, that leads him to feel his position as king makes him a special person who should be indulged, and a self-effacing bargain with his daughters, whom he perceives as recipients of his undying devotion. While dividing characters in *King Lear* into the two camps of arrogant-vindictive, evil characters and self-effacing or perfectionistic, good characters, he does not read them in simple terms, as this division may imply. He argues both Cordelia and Edgar, for example, conceal vindictiveness behind their more noble defences, accounting for Edgar's refusal to reveal his identity to his blind father until it is too late, and Cordelia's leaving her father to her resentful sisters, who she knows will mistreat him.

In *Character as a Subversive Force in Shakespeare: The History and Roman Plays*, the 'subversiveness' of Paris's title refers to the 'conflicting messages' in the plays created by 'rhetorical inconsistencies, disparities between rhetoric and mimesis, and authorial blind spots and inner conflicts', all of which he attempts to unravel through applying Horneyian psychology to the texts.[61] In *Julius Caesar*, for example, Brutus has inner unconscious conflicts between his dominant perfectionistic proclivities and his repressed vindictive side, to which Cassius plays in seducing him to murder Caesar. Although Brutus and Cassius may seem like opposites, they are actually complementary: 'the dominant side of each appeals to the subordinate side of the other'.[62] As the play proceeds, Cassius succumbs to his more compliant side that seeks Brutus's love more than martial success, while Brutus is so dedicated to his perfectionistic side and idealized image of himself that he remains deluded to the very end. Paris regards Antony in *Antony and Cleopatra* as torn between his self-effacing side, which makes him susceptible to the more masterful personalities of both Cleopatra and Octavius, and his perfectionistic side, which compels him to follow his duties as a Roman soldier.

Engaging in the early practice of psychobiography, Paris attempts to infer Shakespeare's personality from that of his characters. Proposing his most powerful conflicts are between his perfectionistic, self-effacing tendencies – his stronger side – and his attraction to vindictiveness and violence, he believes Shakespeare's problem centred on how to vent his sadistic and vindictive urges without compromising his stronger need to be noble and admired. Detecting similarities between Antony and the poet of the sonnets, a man who feels both attraction to a dark lady of questionable reputation and self-disgust for his sexual vulnerability, he claims Antony's rhetoric reflects Shakespeare's own conflict: the first three acts are critical of the lovers' behaviour, while the last two romanticize their union. He believes *The Tempest* embodies his solution: Prospero satisfies his aggressive side by exercising revenge but also serves his more noble side by not hurting anyone and, thus, preserving his innocence. While viewing Shakespeare's characters and Shakespeare himself according to Horney's strategies of defence yields some probing insights, some critics have objected to what they perceive as forcing Shakespeare's characters into neat categories that do not do justice to their psychological complexity. None the less, Paris expands psychoanalytic studies of Shakespeare by illustrating the applicability of yet another theorist to his works.

The French literary theorist René Girard wrote *A Theatre of Envy: William Shakespeare*, based on a seeming contradiction: while taking an oppositional stance to psychoanalysis, he proffers a study of motivation that rests on psychological constructs. In an earlier work entitled *Violence and the Sacred*, he refutes many fundamental psychoanalytic ideas and finds fault with Freudian readings in particular. He argues that the concept of mimetic desire, the topic of his book on Shakespeare, is a stronger foundation for psychoanalytic theory than Freud's ideas about the ego.[63] Even though Klein's ideas about envy would have bolstered his readings, Girard does not make use of them and, instead, proposes his own theory, claiming Shakespeare, like other great writers, has a deep understanding of mimetic or mediated desire, a term he coins that refers to envy and jealousy resulting from imitation. He regards it as the major source of human conflict and a key to unlocking Shakespeare's plays, since he believes Shakespeare discovered it in the early 1590s and from then on it dominated his works. Giving special attention to 14 plays, *The Rape of Lucrece*, and the sonnets, his study begins with *The Two Gentlemen of Verona* and proceeds, chronologically for the most part, through the canon. He believes Shakespeare dramatizes the breakdown of hierarchical order, which makes people dissatisfied and desirous of what another has or wants.

He explores all of the permutations of mimetic desire or 'emulation', as Shakespeare calls it in Ulysses' speech on degree in *Troilus and Cressida*. He examines mimetic rivalry, in which characters imitate each other's desires by wanting what the other one has and competing for the desired object, with the 'interest' in the 'rival' often being more important than the object over which they vie, as reflected in the desires, for example, of Valentine and Proteus, Lysander and Demetrius, Hermia and Helena, and Claudio and Don Pedro. He postulates that 'successful rivalry extinguishes desire, whereas failure exasperates it',[64] the first illustrated by Hermia's lack of interest in Demetrius once he repudiates Helena and chases her, and the second by Helena's indefatigable pursuit of Demetrius when he rejects her and, instead, pursues Hermia. Olivia embodies the 'mimetic fragility of narcissism', when her self-love is shattered by Cesario's indifference to her, and she becomes attracted to Cesario's superior self-love.[65] He elucidates the different types of figures within his construct of mimesis: the self-defeating mimetic lover, who attracts his rival to his lover's charms and his lover to his rival's charms; the 'mimetic seducer', as embodied in Cassius, able to recruit conspirators to the assassination by playing on their need to choose not the same love object but, rather, the same victim; and mimetic doubles, as with Othello and Iago. He asserts 'our desires are not really convincing until they are mirrored by the desires of others' – not just our friends but also our enemies, a situation that establishes a bond in the pursuit of the same object.[66] Devoting significant attention to *Troilus and Cressida*, he describes Pandarus as 'the greatest symbol of mimetic desire and mimetic manipulation in Shakespeare' and the play as the most vivid example of mimetic desire degenerating into political manipulation.[67] He regards *The Winter's Tale* as the landmark play in which the destructiveness of mimetic desire is defeated in the symbolism of the resurrection – not just Hermione's literal one but Leontes' moral one. According to Girard, Shakespeare views envy as a major human characteristic and human motivation as intersubjective. While making incisive points about often elusive character motivation, he reduces Shakespeare's plays to one major theme, with his analyses becoming repetitive.

5

Shakespearean Psychoanalytic Critics in the Twenty-first Century

Feminism and psychoanalysis seem to be intrinsically related to each other, with studies that combine the two continuing to appear in the early twenty-first century. But with the burgeoning of historicism in the new millennium, more psychoanalytic scholars incorporate historical perspectives into their analyses. This new movement seems to be a response, either directly or indirectly, to Greenblatt's urging in his essay 'Psychoanalysis and Renaissance Culture' to provide a historical accounting for Renaissance psychoanalysis, to establish that such approaches have a valid basis in the early modern period. Some of these studies historicize subjects that are typically psychoanalysed; some historicize psychological constructs. But all engage in the debate started by Greenblatt to address the issue of whether psychoanalysis is being superimposed on a time period and culture alien to such concepts. Most set out to prove the early modern period and its literature share attitudes consistent with those of psychoanalytic theory. Lacanian theory also takes a more prominent stance in this period, and while book-length studies of psychological approaches that focus exclusively on Shakespeare continue to be published, studies in this period are typically more expansive, placing Shakespeare within a psychological context in which other authors, often his contemporaries, also fit.

Theresa Krier's *Birth Passages: Maternity and Nostalgia, Antiquity to Shakespeare* responds to much of the psychoanalytic feminist scholarship based on Freud and Lacan that views maternal separation as traumatic, creating in humans both a desire for the mother and 'dread of her mighty, procreative, and engulfing powers'.[1] Enlisting the ideas of Winnicott and Luce Irigaray, she argues that aggressive energy between a mother and child does not have to result in resentment and fear but, rather, can maintain an 'open space', what Winnicott calls a 'transitional' or 'potential space', between the two, allowing for both a psychically healthy connection and separation, and resulting in the child's expression of 'praise, celebration, exultation, exaltation, gratitude' – the subject of the book.[2] She takes an opposite stance from those psychoanalytic critics who emphasize the 'phallic order' in their readings and argues such texts 'repudiate the mother, abject the feminine, marginalize women'.[3]

While Krier's study is not devoted exclusively to Shakespeare, she does look at images of creativity, fertility and gratitude in *Love's Labour's Lost* and *The Winter's Tale*. She argues the aggressive male aristocrats in the former play feel envy, 'a Kleinian form of aggression', for the women and their 'bounty', and refuse to acknowledge their debt to the maternal.[4] She proposes the men learn gratitude, a maturity indicated by the shift in the play from Petrarchanism and humanism to the lyricism of the concluding songs of Spring and Winter that celebrate Mother Nature, reflected in the Princess and her ladies, as 'the good-enough mother who has nurtured us but also left us to our own devices in her presence' and, thus, created a 'transitional space' ... 'for those strong enough to ... entrust themselves to mutability'.[5] With regard to *The Winter's Tale*, she asserts Leontes' jealousy results from his feeling threatened by the fullness of Hermione's pregnancy and articulation of her desires; like the Winnicottian child, he needs a 'transitional space' to discover his own appetite. His repentance allows him to give himself 'over to the realm of generation and maternity' and rediscover his lost appetite.[6] She claims Hermione and Paulina, her surrogate, use aggression 'to hold open a space for the daughter'.[7] Krier's analysis underlines the usefulness of Winnicottian theory to Shakespearean studies and provides a welcome departure from the psychoanalytic feminist view of his mothers as fearful agents of engulfment.

In *Crossing Gender in Shakespeare: Feminist Psychoanalysis and the Difference Within*, James W. Stone begins by noting close readings of 'gendered subjectivity' have significantly waned, a decline he tries to remedy in his study of combining psychoanalysis and new historicism to read gender in Shakespeare by focusing on close readings of language. He critiques the traditional concept that 'man is the principle of sameness-unto-itself (self-identity)', devoid of any connection to women, and establishes its misogynistic foundation.[8] As his title suggests, he explores the troubling 'crossing of the boundaries between the sexes', which includes the transvestism of female protagonists in the comedies, especially Viola, and the debilitating androgyny of some of his tragic male protagonists.[9] The males' determination to define themselves as unrelated to the feminine ultimately proves futile.

In his discussion of *Twelfth Night*, Stone describes Viola's cross-dressing with the term 'hermaphroditic anamorphism, the quality of being and simultaneously not being one sex; of being both male and female and therefore neither one nor the other'.[10] He believes this situation basically 'straitjackets' her, 'confining her to a position of impossible in-betweeness' that traps her in passivity and ineffectuality.[11] Furthermore, he views Malvolio as her 'hermaphroditical complement', a 'castrato', caught in the trap of playing the eunuch.[12] Although creating disorder, transvestism supports the *status quo*, for the only way Viola can escape her double-bind is to dress herself in her female garb and enter into a marriage that reinforces the patriarchy. Likewise, Imogen's transvestism contributes to her 'erasure' and invisibility in a play that propounds parthenogenesis, whereby women are eliminated 'altogether from familial and national genealogies'.[13] He sees this as a pattern in the romances, where women become more and more invisible until they are eliminated altogether. Cleopatra seems to be the exception in this paradigm. Her androgyny is far more impressive and effective: while she can assume dominance and exchange clothing with Antony, she never sacrifices her womanly qualities of nurturance. Interpreting the asp as a symbolic representation of Antony, her child, Stone claims she dies breastfeeding her child while heroically killing herself, dying as a 'warrior mother', who 'remasculinizes Antony (her lover, her child) posthumously'.[14] Shakespeare offers 'a unique resolution to the antagonistic gender binarisms' operative in the other plays Stone analyses.[15]

Stone's reading of *Richard II* is indebted to Hélène Cixous, Irigaray and Freud, and spotlights the many 'un' words in the play, such as 'unborn', 'unking' and 'undo', that signify Richard's femininity. Applying Freud's essay 'The Uncanny', in which he identifies the prefix 'un' with repression, to Richard's use of 'un' words, he argues that because Richard fails to repress the 'lyrical and feminine voice within himself', which society views as unacceptable for a king, he fails.[16] Although critics have noted Hamlet's feminization and viewed it as an asset, Stone regards it as 'debilitating and horrifying' and the ultimate impetus for Hamlet's violence, as he tries to purge the feminine in himself and the realm.[17] He attributes the tragedy in the play to androgyny, as embodied in Hamlet's feminization and Gertrude's masculinization, a lack of difference between the sexes that indicates 'nothing is taboo, including incest, adultery, and murder'.[18] Othello's problems are his age and impotence, both of which feminize him, and, in contrast, Desdemona's masculine qualities that only highlight his inadequacies. Othello fears the consummation of the marriage has feminized him and conversely made his wife sexually insatiable, an unstable situation that he tries to rectify by killing and revirginating her to fend off his 'unconscious sense of male sexual inadequacy'.[19] In agreement with much of the earlier psychoanalytic feminist readings of Shakespeare, Stone's study views the feminine as a negative construct in contrast to Krier's views, as the feminist debate continues about whether Shakespeare takes an appreciative or depreciatory view of the female.

Philip Armstrong's *Shakespeare in Psychoanalysis* is an important study that surveys the progress of psychoanalytic theory in Shakespeare from the beginnings to the twenty-first century and highlights both its advantages and its shortcomings. He assesses the status of 'psychoanalytic Shakespeare', taking a historical approach to illustrate that 'Shakespeare has been both subject *to* psychoanalysis and a constitutive presence *in* psychoanalysis at least since Freud's inaugural formulation of the Oedipus complex'.[20] Concentrating primarily on psychoanalysis in *Hamlet*, he illustrates how psychoanalytic theories have impacted readings of Shakespeare, as well as how Shakespeare has been a seminal influence on the genesis and development of psychoanalytic theory.

The first half of the book resembles a survey, starting with the 'first-wave of psychoanalytic criticism' of Freud, Jones, Rank and Lacan, all of whom were preceded by the intense character analysis of A. C. Bradley, who 'concludes his reading of [*Hamlet*] at the very point at which psychoanalysis will take it up'.[21] Armstrong records how the play informed early psychologists', especially Freud's, conceptions of repression, the unconscious, the oedipal complex, projection, introjection, displacement, condensation, decomposition and the superego. Discussing the second wave of psychoanalytic theory and criticism, he specifies the impact on the reading of Shakespeare by ego psychologists – Erikson, in particular – and Jung, and surveys the approaches of some of the more recent psychoanalytic critics of Shakespeare. His reading of Lacan's seminar on *Hamlet* centres on Lacan's inadvertent allowance for a self-contained feminine pleasure, independent of male desire, with Armstrong ultimately claiming modern feminism derives from psychoanalysis and Shakespeare. But he also clarifies that the 'feminine principle' in psychoanalytic theory has either been 'rendered lifeless by the very system of signification within which the patriarchal order attempts to hold it, or else it manifests as that embrace which is itself both silencing and lethal'.[22]

Armstrong continues to outline the limitations of psychoanalysis by examining Wulf Sachs's application of oedipal theory to *Black Hamlet* (1937) and *Black Anger* (1947), in which Sachs, a medical doctor, tries to prove the universality of psychoanalytic theory, especially the oedipal complex, by applying it to the situation of a black immigrant from what was then Rhodesia. Armstrong explains that psychoanalytic theory leads Sachs to condemn the colonialism of postdepression apartheid in South Africa, yet also to justify the black African's 'continued dependency on white patronage' by postulating the black immigrant feels the same 'internal psychic ambivalence' as Hamlet: he is 'caught between two parent cultures' and, as a result, is unable to rebel against injustice.[23] Demonstrating its limited applicability, Armstrong judges psychoanalytic theory as too Eurocentric to come to terms meaningfully with 'otherness'. Looking at Octave Mannoni's *Prospero and Caliban,* he provides proof that psychoanalytic theory, particularly Freudian, can be used to justify Prospero's 'colonial' power over the island and its inhabitants. He last explores what he sees as another deficiency in psychoanalytic theory – 'a narrative of developmental progress, which is "heteronormative" in its psychosexual attitude', practised primarily by feminist object relations critics who regard homosexuality 'as digressive, immature and incomplete'.[24] He claims these critics, especially Kahn, try to impose a twentieth-century view of adolescence on the early modern period that does not share the same orientation towards sexual maturation. He examines how a heteronormative theory has impacted both the critical and performative response to *Romeo and Juliet*, in particular, by overlooking homoerotically tinged language, aggression and sentiments. While highlighting the intrinsic compatibility of psychoanalysis and Shakespeare, Armstrong asserts psychoanalysis has made a major contribution to the 'normalizing' of Shakespeare's texts, especially by directors, and proposes the surprising idea 'to take the Shakespeare out of psychoanalysis, and the psychoanalysis out of Shakespeare', a strange proposal in a book that devotes almost half of its attention to outlining the complementarity of the two.[25] None the less, he accentuates some of the deficiencies of psycho-analytic Shakespearean criticism that need to be rectified.

In his other book entitled *Shakespeare's Visual Regime: Tragedy, Psychoanalysis, and the Gaze*, Armstrong combines historical and psychoanalytic methods to explore issues of sight in Shakespeare's tragedies. The historical component of his study concerns the early modern technologies and philosophies of vision, such as maps, mirrors, perspective glasses and globes, and the impact 'the emergence of the new scopic order' had on Shakespearean tragedy.[26] The psychoanalytic component involves relating Lacanian concepts of mirrors and gazes to 'classical and medieval optical theory' and Shakespeare.[27] Rather than concentrating on characters' interiority, he applies Lacan to chart the exterior forces that impact identity, such as social class, gender and race.[28] Claiming 'the metaphor of the stage as a mirror appears ubiquitous in the Renaissance', he explains that the 'projection' of spectators' perception of the 'masterful image' of themselves in the mirror (Lacan's the 'Mirror Stage') is comparable to what Lacan calls the Imaginary, whereas the 'introjection' of trying to incorporate the mirrored 'displaced and alien images' renders the self inaccessible, as the subject tries to adapt itself to the gaze of the Other, what Lacan calls the Symbolic.[29] Hamlet 'typifies the theatre-goer confronted by the spectacle of her or his own subjection to an accusing and masculinist gaze' of patriarchal power.[30] The reason Claudius ignores the dumb show and reacts only to the spoken enactment of his crime resides in the difference between the Imaginary and the Symbolic. In the first he projects himself into the dumb show as the king, his exemplary mirror relation, not the poisoner. In the second, he reacts when he introjects, when he becomes aware of himself as the object of an accusing vision. Hamlet reproduces the 'uncanny gaze' of his father's ghost on Claudius.[31]

Presenting so many conflicting responses and gazes that it renders a single and constant subject impossible, *King Lear* reflects back to the audience their exile from themselves and concerns itself with sight and blindness, as represented in the actual blinding of Gloucester. Armstrong explores the 'mirror' identification of the Fool and Lear and claims that 'Lear's identity fractures into a series of uncanny *doppel-gangers*', with Cordelia reappearing at the end 'in the form of the Fool, Lear's "shadow" in the mirror'.[32] Last he concentrates on the scene at Dover when the audience is momentarily unsure if Gloucester jumps from the cliff, a moment in which 'the audience see themselves, as blind, in Gloucester's place, at risk of falling into the abyss between the "representation" and "reality"'.[33] The discussion of *Othello* centres on the concept of 'masquerades', a term introduced to psychoanalysis by Joan Riviere. Desdemona falls in love with the image Othello projects in his wooing narrative, his 'narrative mask', which compels him to incorporate this mask, 'adapted to the gaze of the Other'.[34] In turn, Desdemona introjects a false identity that she imagines occupies her lover's mind, as they both engage in a masquerade. The chapter on *Macbeth* introduces the debate over whether light 'stream[s] from the eye (extramission), or enter[s] the eye from outside (intromission)'.[35] Armstrong argues the play looks at the potentially deadly force of extramissive vision: the air-drawn dagger, Banquo's ghost and the other apparitions turn Macbeth into the object of a gaze, 'no longer the agent of extramissive vision'.[36] The accusing gaze of the ghost enslaves Macbeth to the gaze of the Other and denies him a 'position of scopic mastery'.[37] The audience, like Macbeth, are rapt and disempowered by the gazes of the ghosts. Armstrong contends the subject's attempt to exert 'scopic mastery' embodies the general dilemma of the modern person.[38]

An anthology edited by Carla Mazzio and Douglas Trevor entitled *Historicism, Psychoanalysis, and Early Modern Culture* consists of essays, half of which concentrate on Shakespeare, that explore psychology and history, as the title suggests. Freud and Lacan are the dominant psychoanalytic discourses, and *Hamlet* is the focus of three of the essays. This volume highlights the renewed interest in determining the advent of modern subjectivity, establishing a connection between methodologies that are often seen as incompatible, and giving serious attention to the tendency of historicism to overshadow psychoanalysis as a theoretical approach to Shakespeare.

The following scholars in the anthology historicize psychological concepts. Ann Rosalind Jones and Peter Stallybrass historicize fetishism, claiming it 'developed in the Renaissance on the boundaries of capitalism'.[39] Marjorie Garber labels Shakespeare's 'second-best bed' a 'fetishistic' object and draws parallels between it and Freud's couch to illustrate the linkages between historicism and psychoanalysis.[40] Carla Mazzio in an analysis of *Love's Labour's Lost* claims male melancholia is the outgrowth of a 'marked failure of oral expression linked specifically to an overdependence on books', with lovers being unable to express themselves in ways that had not already been expressed in print.[41] David Hillman explains that early moderns were preoccupied with inner and outer realities, the 'same spatial binary [that] figures centrally in psychoanalytic conceptions of the early stages of identity formation, where the division between self and other is thought to be marked'.[42] It is no more evident than in *Hamlet* where there is an 'unbridgeable gulf' between the exterior and interior of characters.[43] Douglas Trevor finds the roots for key Lacanian concepts in a Protestant interpretive mode that developed in the early modern period.[44] Katharine Eisaman Maus explores the similarities between psychoanalytic theory and early modern witchcraft, claiming both the witchcraft believer and the psychoanalyst are concerned with 'psychosomatic' sickness. Both see the individual as being invaded by 'internalizations of the external world' and being 'permeable to outside influence'.[45] All of these studies provide a historical validity for psychoanalytic theory's application to early modern literature, showing various events and concepts in this period were related to a psychological frame of thought.

While these scholars illustrate that historicist and psychoanalytic approaches can be symbiotically linked and a compatibility between the early modern period and psychology exists, some use historicism to question psychoanalytic interpretations. John Guillory believes, for example, that although psychoanalytic critics read Hamlet's soliloquies as indicators of penetrating interiority, they are more likely performances of philosophy, underscoring philosophy's limitations in comparison to the limitlessness of theology and intended to appeal to an elite faction of the audience. He ultimately agrees with Greenblatt and declares 'Hamlet's interiority cannot anticipate bourgeois subjectivity in advance of the age'.[46] If there is a psychological component, it 'might best be described as the sublimation of aggressivity', but he believes this is based on philosophy's countering the violence instigated by theological dispute.[47] For Guillory historicism takes priority over psychoanalysis. The essay by Jonathan Goldberg explores issues of sexuality, clarifying that while scholars have noted the oral images in *Coriolanus*, they have overlooked the anal imagery, which connotes both 'the dynamics of pleasure and pain that many readers will recognize as crucial throughout the play'.[48] He clarifies that because homosexuality establishes the anus as 'a site of desire', it threatens the 'psychic and capitalist' economies that require its sublimation, but because such 'modern economies' are not yet operable in Renaissance England, the anus may not require a 'civilized covering'.[49] This essay asserts that psychoanalytic studies of Shakespeare, especially of homoerotics, need to historicize their approaches to avoid imposing a modern view of sexuality on a time when viewpoints may have been different.

Carol Thomas Neely's *Distracted Subjects: Madness and Gender in Shakespeare and Early Modern Culture* historicizes the concept of madness, a term that early moderns eschewed because of its pejorative connotation and replaced with the word 'distraction', denoting a temporary, curable illness. Looking at the years 1576–1632, Neely sets out to disprove the opinion specifically of Foucault, who claims that attitudes towards madness in the seventeenth century were static and disparaging, with sufferers of mental maladies being confined to institutions that were visited by those who entertained themselves by gawking at the 'crazy' antics of the inmates. This characterization presents early moderns as barbaric and unsophisticated in their views, shamefully unaware of the nuances of mental imbalances. Examining medical books, doctors' diagnoses and case histories, dramatic texts, and anti-witchcraft tracts, Neely dispels these views and claims there was a 'renaissance of madness', during which early moderns showed marked concern, sensitivity and understanding for the distracted, who were institutionalized only as a last resort and usually for a limited amount of time, and more often were housed at home where they were treated by solicitous family members and doctors, who administered various benign treatments.[50] She argues it was not until the end of the seventeenth and beginning of the eighteenth centuries that the regressive view of mental illness began to develop, an unfortunate reversion fuelled in part by farcical depictions of the distracted in some plays by Shakespeare and his contemporaries. The years she studies are a hiatus in the dehumanization of the mentally ill. Neely credits this more humane attitude in part to the demystifying of exorcisms, witchcraft and possession, a movement that led to the 'secularization and medicalization of distracted subjects, separating them off from the supernatural and theological'.[51] As witchcraft declined, doctors and medical texts increased. She conjectures that, because women were most associated with witchcraft, their mental ailments attracted more attention than those of men, a situation that led to the recategorization of some disorders to include women, in some instances almost exclusively.

Looking at Mr S.'s *Gammer Gurton's Needle* and Thomas Kyd's *Spanish Tragedy*, Neely views these as some of the earliest secular theatrical depictions respectively of farcical and tragic madness, a portrayal that leads to the representation and analysis of madness in subsequent drama. Asserting that 'Shakespeare's plays provide the most numerous, extensive, and richest representations of distracted subjects', she looks at the rendering in *Hamlet*, *Macbeth* and *King Lear* of a specialized language to give voice to the distracted characters' mental conditions, a verbal characterization she believes leads to 'increased emotional intensity and psychological development' and invites the audience to learn how to distinguish between planned suicide and madness-induced self-harm; the distraction of women and the melancholy of men; feigned and genuine mental ailments; and 'natural and supernatural' madness.[52] These plays explore the physical and emotional causes of madness and the standard treatments, both physiological and psychological, the latter reminiscent of exorcisms but within a secularized context, and display the care and compassion with which the ill were treated. Both doctors' and dramatists' studies of women's mental lapses led to an intensified interest in women and a new classified illness – female melancholy – and its treatment, depicted dramatically in the case history of the jailer's daughter in Shakespeare and Fletcher's *The Two Noble Kinsmen*. Early modern doctors explored the interaction between the body and mind by noting how women's menstrual cycles and sexual desires impact their psychological constitution and often prescribing what we today would call placebos to try to cure delusions. With the interest in women's distractions intensifying, lovesickness, delineated as intense and often unconventional erotic desire that requires satisfaction and treatment with sexual therapies, began to be diagnosed more in women than men and explored more openly in dramatic characters such as Rosalind, Olivia and Viola. As a result, the study of women's desires gained recognition and led to the dramatic portrayal of fluid gender roles, more 'permeable subjectivities', and 'loosen[ed] boundaries between homoerotic and heteroerotic desires'.⁵³ These dramatic representations of forms of distraction expand human subjectivity and privilege female desire.

But not all of Shakespeare's plays enhance the knowledge of and sensitivity to the complexity of the human psyche. Neely feels that *The Comedy of Errors*, *The Merry Wives of Windsor* and *Twelfth Night* make fun of and, thus, degrade the mad subjects and the doctors or exorcists, a debasement she feels leads to the negative views of madness that become dominant in the early eighteenth century and other dramatists imitate by depicting demeaning images of bedlam and bedlamites. In reality, Bethlem Hospital in the early modern period was a benign institution that offered treatment intended to help the patients reorient themselves to family and society. She argues that from at least 1576 to 1632 the views towards and treatment of mental illness were enlightened and sufferers were treated with compassion, a perception that we have started to embrace within the last half-century. In fact, she claims 'our representations of madness often appear as mirror images of early modern ones', an observation that illustrates the sophistication of early modern views towards mental disease and their psychological orientation.⁵⁴ Like other twenty-first-century scholars, Neely provides historical evidence that psychological approaches to early modern literature, and Shakespeare in particular, are not anachronistic or erroneous but, rather, compatible in their view of subjectivity and the complexity of the human mind.

Cynthia Marshall's *The Shattering of the Self: Violence, Subjectivity, and Early Modern Texts* proposes a corrective to Stephen Greenblatt's thesis in his groundbreaking book *Renaissance Self-Fashioning* by suggesting the birth of individualism in the Renaissance was not as smooth or complete as he has argued. Her thesis is that there existed a 'counter-force to the nascent ethos of individualism', one that reverted to the old humoral psychology of the self as 'fluid, unstable, and volatile', and viewed individuality with scepticism.⁵⁵ She examines some of the literary instances of reversion that 'shattered' rather than affirmed selfhood, such as Elizabethan sonnet sequences, John Foxe's *Acts and Monuments*, John Ford's *The Broken Heart* and Shakespeare's *Titus Andronicus*. The violence in these works provided an emotional release, or 'psychic fracture or undoing', for an audience coping with the pressures of adapting to an emerging sense of individuality.[56]

The focus of Marshall's study is on a reader's or audience's 'pleasure in projected suffering such as that portrayed in violent Renaissance literature', a pleasure that Lacan calls *jouissance*, or bliss, and signals the negation of selfhood.[57] She combines psychoanalysis – primarily Freudian, Lacanian and post-Lacanian theories – and historical studies of Protestant and Catholic valorization of humility, submission and martyrdom to explicate the concept of sadomasochism, which she sees as a vital part of the theatrical experience in the Renaissance. What the early moderns knew as 'lovesickness, martyrological *jouissance*, or heartbreak, Freud theorized as sadomasochism', a similarity illustrating that psychoanalysis embodies ideas that appeared in the early modern period.[58] Lacan provides the crucial connection between language and masochism that allows for descriptions and performances of violence to permit a subject to vicariously experience the action and be 'pleasurably shattered, lost to himself'.[59] While briefly discussing the onstage mutilation of Gloucester, Cordelia's martyrdom and Hamlet's masochism, she focuses her attention on the eroticized violence in *Titus Andronicus* – in particular the rape and mutilation of Lavinia – to argue Shakespeare presents on stage 'the equivalent of hard-core pornography, pushing the erotics of pain, suffering, and dominance to new limits'.[60] His presentation of the mutilated Lavinia on stage does not allow the audience to identify with her or view her empathetically but, rather, to experience a sadistic identification with her violators. Marshall illustrates that psychoanalysis helped uncover an unstable dimension of early modern selfhood that a historical approach overlooked, a discovery that gives support to the viability of psychoanalytic approaches to the early modern period.

David Lee Miller's *Dreams of the Burning Child: Sacrificial Sons and the Father's Witness* addresses a subject that has always concerned psychoanalytic analyses – the relationship of fathers and sons and its significance to the patriarchal order. His approach is different, though, from earlier studies: while both Freud and Lacan are central to his argument, he enlists a method of historicism that incorporates ideas about desire and the unconscious. He bases his argument on the work of anthropologist Nancy Jay, who has studied how ritual sacrifice of sons ratifies patrilineal descent. He poses the question of why the sacrificial death of sons witnessed by their fathers appears as a motif in major texts of Western literature. The book's title derives from a father's dream about his son burning and returning from the dead to denounce him, a dream recounted in Freud's *The Interpretation of Dreams*. Applying Lacan's ideas about language and other social systems' splitting a subject, Miller professes patriarchy is based on the symbolic signification of the bodiless father. Because a father does not have a bodily relationship to a son as the mother who gives birth to him does, a father's connection 'is always nominal, legal, testimonial, and therefore speculative – in short, fatherhood is language'.[61] Engaging in the ritual of filial sacrifice is seen paradoxically as substantiating fatherhood.

Applying these ideas to Shakespeare, he believes Leontes' frenzy derives from his seeing his wife's pregnant body, which only reminds him of his own lack of a corporeal linkage to his son, whom he is obsessed with seeing as a physical double of himself. He sacrifices his family to validate his fatherhood and sees 'in the dead bodies of his wife and child, divine assurance that he really was a father after all'.[62] Miller claims this 'sacrificial economy' pervades Shakespeare's canon, from the conflicts between fathers and sons and the killing of children in his early history plays to the motif of infanticide in *Macbeth*. He views *Hamlet*, where a father's ghost proves paternity by having his son sacrifice himself to avenge his murder, as connected to *The Winter's Tale*, where Shakespeare finds a resolution to the 'dilemmas of sacrificial manhood' through the resurrection of Hermione, 'an extreme version of Hamlet's desire to sequester Ophelia and reform Gertrude'.[63] Miller provides a psychological and historical basis for the early modern theatre, when he speculates that Mary Tudor's burning of Protestants before an audience created a niche for the theatre where people could 'witness' illusory sacrifices.

When Greenblatt's essay 'Psychoanalysis and Renaissance Culture' appeared in 1986, casting doubt on the applicability of psychoanalytic approaches to Renaissance literature, there was concern about their viability. As this chapter has illustrated, scholars argue both sides of the issue with conviction and persuasion. Since the inception of psychoanalytic theory, there has been a problem with credibility, with Freud attempting to bolster the validity of his ideas by applying them to literature and especially Shakespeare. Greenblatt's urging to scholars to historicize their psychological approaches to the literature has prompted them to see numerous connections between twentieth-century psychology and various early modern concepts, thoughts and events. The debate has provided solid, tangible proof for a close connection between psychoanalysis and the early modern period and Shakespeare in particular, a compatibility that was often only assumed to exist but is now established. It is my firm belief that psychoanalysis and Shakespeare are intrinsically connected to each other, and because astute readers will always detect the interiority of his characters, they will turn inevitably to psychology to help them try to understand their motivations because they sense this is the key to unlocking Shakespearean mysteries. Hopefully, this study has illustrated how psychoanalytic approaches to Shakespeare have evolved from a limited Freudian perspective to a richly diverse discipline enlisting different schools of thought, a method of analysis that will undoubtedly continue to flourish.

6

The Feminine Oedipal Complex in *All's Well That Ends Well*

Both Freud and Lacan consider the oedipal complex as a fundamental construct of psychoanalytic theory, especially of psychosexual development. It is also a compelling topic in some of the greatest literature, including, of course, some of Shakespeare's plays. Using Sophocles' *Oedipus Rex* and Shakespeare's *Hamlet* as foundations for his theories about the phallic stage of infantile development, Freud primarily concentrates on the male experience and only later in his writings directs attention to the 'feminine Oedipus attitude'. Likewise, psychoanalytic studies of the oedipal situation in Shakespeare largely concentrate on the male perspective, on, for instance, Hamlet's repressed desires for his mother; and King Lear, Prospero and Pericles' incestuous feelings for their daughters. The desires of the women receive far less attention from both critics and Shakespeare. For example, Gertrude is regarded as a psychologically skeletal character, an underdeveloped figure on whom Hamlet projects his anxieties and desires. In *All's Well That Ends Well*, though, Shakespeare changes his emphasis by focusing on the oedipal complex as it applies to women, having the Countess in the first line of the play refer to her son as 'a second husband',[1] a reference that resonates with incestuous overtones. Nevertheless, psychoanalytic literary critics direct much of their attention to the oedipal dilemma of her son and slight the Countess and Helena's desires and motivations.[2] I intend to focus on the incestuous nature of both women and their relationship to each other, seeing them as active negotiators of the oedipal complex, not as passive recipients of male desires.

Shakespeare presents the two women as psychological doubles, both having lost significant male figures in their lives – for Helena a father six months earlier, for the Countess a husband – and facing the imminent loss of Bertram, for whom both feel a deep affection. The Countess has an intuitive understanding of Helena that permits her to detect her most hidden designs and desires, some of which the young protagonist herself is not fully conscious. At times Shakespeare uses the mother's knowledge to inform his audience of the deeper psychological recesses of his heroine. For example, it is the Countess who reveals the importance of the deceased Gerard de Narbon to his daughter, who cries at the mere mention of his name: 'The remembrance of her father never approaches her heart but the tyranny of her sorrows takes all livelihood from her cheek' (1.1.45–7). She also senses the young woman loves her son, an intuition Lavatch corroborates by eavesdropping on her.

She can reach the depths of Helena's psyche because she shares a 'likelihood' (1.3.118) with her, a likeness, resemblance or similarity,[3] seeing in her the qualities and situation that remind her of herself in her youth:

> Even so it was with me when I was young;
> If ever we are nature's, these are ours; this thorn
> Doth to our rose of youth rightly belong;
> Our blood to us, this to our blood is born:
> It is the show and seal of nature's truth,
> Where love's strong passion is impress'd in youth.

By our remembrances of days foregone,
Such were our faults, or then we thought them none.
(1.3.123–30)

This passage is undeniably obscure, enlisting vague terminology and indefinite pronouns. To make sense of it, one needs to consider that in the following dialogue between the two women, the Countess taunts her ward with the non-consanguineous, but none the less familial, relationship she shares with her and her son, a situation that smacks of incest. In this passage she seems to be remembering an event that happened in 'days forgone' when she was young, something triggered by Helena's attraction to Bertram. The words 'blood', 'love's strong passion', 'nature' (*OED*, 3b), 'thorn' and 'rose of youth' can all have sexual connotations, by which the Countess references her desires and erotic appetites.[4] She can be saying that in earlier days she, like Helena, had sexual feelings for a family member (perhaps a brother and/or father), someone of the same 'blood' (*OED*, 5, 7a), or of a common family.

Freud recognizes it is natural for a child 'to choose as his sexual objects the same persons whom, since his childhood, he has loved with what may be described as damped-down libido', and there is a '*natural* instinct in favour of' incest (italics mine).[5] Like Freud, the Countess speaks of 'nature' and 'nature's truth', which can refer to the 'natural feelings or affections between a parent and child' (*OED*, 'nature' 2b) that become 'impress'd in youth', or imprinted in one's being from an early age (*OED*, v^1 3). She explains that one develops an intimate affection before one is aware of its wrongness, before one is indoctrinated into societal morality; and that at a later stage the child begins to realize it is a 'fault', a reference perhaps to the 'incest barrier' that society prescribes by enforcing exogamy and criminalizing incest, a prohibition that Freud explores in *Totem and Taboo*.[6] Shakespeare allows for the reading that the Countess's own early incestuous experiences lead her to recognize the same impulses in Helena, who she intrinsically knows is attracted to Bertram for his family connection to her. As psychoanalysts observe, the cycle of incest that may start when one is young will most likely influence one's later behaviour as an adult, an explanation that clarifies why she speaks of her son as a 'second husband' and suggestively refers to his 'shape' (body and sex organ [*OED*, n^1 1c, 16]) and 'blood' (sexual passion [*OED*, *n* 13]) (1.1.58). The 'thorn' may refer to Bertram, whom she sees as 'belong[ing]' to, or being the possession of (*OED*, 3a), both Helena and herself, or the paternal phallus to which the women are attracted. The 'thorn' can be a symbolic representation of the incest that has become a 'natural' component of the women's lives.

When Helena in 1.1 reveals in soliloquy her determination to win Bertram through her own ingenuity rather than a reliance on the 'heaven[s]' or 'fortune', her language sounds similar to that of the Countess:

> What power is it which mounts my love so high,
> That makes me see, and cannot feed mine eye?
> The mightiest space in fortune nature brings
> To join like likes, and kiss like native things.
> Impossible be strange attempts to those
> That weigh their pains in sense, and do suppose
> What hath been cannot be.
>
> (1.1.216–22)

Although she can be speaking of the disparity in social class that separates her from Bertram, the other impediment that creates an obstacle for her, that places him so 'high' out of her reach, is the incest barrier, for she has had her 'breeding' (2.3.114) in his family. 'Breeding' denotes not just coming from the same lineage (*OED*, 1, 2) but also being reared or raised within the same family (*OED*, 3). The situation resembles that in *Totem and Taboo* when Freud examines the sexual mores of tribal members within a totem that make 'sexual intercourse impossible for a man with all the women of his own clan (that is to say with a number of women who are not his blood-relatives) by treating them as though they *were* his blood relatives'.[7] Likewise, Helena and Bertram's relationship may be non-consanguineous, but it is like that of a sister and brother, which makes a sexual relationship taboo. Evoking the power of 'nature' or 'natural affection',[8] she echoes the Countess, who also acknowledges the impact of nature on the passions, and states it does not abide by societal impediments and can 'join' or unite what is separated. Her phrase of 'join like likes, and kiss like native things' highlights the incestuous undertone to her words, of nature bringing together objects that share a 'like[ness]' and are 'native', or closely related to each other (*OED*, *adj* 6a), so melding them together they can hardly be distinguishable. The sexually charged words 'mount' (coital posture), 'eye' (vagina), 'kiss', 'feed' (copulate), and 'join' (copulate) suggest the erotic element of the linking of 'like likes'.[9] Psychoanalyst Pierre Legendre claims the incestuous 'wish is to be omnipotent' because it centres on 'desir[ing] what is impossible',[10] a sentiment that seems to characterize Helena's soliloquy. In the last lines cited above, she tells herself that just because something is 'strange', or out of the ordinary course of societal behaviour, does not mean it cannot become a reality, especially if it 'hath been' before. While perhaps speaking generally, she can also be referring to an experience that happened earlier in her life, just as the Countess alludes to events in 'days foregone'.

While not giving Helena's father stage presence before his death, Shakespeare provides us with vital information about him. Scholar Kent R. Lehnhof clarifies that rather than a Galenic 'accredited physician', he was a 'folk healer', whose learning is not from scholarly study but from 'manifest experience' (2.3.11, 1.3.218), similar to that practised by 'Renaissance quacksalvers', who typically peddled their sham cures in medicine shows with the assistance of women whose reputations verged on the sexually disreputable: 'The notoriously carnal nature of mountebank physic was the source of contempt among its early modern critics'.[11] Thus,

Shakespeare casts a sexual shading on Gerard de Narbon, in whose very name Frankie Rubinstein sees puns on *guerir*, meaning to cure in French, and *de nar-bon*, of the nose bone in French, a bawdy reference to the penis.[12] He seems to have been a sexual healer, who professed to know a cure for the King's disease – ostensibly a carnal ailment. The references to his 'profession' (1.1.24; 1.3.239) also bring to mind the oldest profession of prostitution. The Countess speaks as though she has personally experienced his skill, claiming 'had it stretch'd so far, would have made nature immortal' (1.1.18–19); Rubinstein glosses the phrase 'stretch'd so far' as a reference to coital potency.[13] Associating him with quackery and sexual healing, Shakespeare allows for him to have been a man of questionable morality, and for his relationship with his daughter to have been tainted as well, especially since Shakespeare aligns her with the female 'empirics' (2.1.121), who assisted the disreputable mountebanks.

She seems reluctant to talk of her father, telling the King, 'The rather will [she] spare [her] praises towards him; / Knowing him is enough' (2.1.102–3). Her extreme renunciation of him – she 'think[s] not on [her] father' and she has 'forgot him' (1.1.77, 80) – indicates repression and an attempt at denial, an inability to bring into consciousness the full extent of her relationship with him. When she goes on to say more, her language is cryptic:

> On's bed of death
> Many receipts he gave me; chiefly one,
> Which, as the dearest issue of his practice,
> And of his old experience th' only darling,
> He bade me store up as a triple eye,
> Safer than mine own two;
> (2.1.103–8)

On a surface level she is assuring the King that, right before her father's death, he shared many of his remedies with her, especially his most prized and valuable one that just happens to be the prescription that can cure him. But her word choice is unusual and strangely intimate for the description of a medicinal remedy. With the modification being ambiguous, 'the dearest issue of his practice' and 'only darling' can be references to her, especially if she is his most cherished remedy: she speaks of herself as a 'remed[y]' (1.1.212), and Lafew describes her as 'a medicine' (2.1.71). With the word 'die' in the Renaissance having a bawdy meaning of the 'little death' or orgasm, the reference to the 'bed of death' can mean more than the bed on which the father literally died. She can be alluding to acquiring sensual knowledge from her father during her times in bed with him, skills she can use to cure the King's disease. She was his 'darling', his loved one (*OED*, *n*¹ 1a), his 'dearest' for whom he had great affection (*OED*, *adj*¹ 2). If Gerard de Narbon enlists sexual means to treat people, Shakespeare can be implying she is the 'issue' or offspring (*OED*, *n* 6a) from a sexual encounter with one of his customers, especially since her mother is never mentioned or identified. He has told her to 'store up' herself or reserve herself from sexual contact with others, instructions appropriate to a lover. With the 'eye' having a bawdy meaning of the pudendum, 'a triple eye' seems a fitting description of the female genital, distinguishing it from the visual organs. Shakespeare can mean this ambiguous language to hint at a sexual component to her relationship with her father.

What gives credence to this reading is the plethora of sexual nuances surrounding Helena's 'curing' of the King.[14] The references to the King's 'languish[ing]' (1.1.30; 1.3.224), 'infirmity' (2.1.67) and 'fistula' (1.1.31) imply he is suffering from impotence, most likely resulting from syphilis – infamously known as the 'French disease' and, thus, suitable for a 'French' king. Just as the disease seems to be sexual, so is the cure. There are numerous intimations that Helena applies carnal remedies, including not just 'simple touch[es]' (2.1.74), or intimate caresses,[15] but actual intercourse. The most supportive evidence comes from Lafew both before and after the King submits to Helena's 'skills'. His language suffused with references to erections and orgasm, he claims she can 'breathe life into a stone, / Quicken a rock' (enliven the testes) and make the King 'dance canary / With sprightly fire and motion' (be able to fornicate with vigour) (2.1.72–4); she can 'araise King Pippen' (stir him to an erection) and 'give great Charlemain a pen in's hand / And write to her a love-line' (allow him to use his 'pen' or penis in love-making) (2.1.75–6).[16] In referring to himself as 'Cressid's uncle / That dares leave two together' (2.1.96–7), he clarifies his role as a pander, implying Helena will perform the acts of a prostitute or a 'traitor' (2.1.95), with a homophonous pun on 'trader' (whore or bawd), and attesting to her proficiency in her 'profession' (2.1.82) and readiness to do 'business' (2.1.98), or perform coitus.[17] After her visit he describes the King's restored health in terms of sexual rejuvenation: 'your dolphin is not lustier' (2.3.26); and he is 'Lustique, as the Dutchman says' (2.3.41). Shakespeare parallels this 'treatment' of the king with the other act of 'curing' in the play, when Helena tricks Bertram into having a sexual assignation with her, an act that further characterizes her as engaging in sensual behaviour and once again evokes prostitution.

Casting a libidinous tenor over her 'session' with the King, he creates a strong impression that the remedy Helena has acquired from her father is sexual. Moreover, the sensually charged meeting with the King bolsters this reading, since he functions as a paternal figure – as a father of his country, a surrogate father of Bertram (1.1.7) and by implication of Helena.[18] That the King is on his literal deathbed when she applies her treatment can give a lewd dimension to her father's 'bed of death', which she acknowledges visiting. Her sexually laden interchange with him can be a mirror reflection of her relationship with her biological father, as Shakespeare subtly implies a connection between the two men. The vague, allusive way Shakespeare refers to the father–daughter relationship reflects the secrecy that surrounds the forbidden act, a clandestineness that makes detecting incest a difficult proposition, as psychoanalysts acknowledge. Shakespeare's depiction of this illicit relationship should not be surprising since the topic of incest appeared in much of the literature of the early modern period, and 'incest between fathers and daughters ... is among the most frequent of sexual crimes'.[19]

If she does not act like a virgin, she does not talk like one either, even though she claims to be one. Although knowing of Parolles's lewd and dishonest nature, she engages in a lengthy, indelicate discussion with him about sexual intercourse. When he tells her men 'will undermine [her] and blow [her] up' (1.1.116–17) (penetrate and swell her up by impregnating her),[20] she does not display a naïve inability to comprehend him nor revulsion at his bawdiness. Rather, she enlists his vulgar language to ask a question, showing her understanding of his salacious references and ability to engage in some of her own: 'Is there no military policy how virgins might blow up men?' (1.1.119–20). Instead of being the passive recipient of a man's sexual advances, she wants to assume the dominant role and 'blow up' a man, or induce him to have an orgasm, perhaps by oral stimulation, and tells Parolles she 'will stand for't a little, though therefore [she] die[s] a virgin' (1.1.131–2), obscenely punning on 'stand' and 'die' even while professing her virginity.[21] Her proclamations of chastity are at odds with her libidinous knowledge and language, a contradiction that suggests she only projects a façade of virginity and Parolles is closer to the truth about her when proclaiming virginity 'being once lost, may be ten times found' (1.1.128–9). With chastity being difficult to prove, a woman who has lost her virginity can always proclaim otherwise and still be believed, as may be the case with Helena. Since after this conversation she has a soliloquy that ends with an allusion to a 'project' involving the 'king's disease' (1.1.224), Shakespeare gives us the first clues she is contemplating how to 'blow up' the King without compromising her professions of virginity and her chances of attaining Bertram as her own. The signs of promiscuity in Helena can signify an early indoctrination into sexualization. Psychoanalysts have observed that 'girls who have been victims of incest see very few alternatives to prostitution upon reaching adulthood'.[22]

At the play's beginning the Countess calls attention to Helena's 'excessive grief' (1.1.51–2) for her father, mourning that is so demonstrable she warns her against it. Scholars note the similarity to *Hamlet*, in which Shakespeare underscores the Danish prince's public displays of grief months after his father's death – one of the first signs that Hamlet is suffering from an oedipal complex, just as Helena's grief may indicate the same emotions.[23] Her mourning is excessive because her relationship with her father was more intense than the normal one between child and parent. When Bertram leaves her too, her response is extreme as well:

> I think not on my father,
> And these great tears grace his remembrance more
> Than those I shed for him. What was he like?
> I have forgot him; my imagination
> Carries no favour in't but Bertram's.
> I am undone; there is no living, none,
> If Bertram be away; 'twere all one
> That I should love a bright particular star
> And think to wed it, he is so above me.
> ...
>
> 'Twas pretty, though a plague
> To see him every hour; to sit and draw
> His arched brows, his hawking eye, his curls,
> In our heart's table – heart too capable
> Of every line and trick of his sweet favour.
> But now he's gone, and my idolatrous fancy
> Must sanctify his relics.
>   (1.1.77–85; 90–6)

What makes this passage so difficult to decipher is the ambiguity of pronoun reference. Because she speaks simultaneously of her father and Bertram, we are not certain at times throughout the soliloquy to which man she is referring. Since both men are 'lost' to her, she could very well be referring to either one or both at once. The obscurity permits Shakespeare to reveal her projection or transference of her feelings for her father onto Bertram, the only other male in her life with whom she has a familial connection. Because it is highly doubtful she has 'forgot[ten]' her father, as she claims, she most likely has identified her father with Bertram.[24] With her 'sorrows' for her father having 'tyranny' over 'her heart' (1.1.46), or absolute control over her, she transfers that sovereignty to Bertram, his image becoming impressed, or 'capable', on her 'heart' and replacing that of her father. Idealizing the doubled Bertram and her father as a way of denying the reality of her feelings, she 'sanctif[ies]' them and herself, purging the relationship in her mind of any sinfulness (*OED*, *v* 5a).

Just as the speech begins by melding the two men into one, so it ends, with her ostensibly referring to Bertram in words that more appropriately apply to her dead father: he is 'gone' or deceased (*OED*, *adj* 2), and she consecrates his 'relics', a word that often refers to the 'physical remains' of a deceased person (*OED*, *n* 1a, 3a). She views Bertram as a 'relic', or a 'physical reminder or surviving trace' of her father (*OED*, *n* 4c), just as the Countess regards him as the surviving embodiment of his father. She is attracted to him as a substitute for her father, not for who he actually is. This explains her dedication to a man with whom she shares no compatibility and who displays no redeeming character traits; and her refusal of the King's offer to elevate her social stature by marrying her to a man of more distinction than the Count of Rossillion. She wants only Bertram. Psychoanalysts are aware of the cyclical effects of incest, that 'in many cases the person who commits incest has in turn suffered it, and just as frequently the psychopathological distortions that are the cause of incest are spread throughout the whole family group'.[25] Shakespeare suggests both Helena and the Countess have had inappropriate familial relations that compel them to duplicate them with other family members.

Shakespeare emphasizes Bertram's significance to her by focusing on the exchange of rings at the play's end. Bertram stipulates he will become her true husband only if she can *'show [him] a child begotten of [her] body that [he is] father to'* and *'get the ring upon [his] finger'* (3.2.56–8) – a ring she later explains 'downward hath succeeded in his house / From son to son some four or five descents / Since the first father wore it' (3.7.23–5). With the ring being a bawdy symbol of the pudendum,[26] Shakespeare can be using it to signify that she passes her 'ring' from father to son, who becomes a surrogate for her father, and that incest is part of a family cycle 'closed to consciousness'.[27] There is another ring, given to her by the King, that she, in turn, gives to Bertram after the bed trick, yet again a ring that passes from a father figure to a son. If she has sexual relations with the King, she again passes her 'ring' from father to son, with the rings underscoring the incestuous cycle and the substitution of sons for fathers.

Helena's attitudes and behaviour towards Bertram bear all of the markings of an incestuous attraction. Displaying a fixation typical for people who have not resolved the oedipal stage, she claims to think only of him. She is so desperate to get him that she goes to extreme and subversive lengths: she follows him to Paris and stalks him throughout the play; assumes a typically male role of a healer and places her so-called 'virginity' in jeopardy; oversteps the boundaries of the patriarchy by insisting on choosing her own husband; and tricks him into unknowingly having intercourse with her. Psychoanalysts describe this 'greediness' for the incestuous object as pathological and note the presence of an 'unbearable separation anxiety',[28] which Helena displays when she overreacts to Bertram's removal to Paris and professes to be 'undone; there is no living, none, / If Bertram be away'. They observe that perpetrators of incest tend to 'engulf' the objects of their desire by seeing them as 'mere extension[s] of themselves' and ignoring their wishes; they 'use' and 'possess' them, 'with neither regard nor respect for [their] autonomy and individuality'.[29] Being related to the objects of desire, the perpetrators view them as doubles whom they can control. Psychoanalysts attribute this possessiveness to 'the process of pre-oedipal differentiation [being] too weak and precarious'.[30] Certainly Helena fits this profile: she acts as if she owns Bertram and can do whatever she wants with him, never acknowledging his rejections of her and repeated attempts to be rid of her. She is single-minded in her pursuit and will not stop until she gets him, even though he objects every step of the way. Freud was the first to propose that the trauma of childhood sexual abuse leads to later psychic damage, that 'the Oedipus complex is the nuclear complex of the neuroses'.[31] Helena's obsessive behaviour indicates such damage.

When confronting her about her desires, the Countess bombards her double with the incestuous nature of her attachment to her son and repeatedly calls herself her 'mother' (1.3.132, 134, 135, 136, 137, 142, 143, 145, 148, 155, 163) and Helena her 'daughter' (1.3.147, 163). Although Helena denies the connection, Bertram's mother will not hear of it and ceaselessly reiterates their mother/daughter bond. She claims that while she did not give birth to her, she is so 'native' (1.3.141) to her, or shares such a similar constitution (*OED*, *adj* 1a) and familial situation, that it is as if they are related by birth. Asserting her 'love' could not be 'more rooted' (4.5.12) if she had given birth to her, she feels a deep attachment to her and belabours the family connection because she herself is attracted to the incestuous element of the relationship. She relishes imagining and talking about it and wants it to become a reality. In *Totem and Taboo* Freud refers to an older woman who, because her 'marriage relation has come to a premature end' identifies with her children in order to vicariously experience sexual desire through them.[32] This can be the basis of the Countess's relationship with Helena: both women love Bertram, but because he leaves his mother to avoid the incestuous component of their relationship, she understands her only means of realizing her attraction for her son is through her double, whose youth allows her to pursue him relentlessly and whose lack of a consanguineous connection makes their union less prohibited.[33] She splits off aspects of herself, projects her desires for her son onto her substitute, and encourages sexual relations between him and Helena, whom she views as a daughter.

Recognizing Helena's predisposition to indirectness, she corners her into admitting her love for her son and tries to involve herself in her plans to pursue a romantic relationship with him as a means to make it materialize and, thus, gratify herself vicariously: she claims 'heaven shall work in [her] for [Helena's] avail' (1.3.179) and pledges to assist her in her trip to Paris by giving her 'leave and love, / Means and attendants, and [her] loving greetings / To those of [hers] in court'; 'what[ever] [she] can help [her] to, [she] shalt not miss' (1.3.246–8, 251). When Helena marries her son and returns to her court, she claims 'it hath happen'd all as [she] would have had it, save that he comes not along with her' (3.2.1–2), indicating she views her substitute as a means to maintain a close relationship with her son. Later, when Bertram rejects Helena and goes to Florence to avoid her, the Countess requests to share even in her substitute's misery: 'If thou engrossest all the griefs are thine / Thou robb'st me of a moiety' (3.2.65–6). Merging her identity with that of her protégée, she behaves as if Bertram has rejected her when he writes *'till I have no wife I have nothing in France'* (3.2.73). She overreacts, stating she will 'wash his name out of [her] blood' (3.2.67), and defends her substitute with the fervour of a self-defence: 'There's nothing here that is too good for him / But only she, and she deserves a lord / That twenty such rude boys might tend upon / And call her, hourly, mistress' (3.2.78–82). She cannot differentiate herself from her double. Shakespeare's portrayal of the mother's collusiveness concurs with Freud's placing blame on the maternal figure for her instrumental role in the occurrence of incest: he argues that a mother's poor resolution of her own Oedipus complex can result in her encouraging her daughter to enact her own incestuous desires.[34]

Scholars tend to idealize the relationship between the two women,[35] but Freud claims interchanges between mothers and daughters in oedipal situations are typically riddled with ambivalence: the women both love and resent each other. While speaking glowingly of her ward's 'honesty' and 'goodness' (1.1.42), the Countess also implicitly criticizes her excessive mourning: 'No more of this, Helena; go to, no more; lest it be rather thought you affect a sorrow that to have – ' (1.1.47–9). She implies her 'display' of grief is disingenuous (*OED*, 'affect' *v* 6b), putting her in a difficult situation and making her defend herself. That this criticism resembles that of Claudius, who likewise chides his surrogate child for engaging in elaborate and prolonged bereavement, indicates the tension between the two women.

In 1.3 the Countess displays hostility towards the young woman by pretending not to know about her amorous interests in her son and terrorizing her. Although bringing Helena to tears and 'pale[ness]' (164) and causing her to 'start' as though she has seen a 'serpent' (137, 136), she will not cease hammering at her familial connection to her and her son and seems to savour that she is causing her 'blood' to 'curd' (144). Helena's vehement denials indicate she has repressed the forbidden reality of her desires and deluded herself into thinking the impediment to her attaining Bertram's love derives solely from the disparity of their social standings. The Countess's verbal assault is prosecutorial as she forces her 'daughter' to face her repressed desires. Alluding to her affection for Bertram as taboo, she accuses her of 'sin[fulness]' and 'hellish obstinacy' (174, 175). Because incest is a family secret, a 'shameful stigma', Helena cannot verbalize or share it 'either within the family circle or in the wider world outside of the family'; secrecy is the core of the situation, and 'every family member is always involved in this business of "not saying"'.[36] But the Countess harasses her by breaking the silence between them. She entraps her into admitting her feelings for Bertram by 'catch[ing] [her] fondness' (165) and forcing her to 'confess' (186). If we view Bertram's mother in symbolic psychological terms, she is acting as Helena's id, threatening to come into conflict with the superego.

Helena recognizes the source of the mother's hostility and 'hat[red]', as she calls it: she implores her to 'let not [her] hate encounter with [Helena's] love, / For loving where [she] do[es]' (203–4). Just as the Countess intuits the true nature of the young woman's feelings for her son, Helena senses they are competitors and asks 'pardon' (180, 182) for 'lov[ing]' (183) the same man whom she loves. She turns the tables for a moment, upsetting Bertram's mother by bringing her repressed desires into the open. While having no trouble activating her ward's repressed oedipal desires, she is not so amenable to having her own brought to the surface. When asked if she 'love[s]' her son, she incriminates herself in her overreaction: 'Go not about; my love hath in't a bond / Whereof the world takes note' (184). She falsely differentiates her love from that of her double by professing her love to be sanctioned and refusing to allow the true significance of her affection for her son to enter her consciousness. Shakespeare has Helena hit on the source of the Countess's identification with her, asking if she was ever in a similar situation when she was young, if she 'did ever, in so true a flame of liking, / Wish chastely and love dearly' (206–7).

But the Countess also seems to care deeply for her, agreeing that she "love[s] [her] gentlewoman entirely' (1.3.95–6). If Shakespeare is depicting a 'family' mired in erotic entanglements, the boundaries of appropriate relationships may be hazy, and just as the mother loves her son as though he were a 'husband', she may harbour an erotic attachment to her adopted daughter as well, incestuous attachments both children try to avoid. Like Helena's fixation on Bertram, the Countess has an obsession with her, hiring servants to spy on her, sending her letters and begging to be admitted into her confidence. When Bertram renounces the physician's daughter and implicitly her, she rejects her son and proclaims Helena her only child. She states she will 'wash his name out of [her] blood' and make her 'all [her] child' (3.2.67, 68).

Later correlating her incestuous affection for her son with the feelings she has for her 'daughter', she professes an inability to determine which is 'dearest' to her (3.4.39). When praising her, she speaks effusively – 'the most virtuous gentlewoman that ever nature had praise for creating' (4.5.9–10) – idealizing her and seeming to hold her too dearly. She seeks a familial connection to the young woman in order to establish an intimacy with her that may be as forbidden as her attachment to her son.

While politely addressing Bertram's mother in 1.3, Helena does not embrace her request to become her confidante, a detachment that can indicate her own lack of affection for the mother figure and attempt to avoid an inappropriate closeness with her. The Countess realizes the affection is not reciprocated, stating more love 'shall be paid her than she'll demand' (1.3.100–1). Freud argues that 'being in love with the one parent and hating the other are among the essential constituents of the stock of psychical impulses' that arise in early childhood.[37] Consequently, she may feel some hatred for her surrogate mother and rival for her son, a dislike that causes her to distance herself and repeatedly rebuff the older woman's attempts to form a more intimate bond with her. For example, although referring in her soliloquy at the end of 1.1 to her 'project' (224) and 'intents' (225) to get Bertram as her own, she is not forthright with his mother and only admits to her intention to go to Paris when cornered, and even then she is evasive about her intentions. Not hearing from Helena in Paris, the Countess has Lavatch deliver a letter to her, 'urg[ing] her to a present answer back' (2.2.58). But upon receiving the communication in 2.4, she does not send a letter back with Lavatch, even though he tells her his lady 'is not well' (2–3, 5). With Lavatch clarifying she 'has her health' and is 'merry' (2–3), her lack of 'well[ness]' can derive from Helena's lack of receptivity to her requests for closeness (*OED*, 'well' *adj* 2b, 3c). When Helena returns to Rossillion, it is only because Bertram 'entreat[s]' (2.5.63) her to leave Paris, and upon arrival at the court, she upsets the Countess by showing her the letter in which Bertram rejects and abandons her. In 3.2 when deciding to leave Rossillion, she does not meet with her and share her plans; rather, she delivers the news by letter, an indirect approach that seems to irritate the mother, who tells the steward, 'Might [he] not know she would do as she has done / By sending [her] a letter' (3.4.2–3). Moreover, her message in the letter is less than sincere: she implies she plans to take her own life.

The mother surrogate is pained by the news and confesses 'sharp stings are in her mildest words' (3.4.18) and her 'heart is heavy and [her] age is weak' (3.4.41), as Helena torments her just as the Countess distressed her earlier. Moreover, she gives out false reports of her death, never sending secret messages to inform her otherwise, and in 4.5 the Countess laments her death. She is as much deceived as the others when Helena miraculously appears at the play's end and speaks only a few words to her: 'O my dear mother, do I see you living?' (5.3.313). Sounding almost disappointed the old woman has survived the ordeal of her falsely reported death, she has managed to exclude her from any involvement in her plot to win her son as her husband. That the Countess does not respond to her when she appears at the end must indicate her resentment and grief at being deceived by a woman with whom she has tried repeatedly to establish an affectionate relationship. Helena keeps Bertram all for herself, refusing to share him with her double. She seems to embody Freud's 'criminal' death wish that he felt children with unresolved oedipal issues often feel towards the same-sex parent.[38]

Freud claims the dread of incest turns children away from their first love – the parent of the opposite sex – but they unconsciously choose a love object based on the image of the loved parent or sibling.[39] Shakespeare seems to be making the same point with the bed trick: Bertram thinks he has chosen a sexual partner free of incestuous connections, but she turns out to be the woman who haunts his unconscious – his sister, who ultimately reflects his mother, the basis for his choice of a mate. Moreover, the Countess, who has a dominant voice in the first half of the play, assumes a less prominent role as the play progresses. When Helena and Bertram abandon her in Rossillion, Lavatch claims she would be better off if God sent her to heaven 'quickly' (2.4.12). Once she believes her complement is dead, it is as if she moves closer to death herself: she refers to her demise (4.5.81; 5.3.72), and when Helena asks her if she is still 'living' (5.3.313), she does not respond. Her gradually attenuated role can suggest she symbolically becomes submerged into Helena, as Shakespeare correlates Bertram's having sex with Helena with his consummating his repressed oedipal desires for his mother.

Freud claims 'the manner in which one enters and leaves' the Oedipus complex is different for boys and girls. Because for boys 'the complex is not simply repressed, it is literally smashed to pieces by the shock of threatened castration', its objects are integrated into the ego where they form the centre of the superego – the moralizing and critical component of the psyche. Because castration has already had its effect on girls, the Oedipus complex may not end as early as it does for boys and, consequently, persist into 'women's normal mental life', or it may be repressed, making the superego less 'inexorable', 'impersonal' and 'independent of its emotional origins as we require it to be in men'.[40] It can be Helena's socially unsanctioned relationship with her father that has contributed to her weakened sense of right and wrong and a less forceful superego. She repeatedly engages in questionable, even immoral actions that can be the result of a morally tainted oedipal relationship. For example, Shakespeare implies she resorts to less than reputable means to 'heal' the King and does not cure him for benevolent but, rather, selfish reasons. Moreover, she manipulates him into forcing Bertram into marrying her, even though it is against the young man's will. When Bertram refuses to bed her, she engages in the morally questionable bed trick. She also seems to have manipulated a rector (4.3.56) into disseminating a false report of her death. Last, she again ensnares a humiliated Bertram in the last act by exposing him as a lying rake. Tricking or 'entrap[ping]' the object of one's desire is a common phenomenon in situations of incest.[41] Echoing the title 'all's well that ends well' (4.4.35), she confirms she is willing to resort to any means to achieve her 'ends'; unencumbered by a prohibitive superego, she finds nothing morally objectionable.

Scholars have noted the divergence in Helena's actions – that she displays simultaneously 'aggressive initiative and passivity', that she is both a 'saintly maiden and cunning vixen', both 'sacred' and 'profane'.[42] Some believe such behaviour characterizes her as an arch dissembler, who engages in shrewd plots to manipulate others while she projects a façade of virtue and self-effacing passivity to conceal her real duplicitous nature.[43] While she undeniably plots and dissembles to get Bertram, her vacillating between keen plotting and self-effacing submissiveness, like some of her other actions, indicates she is a psychically troubled character. Her behaviour can suggest she enlists the defence mechanism of splitting, first described by Freud and typically employed by people involved in incestuous bonds to protect themselves from the forbidden significance of their actions.[44] There are different forms of splitting. First, because people have trouble accepting into consciousness contradictory objects or persons, containing qualities both acceptable and unacceptable to them, they will unconsciously split them into two categories – the good and the bad – rather than developing a complex picture of the objects or persons. Second, they can experience a split within consciousness of the two disparate parts of themselves that are difficult to assimilate into a cohesive whole; they can be conscious of each of the halves of the self and even conscious of each of them at the same time, but have no unified consciousness of both of them together. I believe it is the second kind of splitting that accounts for Helena's oscillating between different versions of the self, 'the side-by-side conscious existence of otherwise incompatible psychological attitudes'.[45] Shakespeare highlights this splitting by naming his heroine Helena and making Diana her double. He changes the source name of Boccaccio's Giletta to Helena, to designate the seductive, assertive, cunning, scheming side that can engage in immoral, sinful acts. He has Lavatch mention Helen of Troy (1.3.67–76) to clarify the connection between his protagonist and the mythical figure, an association that brings a sexual dimension to his character. Conversely, he introduces Diana, to underscore the virginal, passive, selfless, pure side, inexperienced in the evil ways of the world.

The split halves can appear at the same time, as when Helena talks to Parolles in 1.1 of both her virginity and 'blowing up men'. But more typically after she executes an assertive act of seduction and manipulation, such as convincing the King to let her 'cure' him and asking for the man of her choice as repayment, she switches to the Diana half, modest, self-effacing and undeserving of the prospective spouses and selflessly devoted to Bertram once the King forces him to marry her. Splitting allows her to engage in unchaste, immoral acts while disavowing them at the same time. The virginal side protects her from accepting into consciousness the full significance of her relationships with both her dead father and Bertram. The Diana half surfaces in soliloquies, such as at the end of 3.2 when she reprimands herself for not thinking of her husband before herself, voluntarily leaves the security of the court of Rossillion and places herself in possible danger to clear the way for her husband to come home. Acting as the self-sacrificing wife who imperils her life in order to save her husband from his own failings, she can deceive herself about the immorality of her own actions. In the last scene, Diana has a much larger part than Helena, who appears only at the very end to announce her fulfilment of the bargain with Bertram. Shakespeare can be indicating that, as Helena enters into a sexual union with Bertram, she slips deeper into the half that denies the reality of the taboo significance of her desires for her husband/father. Miraculously returning from the dead, she awes her audience with a resurrection that has religious resonances, and scholars note that in announcing her pregnancy, she resembles the virgin Mary, since Diana alludes to the bed trick but only in a 'riddle' (5.3.297) that no one, except the theatre audience, understands.[46] Engaging in self-delusion and fooling both herself and others, she sanctifies herself and her relationship to Bertram.

But despite the elaborate defence, she displays guilt throughout the play. Psychoanalysts observe that 'disavowal', 'guilt and the need for atonement' are typical in cases of incest. People involved in incest need to suffer or be punished for an unconscious sense of culpability, which can result in '*deadly* masochism', 'indisputably linked to the death drive'.[47] Helena's description of the bed trick betrays guilt: it is a 'wicked meaning in a lawful act, / And lawful meaning in a lawful act, / Where both not sin, and yet a sinful fact' (3.7.45–7). Although consciously meaning her references to 'wicked meaning' and 'sinful fact' to apply to Bertram's behaviour, she engages in excessive justification of her behaviour, a defence that indicates unconsciously she senses there is something 'wicked' or morally wrong (*OED*, *adj*[1] 1) and 'sinful' about both her means and ends of having sexual relations with her 'brother'. Her receding into desperate hopelessness and misery when both alone and with others can be something other than feigning in order to deceive. She focuses on her desolation to assuage her feeling of sinfulness. This can also explain why she submits to Bertram's mistreatment of her, which involves public humiliation, abandonment and infidelity – abuse that satisfies her need to be punished for forbidden desires. She writes a letter to the Countess that states she is making a pilgrimage to Saint Jacques to 'amend' her 'faults' and implies she may seek death (3.4.7), and although she may not reach the shrine, she seems troubled by a sense of wrongdoing for which she must suffer.

Her guilt may extend to her reputed pregnancy. She produces Bertram's family ring at the play's end to verify she has fulfilled one condition of his bargain by having sex with him. But the other condition – that she is pregnant and by Bertram – is more difficult to prove. Scholars have noted the ambiguity surrounding her supposed maternity.[48] There is always the possibility, of course, that she is not pregnant at all and is merely deceiving him, just as she did when he was made to believe he was having a tryst with Diana. Whether she is physically displaying a pregnant state is uncertain. When stating it is 'plain' (5.3.311) she has fulfilled his stipulations, she can use the word to mean obvious or 'easily perceivable' (*OED*, *adj*¹ 7), which can denote that just as the ring is perceptible so is her pregnancy. If she is visibly pregnant, it seems unlikely Bertram is the father: while the time frame is difficult to decipher in the play, the time between the consummation – between 4.2 and 4.3 – and the last scene does not seem long enough for her pregnancy to be visibly detectable. On the other hand, if her curing of the King involved sexual intercourse, as the bawdy language surrounding the event suggests, he may be the father. Likewise, given the incestuous tenor of the father–daughter relationship, we wonder if Gerard de Narbon could have fathered the child: near the play's beginning, the Countess informs us he has been dead for six months, and if the play transpires over two months or so, it could be possible. If she is promiscuous, as the allusions to prostitution imply, the father could be any number of men. Certainly her pregnancy ignites early modern anxieties about the paternity of children and the power of wives to impact a man's lineage. But the pregnancy is important to a psychoanalytic reading in that Freud contends the female involved in an incestuous relationship typically desires a child with the father or sibling with whom she is sexually involved.[49] Shakespeare seems to detect this forbidden desire as well, and, thus, it is quite pertinent he should draw so much attention to the pregnancy and the ambiguity of the paternity.

He casts the female – both Helena and the Countess – as the initiator of liaisons with paternal and fraternal figures, overturning the standard view of early modern women as always victims and illustrating they can enact their own sexual fantasies, even forbidden ones. If the Countess is not as active, it is not through any lack of initiative on her part; it is because Helena excludes her. In his description of the feminine Oedipus complex, Freud portrays the daughter as the active sexual agent, who desires her father as a lover and seduces the relatively passive father into seeing her as a sexual being.[50] Obviously, psychoanalysts object to the sexist portrayal of girls and the casting of blame on the female child, most likely a victim rather than a perpetrator of sexual relations. But both Shakespeare and Freud offer a controversial portrayal of women in this regard.

As he does in *Hamlet*, Shakespeare permeates the play with an atmosphere of sickness – particularly sexual in nature – to reinforce the incest that causes Bertram, Helena and the Countess to be guided by unconscious desires. Of course the most prominent illness is that of the King, who suffers from a 'fistula', which Helena seems to cure, but her associations with 'empirics', or charlatans, lead us to suspect his improvement is temporary. Although in 4.5 Lafew declares the King 'comes post from Marcellus, of as able body as when he number'd thirty' (77–8), by the play's end he seems to have lost some of his revived vigour and refers to his 'old' age and the 'foot of time' impinging upon his 'quick'st decrees' (5.3.40–1) – references that allow for the strong possibility his illness persists. The death of two fathers – Bertram's and Helena's – can also suggest they have died from a similar disease. By the play's end, Bertram's health also becomes questionable: Lavatch refers to a 'patch of velvet on's face' and implies it is not covering a 'noble scar' but, rather, a 'carbonado' (4.5.90–1, 95, 97), or 'incision made to relieve syphilitic chancres'.[51] Although Lafew proclaims the velvet covers 'a noble scar', his quick response sounds more like an attempt to conceal an embarrassing truth. Furthermore, because Lavatch throughout the play has been an irrepressibly bawdy voice of truth, Shakespeare leads us to put more credence in his words. If Bertram has contracted syphilis, it has to be from Helena, since, as far as we know, she is the only one with whom he has had sexual contact. If this is the case, then either she had the disease all along, perhaps contracted from her father, or she contracted it from the King, a possibility that gives support for the implication her treatment of him involved sexual intercourse. When observing her in 1.3 and knowing she is attracted to her son, the Countess claims 'her eye is sick' (130). The very title of the play directs our attention to 'well[ness]' – not just good welfare (*OED*, *adj* 1a) but also sound health (*OED*, *adj* 5a). With such a marred and tentative last act, we are left to believe, as the King states, 'all yet [only] seems well' (5.3.327) but is not 'well' in actuality, that the diseased familial relations have only intensified in severity by the end. The illness can be concealed literally with a 'patch of velvet' or structurally with a comedic façade, but it festers under the attractive covering, making this play one of the most problematic and troubling of Shakespeare's comedies.

7

A Psychoanalytic Reading of Homoeroticism in *Romeo and Juliet*

Although queer critics have uncovered many of the homoerotic strains in Shakespeare's works, especially his comedies and sonnets, the study of non-normative desire in *Romeo and Juliet* has lagged behind that in other Shakespearean works probably because of the idealization of the normative sexuality, which dominates critical studies and theatrical productions of the play. Romeo and Juliet's hasty wooing and short-lived romance are glorified, even venerated, with the play typically being viewed as one of the greatest love stories ever told and Romeo as the quintessential heterosexual lover. Although bawdy sodomitic language appears throughout the play, even lexicon experts of the early modern word are averse to acknowledge it and, instead, give it a heterosexual significance. There is a widespread reluctance to view the play as other than one of the greatest tributes to heterosexual monogamy ever written. But scholars such as Joseph A. Porter, Jonathan Goldberg and Philip Armstrong have made headway in countering the heteronormative readings and disclosing the homoerotic desire in the play, with the emphasis falling on Mercutio's phallic and anal puns and his desire for Romeo.[1]

Psychoanalytic readings of the homosexual in Shakespeare, however, have typically been controversial, with queer critics objecting to what they perceive in these readings as the misapplication of twentieth-century developmental psychology to the early modern subject, the pathologization of homosexual desire and the marginalization of any sexuality outside the boundaries of heterosexual relations. I hope to offer a psychoanalytic reading of *Romeo and Juliet* that avoids these pitfalls and, instead, does justice to the pervasiveness, depth and authenticity of the homoerotic feelings and relationships within it, and concentrates on uncovering the complex, elusive motivations of characters.

That Romeo and his Montague cohorts enter the Capulet ball in masks signifies both literal and psychological concealment, with the mask being a symbol of repression and defence mechanisms. One of the most dominant defences that appears in the very first scene and continues throughout the play is reaction formation, what Freud calls 'overboarding' because people enlisting this defence go overboard in one direction to conceal the opposite reality of their situation.[2] To protect themselves from what they perceive as unacceptable and anxiety-ridden impulses and feelings, they adopt exaggerated behaviour that is opposite to their actual condition. The rejected impulse does not disappear but, rather, persists in the unconscious, which must be probed to discover what a person is blocking from conscious acknowledgement. This defence is characterized by excessive, exaggerated, intransigent and compulsive behaviour. Gertrude's famous comment in *Hamlet* about the player wife's proclamations of her devotion to her husband – 'Methinks the lady doth protest too much' – is a description of reaction formation defence. Gertrude doubts the legitimacy of the wife's words because they are overdone, affected and overwrought – a defence against her real emotions of betrayal. Such extreme behaviour appears in *Romeo and Juliet* – in Samson's exaggerated professions of manliness; Romeo's inflated love rhetoric; Mercutio's scoffing attitude towards love; and Tybalt's combative response to

Romeo's appearance at the Capulet ball and his subsequent pursuit of him. All of these responses bear signs of being defence mechanisms, by which characters protect themselves from feelings that cause them emotional distress.

Shakespeare begins the play with the least complicated example of reaction formation – that embodied in Samson, who pronounces stridently his sexual and martial prowess: 'I will show myself a tyrant: when I have fought with the men, I will be civil with the maids, I will cut off their heads'.[3] In a culture that is defined by a feud of warring families, the men in Verona cultivate a heightened masculinity that they display through violent attacks on their male adversaries and sexual violations of women, with Samson becoming the arch representative of this world view. Shakespeare gives him the same name as the biblical hero to highlight the superhuman strength he professes to possess and its spuriousness, for his machismo is just as fragile as that of the legendary warrior whose potency was destroyed by a simple haircut. That he rejects any sign of softness in his nature and becomes a caricature of masculinity signifies he is relying on the defence mechanism of reaction formation. Shakespeare undermines his character's declarations of virility by having Gregory debunk them with opposite assertions that are closer to the truth and having Samson immediately recoil and equivocate about challenging the Montagues once they appear. He quickly reveals the male bravado was a defence against his true nature of cowardice, fearfulness and lack of sexual potency with women.

As soon as the men of the house of Montague enter, he tells Gregory, 'My naked weapon is out. Quarrel, I will back thee' (1.1.32–3). The sexually loaded language elicits a sodomitic significance, with the 'naked weapon' connoting the penis with which he can 'back' or penetrate him in the 'hinder part of the body'.[4] The references to 'draw[ing]' a 'tool' (exposing the penis) (3, 30) and 'strik[ing]' (5, 6) (copulating); 'stand[ing]' (27) (being sexually erect); being 'a pretty piece of flesh' (28) (having a well-endowed penis); and being 'moved' to 'strike' (5, 6) (sexually aroused) take on similar significance when we realize all of this talk is a prelude to his martial encounter with other men.⁵ In this context, Samson's assertions that 'A dog of the house of Montague moves' him 'to stand' and he 'will take the wall of any man or maid of Montague's' (7, 10–11) indicate his arousal at engaging with men and 'tak[ing] the wall,' or anally copulating.⁶ Benvolio claims when he entered the scene the men were at 'thrusts and blows' (111), both phallically loaded words, and charges them with 'know[ing] not what [they] do' (63). The sexual subtext suggests Benvolio enters a homoerotically laden scene in which the men have become so aroused they have lost all rational control, and he tries to prevent them from openly doing something forbidden. Armstrong calls this aggressivity 'homoerotically engendered violence (or violently engendered homoerotics),' with the sword fights and the phallic thrusts serving as metaphors for homosexual dynamics.⁷ If Samson serves as a representative of the men in the play, these dynamics can be pervasive. Beneath the defensive posturing of an inflated male bravado and sexual virility with 'maid[s]' lies the opposite inclination – sensitivity, vulnerability and sexual attraction between men. The men do not want to sexually conquer the women and martially attack the men; rather, it is the inverse: they want to attack the women both verbally and physically and be intimate with the men. Shakespeare can have Romeo's comment on the fray – 'Here's much to do with hate, but more with love' (173) – indicate the feud is more about love than hate between men.

The foil to Samson is Romeo: he is as extreme a lover as Samson is a warrior. Shakespeare makes his protagonist an inflated embodiment of a hyperbolic literary convention, one that was considered outmoded and ridiculed even in his own time – the Petrarchan lover. In 1.1 he moans, groans and grieves over unrequited love, delivering a barrage of trite oxymoronic definitions of love: 'O brawling love, O loving hate, / O anything of nothing first create, / O heavy lightness, serious vanity, / Misshapen chaos of well-seeming forms, / Feather of lead, bright smoke, cold fire, sick health, / Still-waking sleep that is not what it is' (174–9). His professions are so exaggerated that even he senses the absurdity of his love declarations, asking Benvolio 'Dost [he] not laugh?' (180) and realizing he evokes hilarity rather than sympathy. After a short intermission, he engages again in artificial discourse, continuing with another string of oxymorons: 'Love is a smoke made with the fume of sighs; / Being purged, a fire sparkling in lovers' eyes; / Being vexed, a sea nourished with loving tears' (188–90). His speech is filled with commonplace sentiments about love and war, Cupid and his arrows, love as madness and a religion, with his extended conceits not coming from the heart but from Petrarch's 'book' (1.5.109) of love and Shakespeare making him into a parodic figure. Arriving at the Capulet ball in 1.4, he is just as lovelorn, being too 'heavy' to dance and 'so stake[d] to the ground [he] cannot move' (12, 16). He repeatedly proclaims his misery in love to his friends, garnering everyone's attention, putting his love on display and generally 'protest[ing] too much'. His behaviour bears all of the markings of reaction formation:

> Reactive love protests too much; it is overdone, extravagant, showy, and affected. It is counterfeit, and its falseness ... is usually easily detected. Another feature of a reaction formation is its compulsiveness. A person who is defending himself against anxiety by means of a reaction formation cannot deviate from expressing the opposite of what he really feels. His love, for instance, is not flexible. It cannot adapt itself to changing circumstances as genuine emotions do; rather it must be constantly on display as if any failure to exhibit it would cause the contrary feeling to come to the surface.[8]

When Mercutio tells him in 1.4 to put aside his love sickness for the moment and enjoy himself at the ball, Romeo refuses to be anything other than a miserable lover, showing an inflexibility that betrays a defence. Once he meets Juliet, he is no better: the overwrought love talk continues as he exchanges Rosaline for Juliet, duplicating his earlier words about Rosaline of women's beauty, saintliness and heavenly auras, and the references to Cupid and his wounding influence over lovers. Shakespeare has Friar Laurence's response to learning of Romeo's fickleness signal to his audience the substitution of one woman for another: the Friar professes the young man has laid one 'love in [a grave], another out to have' (2.3.80). That he can forget Rosaline so quickly and immediately begin fawning over a new lady as lavishly as he did the previous one indicates his love sickness is not a genuine, pliant emotion.

Just as Shakespeare undercuts Samson's masculine bluster with Gregory's sarcasm, he has Mercutio mock the extravagant performance of love, 'conjur[ing]' his friend 'in the likeness of a sigh', imitating his simple rhyming of '"love" and "dove"', and ridiculing his special camaraderie with Venus and her son Cupid (2.1.7–13). With his typical indelicacy, he tells Romeo he 'stickest / Up to the ears' in 'the mire, / Or, save your reverence, love' (1.4.41–3). With 'sir-reverence' being a 'euphemism for human dung',[9] he quibbles on it to claim Romeo has gone so overboard in his love sickness that he is suffocating himself in a disgusting pose. Montague laments that his son during the day 'shuts' himself in his dark room 'mak[ing] himself an artificial night' (1.1.137, 138), with Shakespeare possibly evoking the homophone of 'night' to indicate that his protagonist has transformed himself into an inauthentic 'knight' of love.

At the play's beginning, Benvolio reports that when he saw Romeo out in nature one morning, his friend avoided him by stealing 'into the covert of the wood' (1.1.123), a 'covert' signifying something that serves to conceal or disguise (*OED*, 2a, c): the young man seems to be running away from his true self and, in turn, camouflaging himself in another persona. The lover himself momentarily recognizes his use of a defence to deny his true nature, informing Benvolio he has 'lost [himself]. [He is] not here. / This is not Romeo, he's some otherwhere' (1.1.195–6). With these fleeting self-revelations, Shakespeare has Romeo tell us he has repressed an integral part of himself. The parallels between Samson and Romeo suggest the protagonist's extreme Petrarchan persona, like Samson's extreme machismo, is a defence against same-sex attractions.

Much important scholarship has been done on the status of homosocial and homosexual relationships in early modern England.[10] While clarifying the severity of the laws against sodomy in this period, scholars have also explained that prosecutions for the 'crime' were rare. Moreover, sodomy was a loosely defined term that applied not only to buggery, but also to acts against social order, such as treason and heresy. Since male friendship was considered more meaningful than relations between men and women, and the patriarchy was based on homosocial negotiations, these same-sex relationships often led to homoerotic unions, which some scholars argue were quite widespread. The ambiguity in the definition of sodomy and the value placed on male–male relationships allowed for homosexual bonds to exist without calling too much attention to themselves, as long as they did not threaten the social order by becoming exclusive of heterosexual unions, which perpetuated the patriarchy through reproduction, secured and transferred property, and established lineage. Goldberg calls it an 'open secret' – 'something that existed, something that everyone knew existed, but something that had no name of its own'.[11] While homoerotic relations were not considered deviant or in opposition to heterosexuality, there were both acceptable and transgressive forms: 'When homoerotic exchanges threaten to replace heterosexual bonds, when eroticism is collapsed into anxiety about reproduction, then homoeroticism is exorcised'.[12] Given this relative tolerance towards same sex relations, it is essential to understand why Romeo represses himself so urgently and denies his friendship with Benvolio and Mercutio. His extreme Petrarchanism even gives a homophobic tinge to his character.

Shakespeare intimates that before the play begins Romeo has had close bonds with his male friends: in 2.4 Mercutio makes a vague allusion to playful former times when they went 'for the goose' (75), which Romeo confirms; in the same interchange Romeo joins Mercutio in bawdy punning, suggesting a history of playful verbiage; Mercutio has formed such a strong connection to Romeo that he is willing to defend his friend and risk his life against the dueling Tybalt; and Benvolio cares enough about his friend to dedicate himself to curing his love melancholy. All of these facts indicate the men have spent much time together and care deeply for each other. Yet at the play's beginning Montague reports his son has been acting strangely, spending 'many a morning' (1.1.129) out in nature by himself and cutting himself off from social contact. Benvolio confirms Montague's report, claiming that when his friend saw him in the forest, he ran away from him, a reaction that obviously hurts his feelings: 'Towards him I made, but he was ware of me / And stole into the covert of the wood. / I, measuring his affections by my own', 'Pursued my humour, not pursuing his, / And gladly shunned who gladly fled from me' (1.1.122–4,127–8). Once again a character resorts to reaction formation: since, according to his father, Romeo has established a pattern of spending nights in the woods, Benvolio's going to the same location at the unlikely time of a little before dawn must signify his intention of meeting up with him; but when Romeo slights him, he hides his disappointment and emotional pain behind a defence of indifference, even appreciation for the rejection. Once he gets an opportunity to talk to his friend in private, Romeo is withdrawn and not forthcoming about his feelings, an evasiveness that forces Benvolio to ask several times about the source of his misery. Romeo twice abruptly cuts off the dialogue with a cold 'farewell' (1.1.192, 235), forcing Benvolio at one point to claim his cousin 'wrong[s]' him if he 'leaves [him] so' (194) and to invite himself to accompany a friend who continues to slight him. In 2.1, even though Mercutio and Benvolio call out to him, he 'withdraws' and refuses to come forward and confide in them his new feelings for Juliet. After the balcony scene, he goes to visit Friar Lawrence, not his friends, and the next morning when he meets up with them, he is evasive about his whereabouts the previous evening and never tells them about Juliet or his making plans with the Friar to marry her – big news one would think one would confide to one's close friends. His lack of interest in the feud, phallic sword and his male companions signals his withdrawal from the same-sex world; conversely, his adoption of the Petrarchan lover, who hides his penis in the 'covert' of a woman's privates, designates his entry into the heterosexual world.

Certainly the relationship with Benvolio poses no threat to him and is not causing his alienation from his friends. His cousin is the 'acceptable' male friend, who, although he 'measur[es] [Romeo's] affections by [his] own' (1.1.124), or empathizes with his misery so much that he feels miserable too, is supportive of Romeo's interests in women. Like Antonio of *The Merchant of Venice*, he tries to assist his friend, dedicating himself to alleviating his misery by getting him to 'forget to think of' Rosaline and directing his eyes to 'examine other beauties' (1.1.223, 226). While he might secretly hope his friend would 'turn giddy and be holp by backward turning' (1.2.46) – deviate from social and sexual norms by remaining single, engaging in homosexual sex and 'turning' for love to him in particular[13] – he is willing to share Romeo's attention and affections with a woman and even help him in the attainment of that union. Wearing his heart on his sleeve, he is sensitive to Romeo's feelings and forthcoming about his own.

Mercutio is another matter, however, and is more of a foil to Benvolio than a complement. His language filled with phallic and sodomitic puns, sometimes shocking in nature, he is blatantly transgressive, with Porter labeling him 'Shakespeare's most phallic character' and describing him as a tribute to 'the memory of Christopher Marlowe', noted for a 'subversive' sexuality of 'flaunted homoeroticism'.[14] Since the phallus from the very first scene becomes correlated with same-sex desire, Mercutio's patently phallic nature marks him as clearly homoerotic. He expresses no interest in marriage and speaks pejoratively during the Queen Mab speech of heterosexual sex (1.4.92–4), an indication he most likely finds it undesirable. Unlike Romeo, he does not feel the need to wear either a literal or figurative mask: while his companions are masked at the Capulet ball, he proclaims, 'Give me a case to put my visage in, / A visor for a visor! What care I / What curious eye doth quote deformities?' (1.4.29–31). He asks for a bag (*OED*, 'case' n^2 1a) in which to put his mask, speaking metaphorically about his determination to be true to himself and indifference to societal ostracism.

Mercutio never misses an opportunity to mock, deride and rebuke Romeo's susceptibility to the vagaries of heterosexual love. Porter calls him a 'scoffer at love', who speaks disparagingly of amorous sentiments and advises Romeo, 'If love be rough with [him], be rough with love' (1.4.27).[15] He follows his own advice, speaking so harshly of love that he seems to have made himself impervious to it. Romeo certainly feels his 'jest[ing]' indicates he has 'never felt a wound' (2.2.1), that Mercutio makes fun of his love for Rosaline because he has not himself been hit by Cupid's arrow. But his 'rough' attitude towards both Romeo and passion is too extreme, indicating Shakespeare is giving us another instance of the defence mechanism of reaction formation. He adopts the behaviour of gruffness to conceal his sensitivity and vulnerability to love, specifically his feelings for Romeo. Although Romeo wallows in romantic concepts about women and rightly deserves some of the criticism, Mercutio projects his own covert susceptibility to ardour onto Romeo and derides him for it as a way to try to 'beat [his own] love down' (1.4.28). Finding it too painful to admit his feelings, as Benvolio so readily does, he develops a defensive way to protect himself from emotional pain and rejection. He may not 'mask' his homosexual desires, but he certainly 'masks' his emotions. He has so fully adopted the defence into his consciousness that he seldom reveals his true sensitive nature. Shakespeare shows us only an inkling of it at the beginning of the Queen Mab speech, when he delivers a touching poetic rendering of the deliverer of dreams as a microscopic figure, who visits sleepers at night in her 'hazelnut' ... 'chariot' (1.4.59). But he soon has her degenerate into a malevolent hag, who 'blisters' ... 'ladies lips' (74–5), 'frighte[ns]' a soldier with the noises of war (87), tangles hair into knots, and 'presses' women while they lie on their backs in simulation of sexual intercourse (93). The descent of the speech mirrors Mercutio's gradual coarsening into the sardonic, bitter man whom we meet in the play.

With the majority of his comments centring on Romeo, it seems his young friend has caused him to hide his true feelings behind the defensive mask of jesting mockery. What torments him is Romeo's turning away from him to pursue women. Unlike Benvolio, he is unwilling to subsume his relationship into Romeo's social union with a woman. When Romeo informs him he 'dreamt a dream tonight', Mercutio snaps back, before his friend can tell him of a dream about a woman, that he had a dream as well, 'that dreamers often lie' (1.4.49, 52). He obviously puns on the word 'lie', implying Romeo is a liar, an imposter (*OED*, v^2 1a), who has deceived him (*OED*, v^2 2) by lying (*OED*, v^1 1f), or having sexual relations, most likely with women, an act that he starts to depict crudely in his Queen Mab speech before Romeo stops him. Shakespeare allows for the probability that Mercutio's dream has been about having Romeo as his exclusive lover, especially since he mentions lovers first in his list of dreamers whom Queen Mab visits at night. When Romeo tells him he 'talk'st of nothing' (95), Mercutio agrees, delivering lines that seem laden with a double meaning:

> True, I talk of dreams,
> Which are the children of an idle brain,
> Begot of nothing but vain fantasy,
> Which is as thin of substance as the air,
> And more inconstant than the wind who woos
> Even now the frozen bosom of the north,
> And, being angered, puffs away from thence,
> Turning his side to the dew-dropping south.
>   (1.4.96–103)

He obliquely implies he was childishly foolish (*OED*, 'vain' *adj* and *n* 3) to believe his dreams could come true regarding a 'vain', or conceited (*OED*, 4a), and 'inconstant' young man, who changes his affections at a whim and 'is thin of substance', or without strength of character. By implication he is like 'the wind' in that he has 'woo[ed]' Romeo, but to no avail, since he has become unreceptive to him. This rejection causes him to reverse his wooing into the opposite behaviour of angry rebuffs, as he defends himself from heartache by adopting a harsh exterior.[16]

He speaks pejoratively of Romeo's Petrarchanism, not because he is opposed to love, but because he is opposed to Romeo turning his attentions from him to a woman. He later claims he wants 'to raise up him' (2.1.29), a phrase with several meanings: his purpose is to restore Romeo, who is 'dead' (2.4.13) to him, back to life (*OED*, 'raise' v^1 2b, 3), or back to his former relationship with him; to arouse him erotically in intercourse with him; and to stir him up so that he will stand in revolt (*OED*, v^1 4c) against a heteronormative culture. In glaringly bawdy language, he openly speaks of sodomy when he refers to the fruit of the 'medlar tree' (2.1.34), the slang term for which is '"open-arses"',[17] and wishes Romeo could openly admit what he ponders to himself when he sits alone in the woods under the tree: he is more sexually excited by the prospect of being intimately involved with men than women.

Mercutio aims his loaded language at communicating a special message to Romeo. Rather than commiserating with him or offering to find him another woman, as Benvolio does, he gets 'rough' or harsh with him because Romeo has been 'rough' by rejecting him and causing him misery. He tells him that instead of languishing in the misery of his heterosexual love pose, he should take an aggressive stance, wage a 'thrust' at Cupid who has wounded him, and destroy these emotions by turning away from women: 'Prick love for pricking, and you beat love down' (1.4.28). With 'love' seeming to refer to the boy Cupid, he can be telling Romeo to turn from heterosexual relations to 'prick[ing]', or penetrating, a man

– specifically himself. Claiming he does not 'care' (30) that others might disapprove of his sexual desires, he puts pressure on his friend to have the courage to follow his lead and not conceal his desires for him. He verbally 'pricks', or tries to provoke (*OED*, *v* 9a), Romeo into repudiating his pursuit of women.

Once Romeo appears in 2.4, the morning after the balcony scene and his meeting with Friar Lawrence to arrange the marriage, Mercutio continues to 'prick', or verbally stab, at his friend and assumes his absence the night before was because of a tryst with Rosaline. He is just as aggrieved as earlier and persists in expressing his anguish through the opposite behaviour of hostility by greeting him with pejorative references to his Petrarchanism and implying it is 'slop' (45), or excrement.[18] Because the three men are alone together, they can relax some of their defences and anxieties and be more forthright with each other, and, indeed, Mercutio is able to get Romeo to reveal some of his true nature. Mercutio begins by accusing Romeo of giving them 'the counterfeit', 'the slip' (45, 48), referring literally to his deceiving them by not returning home the night before, but more covertly to his inauthentic Petrarchan defence (*OED*, 'counterfeit' *adj* 7a).[19]

The ensuing exchange between the two men starts out relatively inoffensively, but it gradually becomes more sexually charged with each comment. Romeo begins with his defence well positioned, decorously and evasively declaring he missed meeting his friends the night before because he had to attend to important matters: his 'business was great, and in such a case as [his] a man may strain courtesy' (49–50). But to each of his attempts to hide behind appropriate language, Mercutio delivers lewd replies until Romeo cannot resist and gradually lets his false persona drop and puns on Mercutio's use of the word 'flower' to claim his 'pump [is] well flowered' (59), referring literally to his shoe being nicely decorated with 'flower[s]' but bawdily to his 'pump', or penis, being in impressive working order.[20] Sensing he has broken down his friend's Petrarchan defence for the moment, Mercutio invites him to 'follow [him] this jest now till [he] hast worn out [his] pump, that when the single sole of it is worn, the jest may remain, after the wearing, solely singular' (60–3). He summons him to engage in a verbal race with him, which becomes a metaphor for sexual relations between the two, until they have exhausted their 'wits' (70), or genitals, and all that is left is the good 'jest', or coitus.[21] Romeo throws his defence to the wind and reveals his joviality at exchanging ribald repartee: 'O single-soled jest, solely singular for the singleness!' (64–5). Since Mercutio's words often contain several levels of meaning, his talk of 'single' and 'solely singular' can be appeals to his companion to remain 'single' or unmarried (*OED*, *adj* 8a), to be 'solely' his, and to be 'singular', or different from what custom expects of a young man (*OED*, *adj* 1a, 13) – a recurring entreaty.

Feigning a deficiency in wit, he joyously proclaims he cannot keep up with Romeo's verbal race and subtextually implies he is sexually spent: 'Nay, if our wits run the wild goose chase, I am done, for thou hast more of the wild goose in one of thy wits than, I am sure, I have in my whole five. Was I with you there for the goose?' (70–3). The references to 'goose' lead the dialogue in a different direction, in which the two men keep repeating the word and talk about the 'sauce', most likely apple sauce, that one serves with a dinner of 'sweet goose' (79–80). With a 'goose' being a bawdy designation for a prostitute, scholars have felt the two men are engaging in obscene innuendo about heterosexual relations with a 'girl in the brothel',[22] perhaps indicating they have frequented such a place. But Mercutio's homosexual proclivities make this unlikely, and Romeo's words clarify that he refers to Mercutio when he speaks of a 'goose' (77, 84). Mercutio says he 'will bite [him] by the ear' (76), which can signify a fond caress (*OED*, 'bite' *v* 16), or more graphically anal copulation,[23] and he compares his 'wit' to a 'a very bitter sweeting', 'a most sharp sauce', which Romeo proclaims is 'well served in to a sweet goose' (78–80). Given that Romeo designates his friend, not a female prostitute, as a goose, Mercutio seems to have managed to get his friend to take pleasure in reminiscing about their past sexual experiences with each other, when he released his 'sauce', or semen,[24] into his lover, with both men referring to each other as 'sweet' and 'sweeting' – a sweetheart (*OED*, 'sweeting' n^1 1; 'sweet' *adj* 8a). With a 'wild goose chase' being a race (often involving horses) in which participants had to follow 'behind' the leader 'with precision and at a specific interval', like a 'flight of wild geese', the reference reinforces the sodomitic nuance of following the backside and may bolster Mercutio's double message of encouraging his lover to follow his lead and defy a heteronormative culture.[25] Seeming to speak of Romeo's wit, Mercutio comments on his ability to extend a joke to its full capacity: 'O here's a wit of cheveril, that stretches from an inch narrow to an ell broad' (81–2). But the sexually charged language allows him to laud the size of Romeo's erect penis, which his friend confirms: 'I stretch it out for that word "broad" which, added to the goose, proves thee far and wide – a broad goose' (83–4). With Romeo obviously enjoying the verbal game and the bawdy reaching a height of obscenity, he refers either to penis, or more likely anus, width that can accommodate his 'wit of cheveril'. With the word 'broad' denoting a 'loose, gross, indecent' person (*OED*, *adj* 6c), he can also be jocularly teasing him about his blatantly lewd language and behaviour.

Successfully inducing Romeo to drop his defence of the miserable, unrequited lover of women and reveal his witty, bawdy, lighthearted, homoerotic nature, Mercutio discloses his objective for the lengthy exchange: 'Why, is not this better now than groaning for love? Now art thou sociable, now art thou Romeo, now art thou what thou art, by art as well as by nature' (85–7). He continues to induce Romeo to drop his repression and follow his own 'nature', his inherent sexual proclivities (*OED*, *n* 4b, 7b), and to be what he truly is – one who prefers the sexual company of men rather than women – a decision that will make him happier, more gregarious, and more 'sociable', or less inclined to reject his companionship. Benvolio interrupts when Mercutio intensifies the lewdness of his homoerotic talk about a 'bauble in a hole' (89) because it veers on indecency, but his intrusion into the conversation also indicates his own arousal and excitement at the sexual interchange, bawdily proclaiming if Mercutio had not stopped, he 'wouldst else have made [his] tale large' (93), or experienced penile tumescence. Mercutio answers the opposite is true: 'I would have made it short, for I was come to the whole depth of my tale and meant indeed to occupy the argument no longer' (94–6). The different levels of meaning allow him to make several points: he had reached the apex of ribald punning and, thus, was just about to stop; he was just about to achieve sexual climax and would have withdrawn his detumescent 'tale', or penis, from the 'hole', the verbal interchange representing a physical encounter the two men have had with each other; and he was just about to stop the dialogue because he had finished his attempt to establish his position and try to reason with his friend (*OED*, 'argument' *n* 4) to reject women and be companionable with him.

I believe it is the pressure the uncompromising Mercutio repeatedly places on his friend to drop his pursuit of women and be true to his homosexual nature that compels Romeo to resort to the extreme defence of avoiding his male friends and becoming the paragon of the Petrarchan lover. He is willing to assume his proper social role of marrying a woman while maintaining his male friendships, but not to become a rebel and enter into an exclusively homosexual relationship. The stressful situation plummets him into desolation as he displays some of the qualities that Freud attributes to melancholia – 'a profoundly painful dejection' that verges on suicidal tendencies, 'cessation of interest in the outside world', 'inhibition of all activity' and 'sleeplessness'.[26] As the play continues, he displays more of the symptoms as his melancholia increases. His despondency seems very real: early in the play his father reports he has been seen in the woods, 'With tears augmenting the fresh morning's dew, / Adding to clouds more clouds with his deep sighs' and 'steal[ing] home' at dawn only to 'pen himself' ... 'private in his chamber', 'shut[ting] up his windows, lock[ing] fair daylight out' (1.1.129–31, 135–7). His gloominess is so acute that Montague worries about his son's well-being: 'Black and portentous must this humour prove, / Unless good counsel may the cause remove' (139–40). Shakespeare makes it difficult to believe his sadness at the beginning centres on Rosaline's rejection of his amorous advances, since he never gives her substance as a character and Romeo forgets her instantaneously upon first sight of Juliet. If he were so traumatized by Rosaline's rebuff as he claims, he would not be able to switch off his emotions for her and marry a complete stranger. It seems more likely he is denying the real reason for his sadness and hiding behind an acceptable façade, deceiving even himself about the cause.

Freud explains melancholia is not necessarily, like mourning, the reaction to a loved one who has actually died but, rather, who 'has been lost as an object of love'.[27] Romeo's love object is not Rosalind but his male friends, Mercutio in particular, and a crucial part of himself that he repudiates. As Romeo tells Benvolio, 'In sadness, cousin, [he] do[es] love a woman' (1.1.202). He has felt compelled to choose between either women or men as his love objects and has chosen the former, a situation that makes him unhappy. His situation resembles some of the cases of melancholia Freud describes in which 'the inhibition of the melancholic seems puzzling to us because we cannot see what it is that is absorbing him so entirely'; 'one cannot see clearly what it is that has been lost, and it is all the more reasonable to suppose that the patient cannot consciously perceive what he has lost either ... . This would suggest that melancholia is in some way related to an object-loss which is withdrawn from consciousness'.[28] Thus, Romeo's melancholia shows itself not when he is contemplating Rosaline, but when, for example, Mercutio speaks disparagingly of dreams in the Queen Mab speech and obliquely chides him for his renunciation of him. He immediately returns to his despondency and fatalistic view of existence, saying he 'fear[s]' his 'despised life' will come to an 'untimely death' (1.4.110–11), as if Mercutio's comments have provoked his suicidal impulses.

Melancholia typically takes the form of 'self-torment', which Freud believes the melancholic finds 'enjoyable': it signifies that 'trends of sadism and hate which relate to an object ... have been turned round upon the subject's own self'. Certainly Romeo wallows in his misery, perhaps savouring it. Freud contends his melancholic patients 'by the circuitous path of self-punishment' manage to take 'revenge on the original object and in tormenting their loved one through their illness, hav[e] resorted to it in order to avoid the need to express their hostility to him openly'.[29] Similarly, Romeo secretly resents Benvolio and particularly Mercutio for their ability to enjoy a non-normative lifestyle, one he does not feel he can continue. He is vexed especially at Mercutio for repeatedly chiding him and trying to induce him to join in his renunciation of societal demands to marry. He takes out his covert hostilities on them in various ways: he denies them his company, becoming more distant physically and emotionally, literally running away from them and forcing them to try to locate him and communicate with him; he flaunts his supposed love of Rosaline and belabours his pose of an unrequited, miserable Petrarchan lover in front of them; he refuses to have fun with his friends and dance at the Capulet ball; and he forces them to try to reason with him, but remains unreceptive to their pleas and efforts to relieve his depression. He is making their lives just as miserable as his own.

Shakespeare displays Romeo's passive-aggressive behaviour with Benvolio in 1.1, for example, as his cousin tries earnestly to get him to confide the source of his sadness to him. He frustrates him by prolonging the confession with equivocations, lengthy definitions of love, contrived misunderstandings and puns. When Benvolio expresses his love and sensitivity to his plight, Romeo flippantly rejects it and accuses him of selfishness: 'This love that thou hast shown / Doth add more grief to too much of mine own' (186–7). He so torments his cousin with his indifference and lackadaisical dismissal of him that Benvolio is reduced to begging to follow him. Romeo gets him to dedicate himself to relieving his misery and shows him no appreciation for his efforts. Benvolio openly expresses his hurt when Romeo plays with his emotions, whereas Mercutio expresses his through anger.

Romeo is so threatened by the intensity of his homoerotic nature that he rushes into a marriage with Juliet, whom he has known for only a few days and with whom he has had limited contact, as a way to run away from the natural urge to be with his male friends. By presenting Friar Lawrence as a wise counsellor and having him express incredulity at his impulsive switch from Rosaline to Juliet, Shakespeare leads us to regard Romeo as not displaying genuine affection for Juliet but, rather, infatuation and immaturity: 'Holy Saint Francis, what a change is here! / Is Rosaline, that thou didst love so dear, / So soon forsaken? Young men's love then lies / Not truly in their hearts but in their eyes' (2.3.61–4); 'Thy love did read by rote, that could not spell' (84). Romeo tries desperately to convince himself – and everyone else – he is happily in love with a woman, resorting to extreme proclamations of his amorous devotion, elevating Juliet into a saint and angel, and engaging in heroic actions of defying danger, even death, just to be in her presence: 'My life were better ended by [Juliet's kinsmen's] hate / Than death prorogued, wanting of [her] love' (2.2.77–8). But the extremity of his behaviour suggests defensive strategies.

After he marries and most likely experiences his first intimate relations with a woman on the wedding night, his tone seems to change. We expect Juliet to have a difficult time getting him to leave the next morning – the typical response of a lover. But instead of having the couple express their passion for each other and reluctance to part, Shakespeare begins the scene with Romeo evidently about to exit through the balcony window, for Juliet urges him to stay: 'Wilt thou be gone? It is not yet near day. / It was the nightingale, and not the lark, / That pierced the fearful hollow of thine ear' (3.5.1–3). Undoubtedly he is following the Friar's directions to 'be gone before the watch be set / Or by the break of day disguised from hence' (3.3.166–7) and senses the danger he would face if he were detected in Juliet's bedroom. But in contrast to his earlier behaviour in the balcony scene, when he faced the same danger and yet was willing to stay and brave it, he seems a bit eager to leave here:

> It was the lark, the herald of the morn,
> No nightingale. Look, love, what envious streaks
> Do lace the severing clouds in yonder east.
> Night's candles are burnt out, and jocund day
> Stands tiptoe on the misty mountain tops.
> I must be gone and live, or stay and die.
> (3.5.6–11)

His language is distinctly different from that of the dreamy Romeo in the balcony scene who spoke of heaven, 'lazy-puffing clouds' and 'love's light wings' (2.2.31, 66). Here he has a more assertive voice and stands his ground against Juliet's declarations it is night, citing evidence to support his assertions of the breaking daylight. Although declaring earlier in the balcony scene he would rather die than leave her, he now realizes his life is more important than staying with her. He seems to have both literally and figuratively seen 'the light of day' and is brushing aside the Petrarchan haze. The tone of the interchange sounding almost argumentative, she refuses to back down and refutes him – 'Yond light is not daylight; [she] know[s] it' (12) – telling him to 'stay yet; [he] need'st not to be gone' (16), an attempt at persuasion that suggests his determination to leave. While seeming to capitulate, he actually takes a circuitous route to get his way, making her feel guilty should he stay and die: 'Let me be ta'en, let me be put to death. / I am content so thou wilt have it so'; 'Come, death, and welcome! Juliet wills it so' (17–18, 24). He is no longer deluded and out of touch with reality: he can see the 'grey' of 'the morning's eye' (19) and knows it is dawn. He proclaims he has 'more care to stay than will to go' (23), but this profession certainly lacks the passion of his earlier parting in the balcony scene. After a last kiss, he speaks rather stiltedly: 'Farewell. / I will omit no opportunity / That may convey my greetings, love, to thee' (48–50). He sounds as if he is parting from an acquaintance, not a lover, promising to send his goodwill and kind regard to her (*OED*, 'greet' v^1 3a). Although he tells her he 'doubts it not' (52) they will be together again, as soon as she expresses doubt, he concurs, making it seem as though his reassurances of a future for them were simply a means to appease her so he could leave. This waning of Romeo's passions after the night with Juliet allows Shakespeare to intimate the lovemaking has been less than satisfying for Romeo. Sensing that to 'stay' in this relationship is death, he fears Mercutio was correct about his sexual preference.

The other character who engages in extreme behaviour is Tybalt, with his excessive violence catapulting the play into the realm of tragedy. He can be characterized as just a hothead so deeply invested in the feud that when he enters the play in 1.1 and sees the Montagues and Capulets fighting, he cannot resist entering the fray to defeat the Montagues. But that he resembles Samson in his male bravado and 'flourishes his blade' (1.1.76) in a scene in which aggression is homoerotically charged allows for the probability he is a much more complicated character, who, like Samson, is concealing vulnerability behind an overly belligerent defence and engaging in the defence of reaction formation. Traub clarifies that 'extreme virility' is depicted in Shakespeare as 'consistent with erotic desire for other men', with 'male homoerotic desire [represented] as phallic in the most active sense: erect, hard, penetrating'.[30] Tybalt enters the play as the embodiment of phallic thrusting, immediately drawing his sword and challenging Benvolio, who pleads for peace and describes him as though he and his sword are red hot: he is 'fiery Tybalt', who 'breathed defiance', 'swung [his sword] about his head and cut the winds', and 'hissed him in scorn' (1.1.107–10). Later Mercutio calls him the 'Prince of Cats' (2.4.19). Editor René Weis explains that Q1 refers to him as 'Catso' instead of 'Cats' (2.4.20) and elucidates that the word is from the Italian 'cazzo', which means 'prick', making Tybalt 'King of Cats and Chief Prick'[31] and designating him as homosexually nuanced.

His extreme violence flares up again in 1.5 when he perceives Romeo at the Capulet ball. Again he can be read as simply an enemy to all Montagues, and, as a result, when he realizes Romeo has crashed the Capulet ball, he becomes enraged at the 'intrusion' (90). But that Romeo is wearing a mask and Tybalt can recognize him by 'his voice' (53) suggests some past interactions between them. When he reacts venomously and tells Capulet the masker is 'a Montague' (60), Capulet asks if it is 'young Romeo' (62), as though he knows of a strained past between the two that would cause him to act so violently. Certainly Romeo is accompanied by other Montagues towards whom Tybalt could direct his anger, including his cousin Benvolio, whom he could single out because of their earlier interrupted skirmish. He could direct his anger at the whole lot of them, but he focuses on Romeo. One could argue that he does so because Romeo is the son of the patriarch of the Montagues, but even then his antagonism towards Romeo is excessive. He wants to kill him on the spot for a rather paltry reason: Romeo has come 'with an antic face, / To fleer and scorn at [their] solemnity' (55–6). Shakespeare underscores the excessiveness of his reaction by making the patriarch Capulet accepting of Romeo's presence and having him incredulously ask his nephew 'wherefore storm[s] [he] so?' (59). If father Capulet, who has every reason to dislike Romeo, thinks his nephew is 'storm[ing]' or raging uncontrollably, then he is clearly overreacting. Upon leaving the scene, he claims his 'flesh tremble[s]' (89), a potentially loaded phrase that can mean he is sexually aroused at the prospect of an encounter with Romeo, but he must suppress it and 'withdraw' (90) his phallic sword. He is so heated that he is determined to fight with Romeo, and we learn in 2.4 he has sent a 'challenge' (8) to a duel to him. All of his behaviour is exaggerated. His inflated warrior pose and intense hatred can be a reaction formation, as he represses his true nature as a homosexual lover and covert attraction to Romeo in particular. His situation may be like that of Samson, his double, who states 'a dog of the house [of Montague] shall move [him] to stand' (1.1.10). The 'dog' that 'moves', or sexually excites, Tybalt is Romeo.

Learning from Benvolio of Tybalt's 'challenge', Mercutio speaks of him as a duellist:

> O, he's the courageous captain of compliments: he fights as you sing pricksong, keeps time, distance and proportion. He rests his minim rests, one, two, and the third in your bosom; the very butcher of a silk button, a duellist, a duellist, a gentleman of the very first house, of the first and second cause. Ah, the immortal *passado*, the *punto reverso*, the hay!
>
> (2.4.19–26)

While seeming to praise Tybalt, Mercutio seldom speaks straightforwardly. He is actually derisively characterizing him as fighting by the book in a stilted and predictable fashion and following the precise codes of duelling. His moves are not inventive, spontaneous or fervid, with Mercutio suggesting he typically relies on only three basic strokes. Characterizing him as a 'butcher of a silk button', he ridicules him as a duellist, satirically implying he can annihilate a button and perhaps not much else. He continues to disparage him as an effete, affected fop and ends climactically by speaking facetiously of him as 'a very good blade, a very tall man, a very good whore!' (30). If we apply to Mercutio's characterization the subtext of the phallic significance of duelling established in the first outbreak of the feud in 1.1, then Mercutio expresses a double meaning and describes Tybalt as an uninspired and ineffectual homoerotic lover, more laughable than laudable, more promiscuous than faithful. That he speaks so 'knowingly' of his duelling techniques and specific 'thrusts' can imply Mercutio has had an intimate history with Tybalt and knows his phallic thrusts because he has experienced them himself. Upon learning the 'Prince of Cats' wants to duel with Romeo, an act loaded with homosexual implications, he denigrates Tybalt's sexual expertise, perhaps as a way to assure himself that he poses no threat as a rival for Romeo's affections.

3.1 is a turning point in the play, because the duel takes place, and unlike the sword fight at the beginning of the play, this one ends in fatalities that propel a play that started like a comedy into a tragedy. Mercutio knows Tybalt is looking for Romeo to combat with him, and Benvolio informs him 'the Capels are abroad' (2), which most likely means Tybalt is nearby them. Although accusing Benvolio of being combative, Mercutio is far more bellicose than his companion and projects his fiery spirit onto him: he ironically characterizes himself when he tells his friend he is 'as hot a jack in [his] mood as any in Italy; and as soon moved to be moody, and as soon moody to be moved' (11–13). Mercutio is looking for a battle, most likely with Tybalt, out of anger for his challenge of Romeo. The sexually loaded words 'hot' (sexually passionate), 'jack' (penis) and 'moved' (sexually aroused), as in Samson's use of the same word, add a homoerotic subtext to the imminent meeting of the men.[32]

Mercutio is so 'hot' he provokes Tybalt by claiming he does not want to talk but, rather, deliver a 'blow' (39), with a double meaning of a fencing thrust and a 'stroke of the penis',[33] and instructs him to give a reason for them to fight. Tybalt has a ready answer: 'Mercutio, thou consortest with Romeo' (44). Since he will later make the same allegation to Romeo's face and it seems to be a major reason for the fatal duel, the meaning of the verb 'consort' takes on significant importance. The verb has several meanings that could apply: *1* 'to associate oneself (with), to keep company' (*OED*, 4); *2* 'to have intercourse with' (*OED*, 6c); and *3* 'to combine in musical harmony; to play, sing or sound together' (*OED*, 7).[34] Mercutio's reply suggests he responds to the second and third meaning, a reply that hides the sexual significance behind the musical one. He threatens him with his 'fiddlestick' (47), a bow with which to play the fiddle, and a bawdy designation for a penis.[35] But the outrage expressed in Mercutio's 'Zounds'

(48) bolsters the sexual meaning of 'consort' and indicates he understands the real reason for the duel. Benvolio tells them to 'withdraw unto some private place, / Or reason coldly of [their] grievances' (50–1), not just because of the Prince's warning to cease the feud but also because their homoerotic subtext is becoming too explicit and 'all eyes gaze on' them (52). Mercutio responds to both Benvolio's instruction and Tybalt's accusation, speaking again on two levels when he says he 'will not budge for no man's pleasure' (54): he will not move from where he stands, and he will not 'bugger for any man's pleasure'.[36]

Tybalt's accusing Mercutio of having sexual relations with Romeo and his consideration of it as a basis for a confrontation between them can indicate his jealousy. His reactions fit what Freud calls delusional jealousy, which he associates with 'a homosexuality that has run its course' and defines 'as an attempt at defence against an unduly strong homosexual impulse'. Freud believes a man who feels this jealousy is actually projecting his feelings onto his female mate and saying, '"*I* do not love him, *she* loves him!"'[37] In this case, Tybalt is saying, 'I do not love Romeo, Mercutio loves him!' Porter notes that Capulet's guest list to the ball includes 'Mercutio and his brother Valentine' and 'Signor Valentino and his cousin Tybalt' (1.2.67, 70), calling 'Valentino' a variant of 'Valentine', which signifies lover and in particular Romeo, the paradigmatic lover.[38] This early association of both men with Valentine can be Shakespeare's cue to his audience to see them as men who are in love with the same man, a situation that makes them rivals and prepares for the crucial scene when they will come to arms over him.

Once Romeo enters, Tybalt directs his attention to him, calling him his 'man' (55), a term that can apply to a homosexual[39] and a signification of intimacy Mercutio chooses to overlook. He instead interprets it as a servant or retainer: 'But I'll be hanged, sir, if he wear your livery' (56). Tybalt also twice calls Romeo 'boy' (65, 132), which can designate a 'passive homosexual'.[40] Ignoring Mercutio's interjection, Tybalt clearly wants to talk to Romeo, proclaiming 'the love [he] bear[s] [him] can afford / No better term than this: [he is] a villain' (59–60) and saying he cannot 'excuse the injuries / That [he] hath done' him (65–6). Scholars see in the word 'injuries' an allusion to 'Romeo's uninvited appearance at the Capulets' feast, which resulted in Tybalt's being humiliatingly reproved by Juliet's father', and sarcasm in his contention that he 'love[s]' him.[41] While he most likely is speaking ironically, his words could reflect a truth he is not willing to admit to himself and others – that he truly does 'love' him, which has caused him to pursue the young man and accuse him of 'injur[ing]' or hurting him personally, not physically but emotionally. He does not make a reference to Romeo's 'intrusion' at the ball or an insult to the Montague family by this act; rather, he alludes vaguely to some private wrong done to him alone. Romeo states three times that he 'love[s]' him (61, 68, 69), at least consciously alluding to his new familial connection to him through marriage, but subconsciously referring to more personal feelings.

Overhearing the talk of 'love' between the men and fearing the two men have had intimate relations, Mercutio explodes in what most likely is a jealous rage – 'O calm, dishonourable, vile submission! / *Alla stoccada* carries it away' (72–3) – and draws his weapon on Tybalt, who, in turn, draws his. The intimate talk must make him fear Romeo has been pierced by Tybalt's 'butt-shaft' (2.4.16) – and perhaps he has. As the two men engage in the sword fight, Romeo steps in between them to try to get them to cease the battle, but Tybalt takes advantage of the 'intrusion' and stabs Mercutio under Romeo's arm. Although Mercutio blames his wound on the feud – 'A plague a' both houses!' (92) – the fight has little to do with it; rather, it is a personal battle over Romeo between the two men, both of whom care deeply for him. If one considers the homoerotic significance of the first duel in the play, and if one reads this present battle metaphorically, it can represent a homoerotic relationship that transpired between Mercutio and Tybalt in the play's history, with the fencing moves standing for phallic thrusts. Mercutio's asking Romeo 'Why the devil came you between us?' (104–5) can indicate more than Romeo's physically stepping in between the men; it can signify his causing the men's relationship to break up over him, with both men developing feelings for him.

Although escaping unharmed from a confrontation that leaves Mercutio dead, Tybalt returns to confront Romeo, the focus of his attention from the beginning. That he returns indicates the intensity of his feelings for him: Benvolio describes him as 'furious' (123), mad with both passion and anger (*OED*, *adj* 1a). Making the same allegation he did earlier to Mercutio – 'Thou wretched boy, that didst consort [Mercutio] here, / Shalt with him hence' (131–2) – he might look like a homophobe, but such extreme actions are a defence against his opposite true feelings of desiring Romeo so much that he is obsessed with him. Benvolio describes Tybalt's wounding of Mercutio as 'an envious thrust' (170), a characterization that underscores the jealousy he felt towards his rival for 'consort[ing]' with Romeo. The metaphoric significance of their turning their phallic swords on each other can indicate the two men have had sexual relations. The dynamics of the interactions between the three men suggest that, just as Romeo has turned from Mercutio to deny his homosexual nature, so has he from Tybalt, who follows Mercutio's adage, 'If love be rough with you, be rough with love' (1.4.27). Mercutio turns to 'rough' words to express his 'injuries'; Tybalt to 'rough' actions. Both men behave similarly to those patients whom Freud describes as reacting poorly to the loss of love, which results in a form of melancholia: 'An object choice, an attachment of the libido to a particular person, had at one time existed; then, owing to a real slight or disappointment coming from this loved person, the object-relationship was shattered. The result was not the normal one of a withdrawal of the libido from this object and a displacement of it on to a new one, but something different ... But the free libido was not displaced on to another object; it was withdrawn into the ego.' He goes on to explain that 'strong fixation to the loved object must have been present'.[42]

All of the men, not just Romeo, show signs of suffering from melancholia caused by the loss of a love object and seem suicidal, with the pun embedded in the word 'sycamore' (1.1.119) highlighting the 'amor[ous]' sickness from which they all suffer. While Benvolio's fate is uncertain, the last word he utters before he mysteriously leaves the play is 'die' (3.1.177), as Shakespeare leads us to infer he ends his own life. Tybalt does not need to return after the battle with Mercutio, but he is willing to endanger and lose his life over his feelings for Romeo. Likewise, Mercutio does not need to provoke Tybalt, who 'walk[s]' (3.1.74) away from the passive Romeo, but he puts his life on the line and ultimately loses it. Before his death Mercutio tells Romeo he is 'hurt' (3.1.91), a word that suggests not just physical but also emotional distress and echoes Tybalt's 'injuries'. The fatal wounds both Mercutio and Tybalt suffer represent their emotional anguish at the loss of love, of which Romeo seems unaware. He is so narcissistic, preoccupied with his own misery, and dedicated to maintaining his defences that he is oblivious to the impact his withdrawal has had on the men in his life and says he 'thought all for the best' (3.1.106). He may even secretly enjoy the men's attentions as they fight over him. When Mercutio says he is 'hurt', Romeo claims 'the hurt cannot be much' (3.1.97), insensitive to the misery he has caused him. Mercutio's provoking a duel he could easily have avoided, and his losing the swordfight despite his familiarity with Tybalt's duelling techniques, may indicate an element of self-destructiveness. Romeo describes him as one 'that God hath made, himself to mar' (2.4.111–12), and, indeed, Mercutio seems deliberately to put himself in harm's way. His ability in the last moments of his life to pun on being a 'grave man' (3.1.100) and his describing the wound as being 'enough' and ''twill serve' (3.1.99) can signify he does not fear death, and the physical injury will serve the purpose of accomplishing his plan to end his life. Beneath the scoffing, joking exterior lies a 'grave' man, sombre, serious and unhappy. He most likely senses that, despite his best efforts to get Romeo exclusively for himself, his beloved 'is already dead' (2.4.13), unreceptive and unfaithful. His refusal to compromise in a heteronormative world has taken great emotional toll on him, as it has on Tybalt.

Once Mercutio dies and places blame on his friend for his death, Romeo seems less susceptible to his Petrarchan stupor. Stressing the injustice of his receiving a fatal wound while the 'villain' Tybalt walks away unscathed, Mercutio encourages Romeo to rectify the injustice and kill his murderer, perhaps a last attempt to ensure an end to whatever relationship existed between the two. Romeo sinks deeper into melancholia after Mercutio's death and suicidal thoughts obsess him: 'This day's black fate on moe days doth depend / This but begins the woe others must end' (3.1.121–2). Although he claims his melancholia derives from being banished from Juliet's company, he refuses to cheer up when the Friar reminds him he should be 'happy' (3.3.136, 137, 139) that the Prince showed him mercy rather than sentencing him to death and assures him he will soon be reunited with Juliet. He petulantly clings to his despair and refuses to see that banishment is better than death. Wanting death more than life, he 'fall[s] upon the ground', 'taking the measure of an unmade grave' (3.3.69–70). Cursing and rebuking himself, he tells the Nurse that Juliet must hate his very name and asks the Friar to 'tell [him], / In what vile part of this anatomy / Doth [his] name lodge? Tell [him], that [he] may sack / The hateful mansion' (3.3.104–7). Despite spending a night with Juliet, he returns to his morbid mood. His behaviour is characteristic of the melancholic, who Freud contends displays 'an extraordinary diminution in his self-regard, an impoverishment of his ego on a grand scale. In mourning it is the world which has become poor and empty; in melancholia it is the ego itself. The patient represents his ego to us as worthless, incapable of any achievement and morally despicable; he reproaches himself, vilifies himself and expects to be cast out and punished. He abases himself before everyone and commiserates with his own relatives for being connected with anyone so unworthy'.[43] Romeo's persistent unhappiness indicates the source of his misery is not as he professes. He more likely mourns the death of his male companions, particularly Mercutio, and the figurative death of a vital part of his own sexual identity – losses that are so painful he cannot even consciously acknowledge them.

Although the Friar assures him he will work everything out to his advantage while he is in Mantua and inform him periodically of 'Every good hap to [him] that chances here' (3.3.170), once he arrives in Mantua he is still suicidal and notices an old, penurious apothecary, who he thinks would be desperate enough to sell him poison. After learning of Juliet's reputed death, he tracks the man down, purchases the poison and rushes to the Capulet crypt without first consulting with the Friar. He deludes himself into thinking he dies for Juliet, but he has been determined to kill himself before meeting her. Addressing her in the tomb, he continues to utter Petrarchan superficialities, hyperbolically addressing her beauty, indications his feelings for her are superficial as well. The more authentic sentiments occur when he addresses Tybalt's corpse, claiming he will kill himself to avenge his murder and implying he is 'merry' as he approaches his suicide: 'How oft, when men are at the point of death, / Have they been merry, which their keepers call / A lightening before death' (5.3.88–90). Since this is an apt description of Mercutio's last moments of life, when he punned on being a 'grave' man, Romeo most likely thinks of his friend immediately before his own demise, and his death, which Mercutio blamed on him, weighs heavily on his conscience. But his very last words are directed to the agent of death – the apothecary and his poison – and death itself, with whom he has had a 'dateless bargain' (5.3.115) since the beginning of the play.

Romeo's turning to women and the prospect of his marriage create heartache for both him and his male companions. His unwillingness or inability to defy the demands of a society that requires he marry and relegate his same-sex relationships to a less important role in his life causes the tragedy. Marriage in Shakespeare's plays seldom amicably coexists with male–male relationships. There is no societal niche for the homosexual who refuses to live a double life. In the comedies he is consigned to the periphery of the play world, while the others celebrate impending or completed nuptials. At the end he typically stands alone, isolated, broken-hearted and slighted. In the tragedies he dies, unable to bear the societal and personal pressures that crush his mental health.[44] The ubiquity of the defence mechanism of reaction formation among the male characters in *Romeo and Juliet* indicates the extensiveness of emotional pain and anxiety, and the attempts to deny their impact on the psyche. What is also tragic is for years scholars have brought their heteronormative mindset to the play and have overlooked the tribulations of the male characters by focusing exclusively on the relationship of Romeo and Juliet. But as queer and psychoanalytic studies become more compatible, the psychic toll of a heteronormative world on the homosexual in *Romeo and Juliet* and other Shakespearean plays undoubtedly will command the recognition it deserves.

EPILOGUE

This short conclusion sums up some of the highlights of the study, clarifying areas that need further development and anticipating the directions psychoanalysis in Shakespeare will take. This study has charted the genesis and development of psychoanalytic responses to Shakespeare and established his formative impact on the theory. Harold Bloom rightly claims 'the anxiety of influence has no more distinguished sufferer in our time than the founder of psychoanalysis, who always discovered that Shakespeare had been there before him, and all too frequently could not bear to confront this humiliating truth'.[1] Freud places Shakespeare at the centre of his theories by referencing *Hamlet* as the embodiment of his ideas about the Oedipus complex and has always been present in one form or another in psychoanalytic approaches to his works, a connection that establishes an enduring bond. We have seen that early approaches to Shakespeare are heavily indebted to Freud, and because his theory pivots around the oedipal situation, they primarily emphasize family connections, especially relations between fathers and sons, with repression, unconscious desires, oedipal conflicts, castration anxieties, jealousy, primal scene fantasies and incest being the dominant areas of analysis. The approach begins to expand as critics become more familiar with other psychoanalytic theorists and emphasize more the integral importance of the mother to a child's psychic well-being and development by exploring separation anxieties from the mother and male insecurities with female sexuality and corporeality. With the growing awareness of Lacan's theoretical difference from Freud, some Shakespearean scholars expand their attention to discourse and social forces as a means to probe characters' psyches.

While family relations are central concerns in Shakespeare's drama, psychoanalytic scholars since the 1980s have extended their analysis to explore different topics, such as identity development, psychosexual maturation, dream theory and, more recently, transgenderism, transvestism and female-to-female desire. Undoubtedly, the approaches and topics will continue to expand, even while the standard ones continue to pique scholars' interests.

Perhaps because psychology figures so prominently in his works, psychoanalytic theory has shown itself compatible with other theoretical approaches to Shakespeare. It has been paired with gender studies, anthropology, philosophy, theology, semiotics, deconstructionism and cultural materialism – just to name a few. Even those approaches that started out as oppositional to psychoanalysis have gradually developed a productive connection. For example, feminists first vehemently objected to what they perceived as a male-centred model, but with a growing appreciation of Lacan's focus on the influence of culture and patriarchy on the development of the psyche, they began to find such theories instrumental to their analyses. Likewise, the development of new historicism initially led to a marginalization of psychoanalysis in Shakespeare, but as psychoanalytic scholars began to historicize their concepts and readings, the two theories found a common ground. Some approaches, such as postcolonial and queer studies, for example, have not yet established a congenial relationship with psychoanalysis. Queer scholars often object to what they perceive as a heteronormative bias and a tendency to pathologize non-normative sexuality. But some of the earliest analyses of Shakespeare, as we have seen, focus on uncovering homosexual elements in his works, such as Iago's homoerotic feelings for Othello, or Leontes' for Polixenes, an approach that illustrates the interconnection between the two theories. While early psychoanalytic theory may seem limited and misdirected in its view of non-normative sexualities, other components of psychoanalysis, such as I have shown by applying defensive mechanisms to a reading of *Romeo and*

Juliet, can be useful in uncovering and exploring queerness in Shakespeare. That several other theories started out at odds with psychoanalytic theory and ultimately developed an affinity suggests the same will most likely develop with what may initially seem like less compatible theories.

We have also seen that the first studies are often limited in length and purview of Shakespeare's canon. Many of the earliest publications appear as essays in psychoanalytic journals. In large part because of Freud's fascination with *Hamlet*, early psychological studies focus on it. But with the evolution of the approach, practitioners have extended their interest to the romances and the problem comedies, perhaps because their problematical nature seems to derive from psychic dilemmas. Starting in the 1980s, book-length psychoanalytic studies of Shakespeare began to appear more frequently. Because later critics often apply more than one psychoanalytic theory to their approaches, their broader concerns allow them to analyse a larger body of plays, although typically the tragedies still loom large in these studies. While the comedies, sonnets and long poems have attracted some attention, especially in more recent years, they still substantially lag behind the other works in garnering psychological interest. They are often seen as gateways to the tragedies and critics quickly dispense with them in their analyses. For example, Freud examines the psychological significance of the casket motif in *The Merchant of Venice* but only as it leads to a more informed understanding of the psychic symbolism of the three daughters in the tragedy of *King Lear*.

I believe psychoanalytic theory will continue to be at the forefront of Shakespearean studies because it is intrinsic to detecting the depth of his characterization of the human mind. Future studies need to recognize, however, that while the comedies and poems may not pose mental fractures as complex and challenging as those in the tragedies, their psychological content has been slighted and warrants analysis like that directed to the more standard psychologized plays. What particularly deserves more attention is the psychology of Shakespeare's women. Feminist psychoanalytic scholars attempt to rectify this oversight, but even many of their analyses have been largely male-centred, concentrating on male characters' relationship and reaction to the feminine. Female characters in Shakespeare continue to be marginalized, as many of the major psychoanalytic approaches look at male anxieties, insecurities and even hatred of the feminine element. We need to come to a fuller assessment of Shakespeare's attitudes towards women and explore them in their own psychic dimensions rather than view them as conduits through which to psychoanalyse his male characters. Hopefully, the study that I have offered in Chapter 6 of Helena and the Countess of *All's Well* illustrates the psychological depth of some of the women in his comedies. Once studies of Shakespeare move further in this direction, feminism will develop an even more productive union with psychology.

Like other theories, psychoanalysis sometimes has been misapplied, with some judging the mis-readings as more egregious than those that result from other theories. This may very well be the case, but when psychoanalysis is expertly applied to the Shakespearean text, the readings are often groundbreaking and help to unravel unsolved mysteries that have vexed non-psychoanalytic critics for years. Undoubtedly, such innovative readings will continue to result from the application of the theory to the works of the master of human psychology. Psychoanalytic approaches to the canon will always find an essential place in Shakespearean criticism, and once they more frequently move beyond concentration on the tragedies to the other genres, they will illustrate the ubiquity of psychological concepts in all of his works.

NOTES

Introduction

1 Freud, Sigmund (1953–74), 'Delusions and Dream in Jensen's *Gradiva*' in James Strachey (trans. and ed.), *The Standard Edition of the Complete Psychological Works of Sigmund Freud*, 24 vols. London: Hogarth Press and the Institute of Psycho-Analysis, vol. 9, 8, 43–4.

2 Armstrong, Philip (2001), *Shakespeare in Psychoanalysis*. London and New York: Routledge, 88.

3 Dryden, John (1821), *An Essay of Dramatic Poesy* in Sir Walter Scott (ed.), *The Works of John Dryden*, 2nd edn, 18 vols. Edinburgh: Constable, vol. 15, 350.

4 Johnson, Samuel (1952), 'Preface to Shakespeare' in Walter Raleigh (ed.), *Johnson on Shakespeare*. London: H. Frowde, 11, 37.

5 Coleridge, Samuel Taylor (1904), *Lectures and Notes on Shakspere and Other English Poets*. London: G. Bell and Sons, 353, 343.

6 Pope, Alexander (1958), 'Preface to Shakespeare' in D. Nichol Smith (ed.), *Shakespeare Criticism: A Selection (1623–1840)*. London: Oxford University Press, 43.

7 Goethe, Johann Wolfgang von (1998), *Conversations of Goethe with Johann Peter Eckermann*, J. K. Moorhead (ed.), John Oxenford (trans.). New York: Da Capo Press, 132.

8 Bloom, Harold (1999), *Shakespeare: The Invention of the Human*. London: Harcourt Brace, 714.

9 Sulloway, Frank J. (1991), 'Reassessing Freud's case histories: The social construction of psychoanalysis', *Isis*, 82, 245–6.

10 Vickers, Brian (1993), *Appropriating Shakespeare: Contemporary Critical Quarrels*. New Haven and London: Yale University Press, 272–324.

11 Crews, Frederick C. (1986), *Skeptical Engagements*. New York: Oxford University Press, 97.

12 Vickers (1993), 285.

13 Greenblatt, Stephen (1986), 'Psychoanalysis and Renaissance Culture' in Patricia Parker and David Quint (eds), *Literary Theory/Renaissance Texts*. Baltimore: Johns Hopkins University Press, 210–24.

14 The anthologies are respectively: Schwartz, Murray M. and Coppélia Kahn (eds) (1980), *Representing Shakespeare: New Psychoanalytic Essays*. Baltimore and London: Johns Hopkins University Press, 265–86; and Sokol, B. J. (ed.) (1993), *The Undiscover'd Country: New Essays on Psychoanalysis and Shakespeare*. London: Free Association Books, 218–45.

15 Coleridge, Samuel Taylor (1987), *Lectures 1808–1819: On Literature*, R. A. Foakes (ed.), 2 vols. Princeton: Princeton University Press, vol. 2, 315.

16 Freedman, Barbara (1991), *Staging the Gaze: Postmodernism, Psychoanalysis and Shakespearian Comedy*. Ithaca: Cornell University Press, 29.

17 Armstrong (2001), 12.

Chapter 1

1 Consult Freud, Sigmund (1953–74), 'The Unconscious' in James Strachey (trans. and ed.), *The Standard Edition of the Complete Psychological Works of Sigmund Freud*. London: Hogarth Press and the Institute of Psychoanalysis, vol. 14, 159–204. The following discussion of Freud's key concepts is informed by Levin, Gerald (1975), *Sigmund Freud*. Boston: Twayne.

2 Consult Freud, Sigmund (1953–74), 'The Ego and the Id' in *Complete Psychological Works*, vol. 19, 1–59.

3 Consult Freud, Sigmund (1953–74), 'Repression' in *Complete Psychological Works*, vol. 14, 141–58.

4 Freud, Anna (1946), *The Ego and the Mechanisms of Defense*. New York: International Universities Press.

5 Freud, Sigmund (1953–74), *The Interpretation of Dreams* in *Complete Psychological Works*, vol. 4, 279–309.
6 Consult Freud, Sigmund (1953–74), 'The Dissolution of the Oedipus Complex' in *Complete Psychological Works*, vol. 19, 173–82.
7 Freud, Sigmund (1953–74), *Totem and Taboo* in *Complete Psychological Works*, vol. 13, 156.
8 Freud, Sigmund (1953–74), *The Interpretation of Dreams* in *Complete Psychological Works*, vol. 4, 265.
9 Freud, Sigmund (1953–74), 'On Psychotherapy' in *Complete Psychological Works*, vol. 7, 262.
10 Consult Freud, Sigmund (1953–74), 'Creative Writers and Day-Dreaming' in *Complete Psychological Works*, vol. 9, 141–54.
11 Freud, Sigmund (1953–74), 'An Outline of Psycho-analysis' in *Complete Psychological Works*, vol. 23, 192.
12 Freud, Sigmund (1953–74), 'The Theme of the Three Caskets' in *Complete Psychological Works*, vol. 12, 291–301.
13 Letter to James S. H. Bransom, 25 March 1934, quoted in Jones, Ernest (1953–7), *The Life and Works of Sigmund Freud*, 3 vols. New York: Basic Books, vol. 3, 457–8.
14 The items in the listing are respectively from the following sources: Freud, Sigmund (1953–74), *The Interpretation of Dreams* in *Complete Psychological Works*, vol. 4, 266; Freud, Sigmund (1953–74), 'Obsessions and Phobias,' Case 11 in *Complete Psychological Works*, vol. 3, 79; Jones (1953–7), 'The Fate of Two Women', vol. 2, 350; and Freud, Sigmund (1953–74), 'Some Character-types met with in Psycho-Analytic Work' in *Complete Psychological Works*, vol. 14, 324.
15 The above discussion is informed by Holland, Norman N. (1960), 'Freud on Shakespeare', *PMLA: Publications of the Modern Language Association of America*, 75, 163–73.
16 Jones, Ernest (1910), 'The Oedipus-complex as an explanation of Hamlet's mystery: A study in motive', *The American Journal of Psychology*, 21, 72–113: and (1976), *Hamlet and Oedipus*. New York and London: Norton.
17 Jones (1976), 19.

18 Ibid., 70.

19 Rank, Otto (1992), *The Incest Theme in Literature and Legend: Fundamentals of a Psychology of Literary Creation*, Gregory C. Richter (trans.). Baltimore and London: Johns Hopkins University Press, esp. 165–88.

20 Quoted in Jones (1976), 28.

21 Rank (1992), 168–9.

22 The quotations belong respectively to Krims, Marvin Bennett (2006), *The Mind According to Shakespeare: Psychoanalysis in the Bard's Writing*. London: Praeger, ix; and Holland, Norman N. (1966), *Psychoanalysis and Shakespeare*. New York: McGraw-Hill, 3.

Chapter 2

1 Faber, M. D. (1970), Introduction in M. D. Faber (ed.), *The Design Within: Psychoanalytic Approaches to Shakespeare*. New York: Science House, 7.

2 Sachs, Hanns (1970), 'The Measure in *Measure for Measure*' in M. D. Faber (ed.), 479–97.

3 Ibid., 493.

4 Wangh, Martin (1970), '*Othello*: The Tragedy of Iago' in M. D. Faber (ed.), 157–68.

5 Freud, Sigmund (1953–74), 'Some Neurotic Mechanisms in Jealousy, Paranoia and Homosexuality' in Strachey (trans. and ed.), *The Standard Edition of the Complete Psychological Works of Sigmund Freud*, vol. 18, 225.

6 Wangh, 164.

7 Faber (ed.) (1970), 387 and 233. The two studies, both also in this book, are Ernst Kris, 'Prince Hal's conflict', 389–407; and Ludwig Jekels, 'The Riddle of Shakespeare's *Macbeth*', 235–49.

8 Jekels (1970), 241.

9 Jung, Carl G. (1959), *The Archetypes and the Collective Unconscious*, R. F. C. Hull (trans.). London: Pantheon Books. The discussion of Jung is informed by Hall, Calvin S. (1973),

A Primer of Jungian Psychology. New York: New American Library.
10 Jekels (1970), 238.
11 Bodkin, Maud (1934), *Archetypal Patterns in Poetry: Psychological Studies of Imagination*. London: Oxford University Press, H. Milford, 13.
12 Ibid.
13 Ibid., 21.
14 Ibid., 23.
15 Reik, Theodor (1970), 'Jessica, My Child' in M. D. Faber (ed.), 440, 454.
16 Auden, W. H. (1948), *The Dyer's Hand and Other Essays*. New York: Random House, 195–6, 253, 266.
17 Stewart, J. I. M. (1949), *Character and Motive in Shakespeare: Some Recent Appraisals Examined*. London and New York: Longmans, Greene and Co.
18 Ibid., 93.
19 Ibid., 104.
20 Ibid., 137
21 Ibid., 139.
22 Frye, Northrop (2006), *Anatomy of Criticism: Four Essays*, Robert Denham (ed.). Toronto: University of Toronto Press, 146–223.
23 Frye, Northrop (1965), *A Natural Perspective: The Development of Shakespearean Comedy and Romance*. New York: Columbia University Press, 56, 58.
24 Ibid., see especially 121–2, where Frye says comedy, in particular Shakespearean, is based on the movement 'from death to rebirth, decadence to renewal, winter to spring, darkness to a new dawn'.
25 Lacan, Jacques (1977), *Ecrits*, Alan Sheridan (trans.). New York: Norton. The discussion of Lacan is informed by Evans, Dylan (1966), *An Introductory Dictionary of Lacanian Psychoanalysis*. London and New York: Routledge.
26 Lacan, Jacques (1982), 'Desire and the Interpretation of Desire in *Hamlet*' in Shoshana Felman (ed.), *Literature and*

Psychoanalysis: The Question of Reading, Otherwise. Baltimore: Johns Hopkins University Press, 11–52.

27 Ibid., 36.

28 Ibid., 19.

29 Holland, Norman N. (1966), *Psychoanalysis and Shakespeare*. New York: McGraw-Hill, 220.

30 Wheeler, Richard P. (1987), 'Psychoanalytic criticism and teaching Shakespeare', *ADE Bulletin*, 87, 20.

31 Eissler, K. R. (1971), *Discourse on Hamlet and 'Hamlet': A Psychoanalytic Inquiry*. New York: International Universities Press; and Avi Erlich (1977), *Hamlet's Absent Father*. Princeton: Princeton University Press.

32 Eissler, 296.

33 Reid, Stephen (1970b), 'In defense of Goneril and Regan', *American Imago*, 27, 242, 244.

34 Reid (1970a), 'Desdemona's guilt', *American Imago*, 27, 245–62.

35 Reid (1968), 'Othello's jealousy', *American Imago*, 25, 274–93.

36 Reid (1974), 'Hamlet's melancholia', *American Imago*, 31, 378–400.

37 Reid (1970c), 'The Winter's Tale', *American Imago*, 27, 277.

38 Reid (1970b), 237.

39 Reid (1976), 'Othello's occupation: Beyond the pleasure principle', *Psychoanalytic Review*, 63, 555.

40 Quoted by Stephen Reid (1970), 'A psychoanalytic reading of *Troilus and Cressida* and *Measure for Measure*', *Psychoanalytic Review*, 57, 266.

41 Reid (1969), '"I am Misanthropos" – A psychoanalytic reading of Shakespeare's *Timon of Athens*', *Psychoanalytic Review*, 56, 444.

42 Klein, Melanie (1975), 'Notes on some Schizoid Mechanisms' in *Envy and Gratitude and Other Works 1946–63*. New York: Free Press, 1–24.

43 Reid (1969), 444.

44 Schwartz, Murray M. (1970), 'Between Fantasy and Imagination: A Psychological Exploration of *Cymbeline*' in

Frederick C. Crews (ed.), *Psychoanalysis and Literary Process*. Cambridge, MA: Winthrop Publishers, 219–83.
45 Adelman, Janet (1992), *Suffocating Mothers: Fantasies of Maternal Origin in Shakespeare's Plays, 'Hamlet' to 'The Tempest'*. New York: Routledge, 355.
46 Schwartz (1973), 'Leontes' jealousy in *The Winter's Tale*', *American Imago*, 30, 272.
47 Schwartz (1975), '*The Winter's Tale*: Loss and transformation', *American Imago*, 32, 158.
48 Schwartz (1980),'Shakespeare through Contemporary Psychoanalysis' in Murray M. Schwarz and Coppélia Kahn (eds), *Representing Shakespeare: New Psychoanalytic Essays*. Baltimore and London: Johns Hopkins University Press, 21–32.
49 Winnicott, D. W. (1971), *Playing and Reality*. London: Basic Books.
50 Schwartz (1980), 26, 27, 29.
51 Ibid., 31.
52 Aronson, Alex (1972), *Psyche and Symbol in Shakespeare*. Bloomington: Indiana University Press.

Chapter 3

1 Sundelson, David (1983), *Shakespeare's Restorations of the Father*. New Brunswick: Rutgers University Press, 5.
2 Ibid., 70.
3 Ibid., 18.
4 Ibid., 88.
5 Ibid., 109.
6 Ibid., 108.
7 Kirsch, Arthur (1981), *Shakespeare and the Experience of Love*. Cambridge: Cambridge University Press, 177.
8 Ibid., 37–8.
9 Quoted ibid., 65.

10 Ibid., 98.

11 Ibid., 165.

12 Quoted by Cavell, Stanley (1987), *Disowning Knowledge in Six Plays of Shakespeare*. Cambridge: Cambridge University Press, 182.

13 Ibid., 184.

14 This explication is informed by Altman, Joel B. (1993), 'Review of *Disowning Knowledge in Six Plays of Shakespeare* by Stanley Cavell', *Medieval and Renaissance Drama in England*, 6, 231–2.

15 Ibid., 186.

16 Ibid., 188–9.

17 This is informed by Altman (1993), 227.

18 Ibid., 47.

19 Ibid., 55.

20 Ibid., 165.

21 Coursen, H. R. (1986), *The Compensatory Psyche: A Jungian Approach to Shakespeare*. Lanham, MD: University Press of America, xi.

22 Holland, Norman N. (1980), 'Hermia's Dream' in Murray M. Schwartz and Coppélia Kahn (eds), *Representing Shakespeare: New Psychoanalytic Essays*. Baltimore and London: Johns Hopkins University Press, 11.

23 Ibid., 7, 9, 12.

24 Barber, C. L. (1980), 'The Family in Shakespeare's Development: Tragedy and Sacredness' in Schwarz and Kahn (eds), 196.

25 Fineman, Joel (1980), 'Fratricide and Cuckoldry: Shakespeare's Doubles' in Schwarz and Kahn (eds), 84, 103, 100.

26 Adelman, Janet (1980), '"Anger's my Meat": Feeding, Dependency, and Aggression in *Coriolanus*' in Schwarz and Kahn (eds), 129–49.

27 Leverenz, David (1980), 'The Woman in Hamlet: An Interpersonal View' in Schwarz and Kahn (eds), 110–28.

28 Skura, Meredith Anne (1980), 'Interpreting Posthumus' Dream from Above and Below: Families, Psychoanalysis, and Literary Critics' in Schwarz and Kahn (eds), 211, 213.

29 Skura, Meredith Anne (1981), *The Literary Use of the Psychoanalytic Process*. New Haven: Yale University Press, 264.

30 Skura, Meredith Anne (1989), 'Discourse and the individual: The case of colonialism in *The Tempest*', *Shakespeare Quarterly*, 40, 42–69.

31 Ibid., 64.

32 Ibid., 65, 67.

33 Westlund, Joseph (1984), *Shakespeare's Reparative Comedies: A Psychoanalytic View of the Middle Plays*. Chicago: University of Chicago Press, 2.

34 Ibid., viii.

35 Ibid., 91.

36 Wheeler, Richard P. (1981), *Shakespeare's Development and the Problem Comedies: Turn and Counter-Turn*. Berkeley: University of California Press, 199, 150, 116.

37 Erikson, Erik (1968), *Identity: Youth and Crisis*. New York: W. W. Norton, 96–7, 103–6.

38 Wheeler (1981), 200.

39 Mahler, Margaret (1969), *On Human Symbiosis and the Vicissitudes of Individuation*. London: International Universities Press; and (1975), *The Psychological Birth of the Human Infant*. New York: Basic Books.

40 Barber, C. L. (1959), *Shakespeare's Festive Comedy: A Study of Dramatic Form and Its Relation to Social Custom*. Princeton: Princeton University Press, 15.

41 Barber, C. L. and Richard P. Wheeler (1986), *The Whole Journey: Shakespeare's Power of Development*. Berkeley: University of California Press, 280.

42 Ibid., 298, 333.

43 Ibid., 336.

44 Fineman, Joel (1986), *Shakespeare's Perjured Eye: The Invention of Poetic Subjectivity in the Sonnets*. Berkeley: University of California Press, 45.

45 Ibid., 16, 297.

46 Ibid., 122.

47 Ibid., 243.

48 Ibid., 295.

49 Ibid., 292.

50 Berger, Harry Jr (1985a), 'Psychoanalyzing the Shakespeare Text: The First Three Scenes of the *Henriad*' in Patricia Parker and Geoffrey H. Hartman (eds), *Shakespeare and the Question of Theory*. New York and London: Methuen, 214.

51 Ibid., 213.

52 Ibid., 226, 227.

53 Berger, Harry Jr (1985b), 'Text Against Performance: The Gloucester Family Romance' in Peter Erickson and Coppélia Kahn (eds), *Shakespeare's 'Rough Magic': Renaissance Essays in Honor of C. L. Barber*. Newark: University of Delaware Press, 221.

54 Berger, Harry Jr (2004), 'What Did the King Know and When Did He Know It? Shakespearean Discourses and Psychoanalysis' in Russ McDonald (ed.), *Shakespeare: An Anthology of Criticism and Theory 1945–2000*. Oxford: Blackwell, 381, 379–81.

55 Ibid., 380.

56 All of Berger's previously mentioned essays, as well as others, appear in Berger (1997), Peter Erickson (ed.), *Making Trifles of Terrors: Redistributing Complicities in Shakespeare*. Stanford: Stanford University Press.

57 Nevo, Ruth (1987b), *Shakespeare's Other Language*. London and New York: Methuen, 25. Roberts, Jeanne Addison (1993), 'Review of *Shakespeare's Other Language* by Ruth Nevo', *Shakespeare Studies*, 21, 287–90, makes similar points as I do throughout this synopsis of Nevo's book.

58 Ibid., 24

59 Lacan, Jacques (1977), *Ecrits*, Alan Sheridan (trans.). New York: Norton, 93.

60 Nevo (1987a), 118.

61 Stockholder, Kay (1987), *Dream Works: Lovers and Families in Shakespeare's Plays*. Toronto: University of Toronto, 5.

62 Ibid., 20.

63 Ibid., 5, 220.

64 Ibid., 227.

65 Holland, Norman N., Sidney J. Homan and Bernard J. Paris (eds) (1989), *Shakespeare's Personality*. Berkeley: University of California, 1.

66 Ibid., 7.

67 Barber, C. L. and Richard P. Wheeler (1989), 'Shakespeare in the Rising Middle Class' in Holland et al. (eds), 17–40.

68 Farrell, Kirby (1989), 'Love, Death, and Patriarchy in *Romeo and Juliet*' in Holland et al. (eds), 86–102.

69 Hawkins, Sherman (1989), 'Aggression and the Project of the Histories' in Holland et al. (eds), 41–65.

70 Holland, Norman N. (1989a), 'Sons and Substitutions: Shakespeare's Phallic Fantasy' in Holland et al. (eds), 66–85.

71 Paris, Bernard J. (1989), '*The Tempest*: Shakespeare's Ideal Solution' in Holland et al. (eds), 206–25.

72 Novy, Marianne (1989), 'Shakespeare and the Bonds of Brotherhood' in Holland et al. (eds), 103–15.

73 Willbern, David (1989),'What is Shakespeare?' in Holland et al. (eds), 225–43; and Barbara Freedman, 'Misrecognizing Shakespeare' in Holland et al. (eds), 244–60.

74 Holland, Norman N. (1989), 'Introduction' in Holland et al. (eds), 9.

75 Neely, Carol Thomas (1989), 'Shakespeare's Women: Historical Facts and Dramatic Representations' in Holland et al. (eds), 116–34.

76 Adelman, Janet (1989), 'Bed Tricks: On Marriage as the end of Comedy in *All's Well That Ends Well* and *Measure for Measure*' in Holland et al. (eds), 151–74; and William Kerrigan (1989), 'The Personal Shakespeare: Three Clues' in Holland et al. (eds), 175–90.

77 Garner, Shirley Nelson (1989), 'Male Bonding and the Myth of Women's Deception in Shakespeare's Plays' in Holland et al. (eds), 135–50.

78 Gohlke (Sprengnether), Madelon, '"I wooed thee with my sword": Shakespeare's Tragic Paradigms' in Murray M. Schwartz and Coppélia Kahn (eds), 183.

79 Ibid., 180.

80 Sprengnether, Madelon (née Gohlke), 'The Boy Actor and Femininity in *Antony and Cleopatra*' in Holland et al. (eds), 191–205.

81 Kahn, Coppélia (1981), *Man's Estate: Masculine Identity in Shakespeare*. Berkeley: University of California Press, 17.

82 Ibid., 55 n. 12.

83 Ibid., 10.

84 Ibid., 11, 10.

85 Ibid., 18.

86 Ibid., 70.

87 Ibid., 110, 104.

88 Ibid., 19.

89 Ibid., 151.

90 Ibid., 194.

91 Ibid., 202.

92 Ibid., 225.

93 Kahn, Coppélia (1986), 'The Absent Mother in *King Lear*' in Margaret W. Ferguson, Maureen Quilligan and Nancy J. Vickers (eds), *Rewriting the Renaissance: The Discourse of Sexual Difference in Early Modern Europe*. Chicago and London: University of Chicago Press, 35, 36.

94 Ibid., 49

95 Greenblatt, Stephen (1986), 'Psychoanalysis and Renaissance Culture' in *Literary Theory/Renaissance Texts*, Patricia Parker and David Quint (eds). Baltimore: Johns Hopkins University Press, 221.

96 Holland, 1989, 'Introduction' in Holland et al. (eds), 4.

97 Ibid., 6.

Chapter 4

1 Adelman, Janet (1982), *Suffocating Mothers: Fantasies of Maternal Origin in Shakespeare's Plays, 'Hamlet' to 'The Tempest'*. New York: Routledge, 36.

2 Ibid., 33.

3 Ibid., 36.

4 Ibid.

5 Ibid., 128.

6 Ibid., 83.

7 Ibid., 191, 235.

8 Traub, Valerie (1992), *Desire and Anxiety: Circulations of Sexuality in Shakespearean Drama*. London: Routledge, 3.

9 Ibid., 26.

10 Ibid., 28, 33.

11 Ibid., 51.

12 Ibid., 53.

13 Ibid., 68.

14 Ibid., 92.

15 Ibid., 124, 141–2.

16 Schiesari, Juliana (1992), *The Gendering of Melancholia: Feminism, Psychoanalysis, and the Symbolics of Loss in Renaissance Literature*. Ithaca: Cornell University Press, 10.

17 Ibid., 7, 4.

18 Ibid., 53.

19 Ibid.

20 Ibid., 21.

21 Ibid., 239.

22 Ibid., 265.

23 Sokol, B. J. (ed.) (1993), 'Introduction' in *The Undiscover'd Country: New Essays on Psychoanalysis and Shakespeare*. London: Free Association Books, 2.

24 Bock, Philip K. (1993), '"Neither two nor one": Dual Unity in *The Phoenix and the Turtle*' in *The Undiscover'd Country: New Essays in Psychoanalysis and Shakespeare*, 40.

25 Faber, M. D. (1993), '*Hamlet* and the Inner World of Objects' in *The Undiscover'd Country: New Essays on Psychoanalysis and Shakespeare*, 58, 90.

26 Stephens, Lyn (1993), '"A wilderness of monkeys": A Psychodynamic Study of *The Merchant of Venice*' in *The Undiscover'd Country: New Essays on Psychoanalysis and Shakespeare*, 120.

27 Ibid., 101, 93.

28 Sheppard, Angela (1993), '"Soiled mother or soul of woman?": A Response to *Troilus and Cressida*' in *The Undiscover'd Country: New Essays on Psychoanalysis and Shakespeare*, 137–8.

29 Ibid., 141.

30 Ibid., 148.

31 Sokol, B. J. (1993), '*The Tempest*, "All torment, trouble, wonder and amazement": A Kleinian Reading' in *The Undiscover'd Country: New Essay on Psychoanalysis and Shakespeare*, 191.

32 Ibid., 209, 210.

33 Rogers, Robert (1991), *Self and Other: Object Relations in Psychoanalysis and Literature*. New York: New York University Press, 161.

34 Ibid., 165.

35 Ibid., 166.

36 Ibid., 169, 170.

37 Ibid., 175.

38 Reinhard Lupton, Julia and Kenneth Reinhard (1993), *After Oedipus: Shakespeare in Psychoanalysis*. Ithaca and London: Cornell University Press, 11.

39 Ibid., 24.

40 Ibid., 147.

41 Ibid., 148.

42 Ibid., 152.

43 Ibid., 153.

44 Coursen, H. R. (1992), *Shakespearean Performance as Interpretation*. Newark: University of Delaware Press, 14.

45 Ibid., 75.

46 Ibid.

47 Ibid., 117.

48 Plasse, Marie A. (1992), 'Review of *Staging the Gaze: Postmodernism, Psychoanalysis, and Shakespearean Comedy* by Barbara Freedman', *College Literature*, 19, 145, describes Freedman's concept of theatricality in similar terms.

49 Freedman, Barbara (1991), *Staging the Gaze: Postmodernism, Psychoanalysis, and Shakespearean Comedy*. Ithaca: Cornell University Press, 1.

50 Ibid., 2.

51 Ibid., 3.

52 Ibid., 6.

53 Ibid., 94.

54 Ibid., 139.

55 Ibid., 183.

56 Ibid., 200.

57 Ibid., 205.

58 Ibid., 226.

59 Paris, Bernard J. (1991a), *Bargains with Fate: Psychological Crises and Conflicts in Shakespeare and His Plays*. New York: Plenum Press, 9.

60 Horney, Karen (1950), *Neurosis and Human Growth: The Struggle Toward Self-Realization*. New York: Norton, 15. Maver, Igor (1994), 'Review of *Character as a Subversive Force in Shakespeare: The History and Roman Plays* by Bernard J. Paris', *The Review of English Studies*, 45, 565, describes the strategy in similar terms.

61 Paris, Bernard J. (1991b), *Character as a Subversive Force in Shakespeare: The History and Roman Plays*. London: Associated University Presses, 194.

62 Ibid., 122.
63 Sanderson, Richard K. (1992), 'Review of *A Theater of Envy: William Shakespeare* by Rene Girard', *Rocky Mountain Review of Language and Literature*, 46, 78.
64 Girard, René (1991), *A Theater of Envy: William Shakespeare*. New York: Oxford University Press, 46.
65 Ibid., 103.
66 Ibid., 14.
67 Ibid., 91.

Chapter 5

1 Krier, Theresa (2001), *Birth Passages: Maternity and Nostalgia, Antiquity to Shakespeare*. Ithaca: Cornell University Press, ix.
2 Ibid., xiv.
3 Ibid., 52.
4 Ibid., 140, 155.
5 Ibid., 161.
6 Ibid., 245.
7 Ibid., 247.
8 Stone, James W. (2010), *Crossing Gender in Shakespeare: Feminist Psychoanalysis and the Difference Within*. New York: Routledge, 1
9 Ibid.
10 Ibid., 24.
11 Ibid., 25, 28.
12 Ibid., 36.
13 Ibid., 112, 127.
14 Ibid., 21.
15 Ibid.
16 Ibid., 18.
17 Ibid., 19.
18 Ibid., 62.

19 Ibid., 20.

20 Armstrong, Philip (2001), *Shakespeare in Psychoanalysis*. London and New York: Routledge, 5.

21 Ibid., 40, 17.

22 Ibid., 92.

23 Ibid., 99, 101, 106.

24 Ibid., 187.

25 Ibid., 224.

26 Armstrong, Philip (2000), *Shakespeare's Visual Regime: Tragedy, Psychoanalysis, and the Gaze*. New York: Palgrave, 3.

27 Ibid.

28 Marshall, Cynthia (2003), 'Review of *Shakespeare's Visual Regime: Tragedy, Psychoanalysis and the Gaze* by Philip Armstrong', *Shakespeare Quarterly*, 54, 235, makes the same point in similar terms.

29 Ibid., 8, 10, 11.

30 Ibid., 13.

31 Ibid., 17.

32 Ibid., 42, 45.

33 Ibid., 51.

34 Ibid., 74, 75.

35 Ibid., 177.

36 Ibid., 183.

37 Ibid., 202.

38 Marshall (2003), 237, makes a similar observation.

39 Jones, Ann Rosalind and Peter Stallybrass (2000), 'Fetishisms and Renaissances' in Carla Mazzio and Douglas Trevor (eds), *Historicism, Psychoanalysis, and Early Modern Culture*. New York: Routledge, 31.

40 Garber, Marjorie (2000), 'Second-best Bed' in Mazzio and Trevor (eds), 376–96.

41 Mazzio, Carla (2000), 'The Melancholy of Print: *Love's Labour's Lost*' in Mazzio and Trevor (eds), 188.

42 Hillman, David (2000), 'The Inside Story' in Mazzio and Trevor (eds), 300.

43 Ibid., 312.

44 Trevor, Douglas (2000), 'George Herbert and the Scene of Writing' in Mazzio and Trevor (eds), 228–58.

45 Maus, Katherine Eisaman (2000), 'Sorcery and Subjectivity in Early Modern Discourses of Witchcraft' in Mazzio and Trevor (eds), 325–48.

46 Guillory, John (2000), '"To please the wiser sort": Violence and Philosophy in *Hamlet*' in Mazzio and Trevor (eds), 97.

47 Ibid., 84.

48 Goldberg, Jonathan (2000), 'The Anus in *Coriolanus*' in Mazzio and Trevor (eds), 264.

49 Ibid., 266.

50 Neely, Carol Thomas (2004), *Distracted Subjects: Madness and Gender in Shakespeare and Early Modern Culture*. Ithaca and London: Cornell University Press, 2.

51 Ibid.

52 Ibid., 7, 46

53 Ibid., 117.

54 Ibid., 213.

55 Marshall, Cynthia (2002), *The Shattering of the Self: Violence, Subjectivity, and Early Modern Texts*. Baltimore: Johns Hopkins University Press, 2, 4.

56 Ibid., 1.

57 Ibid., 5.

58 Ibid. 36.

59 Ibid., 53.

60 Ibid., 11.

61 Miller, David Lee (2003), *Dreams of the Burning Child: Sacrificial Sons and the Father's Witness*. Ithaca: Cornell University Press, 94.

62 Ibid., 95.

63 Ibid., 118, 119.

Chapter 6

1 Shakespeare, William (1967), *All's Well That Ends Well*, G. K. Hunter (ed.). London: Methuen, 1.1.1. All further references in this chapter will be to this edition and will be noted in the text by act, scene and line numbers.

2 Wheeler, Richard P. (1981), *Shakespeare's Development and the Problem Comedies: Turn and Counter-Turn*. Berkeley: University of California Press, for example, emphasizes Bertram's 'deep psychological conflict', 55; his struggle to assert 'a masculine identity independent of infantile conflict', 43; and to prove 'his potency has survived the threat aroused by the incestuous dimension of his marriage', 53. While Adelman, Janet (1992), *Suffocating Mothers: Fantasies of Maternal Origin in Shakespeare's Plays, 'Hamlet' to 'The Tempest'*. New York: Routledge, highlights the maternal power embodied in Helena, she, too, spotlights Bertram's desires, in particular his fantasies of despoiling virginity, 76–86. Stockholder, Kay (1987), *Dream Works: Lovers and Families in Shakespeare's Plays*. Toronto: University of Toronto, explores Bertram's oedipal desires and clarifies that the bed trick allows him to fulfil these desires yet evade the guilt, 74–7.

3 Simpson, John and Edmund Weiner (eds) (2011), *Oxford English Dictionary*. Oxford: Oxford University Press, 'likelihood' *n* 1. All further references to this work will be designated in the text as *OED*.

4 Partridge, Eric (1990), *Shakespeare's Bawdy*. London and New York: Routledge, 244, 176, glosses 'thorn' as 'penis' and 'rose' as 'pudend, maidenhead'.

5 The quotations are respectively from Freud, Sigmund (1953–74), *Three Essays on the Theory of Sexuality*, 'III, The Transformations of Puberty' in James Strachey (trans. and ed.), *The Standard Edition of the Complete Psychological Works of Sigmund Freud*, vol. 7, 225; and *Totem and Taboo*, vol. 13, 123.

6 Freud, (1953–74), 'Totem and Taboo', *Complete Psychological Works*, vol. 13, 119–26.

7 Ibid., 5–6.

8 Shakespeare, William (2006), *Measure for Measure, All's Well That Ends Well, and Troilus and Cressida*, David Bevington and David Scott Kastan (eds). New York: Bantam Dell, 216.

9 Henke, James T. (1974), *Renaissance Dramatic Bawdy (Exclusive of Shakespeare): An Annotated Glossary and Critical Essays*, 2 vols. Salzburg: Institut für Englische Sprache und Literatur, Universität Salzburg, vol. 2, 217, 147, 150, 191.

10 Quoted by Tesone, Juan Eduardo (2005), 'Incest(s) and the Negation of Otherness' in Giovanna Ambrosio (ed.), *On Incest: Psychoanalytic Perspectives*. London and New York: Karnac, 54.

11 Lehnhof, Kent R. (2007), 'Performing Woman: Female Theatricality in *All's Well, That Ends Well*' in Gary Waller (ed.), *'All's Well, That Ends Well': New Critical Essays*. New York and London: Routledge, 115, 119.

12 Rubinstein, Frankie (1989), *A Dictionary of Shakespeare's Sexual Puns and their Significance*, 2nd edn. London: Macmillan, 101.

13 Ibid.

14 The following scholars highlight the sexual component of the cure: Hodgdon, Barbara (1987), 'The making of virgins and mothers: Sexual signs, substitute scenes and doubled presences in *All's Well That Ends Well*', *Philological Quarterly*, 66, 48, 52; and Field, Catherine (2007), '"Sweet practicer, thy physic I will try": Helena and her "good receipt" in *All's Well, That Ends Well*' in Gary Waller (ed.), *'All's Well, That Ends Well': New Critical Essays*. New York and London: Routledge, 195–202.

15 Partridge (1990), 203.

16 The glosses are provided respectively by Partridge (1990), 192, 171, and 158; and Rubinstein (1989), 70.

17 Rubinstein (1989), 280, 40.

18 Bergeron, David (2007), '"The credit of your father": Absent Fathers in *All's Well, That Ends Well*' in *'All's Well, That Ends Well': New Critical Essays*, 175, 176, claims Helena 'becomes the "child/daughter" for the King', and 'the King functions as father as well as king'.

19 Rank, Otto (1971), *The Incest Theme in Literature and Legend: Fundamentals of a Psychology of Literary Creation*, Gregory C.

Richter (trans.). Baltimore and London: Johns Hopkins University Press, 301. Forker, Charles R. (1989), '"A little more than kin, and less than kind": Incest, intimacy, narcissism, and identity in Elizabethan and Stuart drama', *Medieval and Renaissance Drama in England*, 4, 13, contends, 'That Renaissance culture was fascinated by forbidden forms of sexuality – especially desire within the confines of the family – is attested by the popularity of the subject in the poetry, prose fiction, and drama of the period.'

20 Colman, E. A. M. (1976), *The Dramatic Use of Bawdy in Shakespeare*. London: Longman, 221, 185.

21 Shakespeare, William (1967), *All's Well That Ends Well*, Hunter (ed.). London: Methuen, 11. Henke (1974), vol. 2, 94, clarifies that 'As a verb "blow" apparently also possessed the contemporary bawdy sense of to perform fellatio.'

22 Welldon, Estela V. (2005), 'Incest: A Therapeutic Challenge' in Ambrosio (ed.), 86.

23 Consult, for example, Magee, William H. (1971), 'Helena, a female Hamlet', *English Miscellany*, 22, 31–46; Nevo, Ruth (1987), 'Motive and Meaning in *All's Well That Ends Well*' in John W. Mahon and Thomas A. Pendleton (eds), *'Fanned and Winnowed Opinions': Shakespearean Essays Presented to Harold Jenkins*. London and New York: Methuen, 35; and Bergernon (2007), 169.

24 Nevo (1987a), 36, concurs that 'her love for Bertram has ... taken the place of her love for her father, the one image overlaying the other'.

25 Argentieri, Simona (2005), 'Incest Yesterday and Today: From Conflict to Ambiguity' in Ambrosio (ed.), 23.

26 Partridge (1990), 175.

27 Glass, James M. (1993), *Shattered Selves: Multiple Personality in a Postmodern World*. Ithaca and London: Cornell University Press, 54.

28 Ambrosio, Giovanna (2005), 'Introduction' in Ambrosio (ed.), 7.

29 Tesone (2005), 59; and Alizade, Mariam (2005), 'Incest: The Damaged Psychic Flesh' in Ambrosio (ed.), 108.

30 Argentieri (2005), 32.

31 Freud (1953–74), *Three Essays on the Theory of Sexuality*, 'III, The Transformations of Puberty', in *Complete Psychological Works*, vol. 7, 226.

32 Freud (1953–74), 'Totem and Taboo' in *Complete Psychological Works*, vol. 13, 15.

33 Nevo (1987), 'Motive and Meaning in *All's Well That Ends Well*', 35, claims that because 'she cannot have a husband in her son, she will identify with the girl who would be his wife, and so transform her love for Bertram into a double maternal solicitude'.

34 Freud (1953–74), *New Introductory Lectures on Psycho-Analysis*, '33, Femininity' in *Complete Psychological Works*, vol. 22, 120.

35 For example, Ellerbeck, Erin (2011), 'Adoption and the language of horticulture in *All's Well That Ends Well*', *SEL: Studies in English Literature*, 51, 318, argues it is 'the Countess's interconnective relationship with Helena that the play endorses as a model for parent–child relations'.

36 The quotations belong respectively to Alizade (2005), 109, and Ambrosio (2005), 10.

37 Freud (1953–74), *The Interpretation of Dreams* in *Complete Psychological Works*, vol. 4, 260–1.

38 Rank (1971), 22.

39 'Totem and Taboo' in *Complete Psychological Works*, vol. 13, 16.

40 Freud (1953–74), 'Some Psychical Consequences of the Anatomical Distinction Between the Sexes' in *Complete Psychological Works*, vol. 19, 257.

41 Tesone (2005), 59.

42 The quotations belong respectively to Snyder, Susan (1988), '*All's Well that Ends Well* and Shakespeare's Helens: Text and subtext, subject and object', *English Literary Renaissance*, 18, 66; McCandless, David (1994), 'Helena's bed-trick: Gender and performance in *All's Well That Ends Well*', *Shakespeare Quarterly*, 45, 455; and Hunter, Robert Grams (1965), *Shakespeare and the Comedy of Forgiveness*. New York: Columbia University Press, 114.

43 Consult, for example, Evans, Bertrand (1960), *Shakespeare's Comedies*. Oxford: Clarendon Press, 145–66; and Levin, Richard A. (1980), '*All's Well That Ends Well*, and "All seems well"', *Shakespeare Studies*, 13, 131–44.

44 Consult Freud, Sigmund, 'Splitting of the Ego in the Process of Defence' in *Complete Psychological Works*, vol. 23, 271–8. Welldon (2005), 86, contends that incest participants typically engage in 'primitive defence mechanisms such as splitting and denial'. Argentieri (2005), 25; and Alizade (2005), 104, 110, concur.

45 Kohut, Heinz (1971), *The Analysis of Self: A Systematic Approach to the Psychoanalytic Treatment of Narcissistic Personality Disorders*. Madison: International Universities Press, 176–7.

46 For example, see Waller, Gary (2009), 'Shakespeare's Reformed Virgin' in Konrad Eisenbichler (ed.), *Renaissance Medievalisms*. Toronto: Centre for Reformation and Renaissance Studies, 110.

47 The quotations belong respectively to Tesone (2005), 54; and Alizade (2005), 107, 109.

48 See, for example, Mukherji, Subha (1996), '"Lawful deed": Consummation, custom, and law in *All's Well That Ends Well*', *Shakespeare Survey*, 49, 197; Traister, Barbara Howard (2003), '"Doctor She": Healing and Sex in *All's Well That Ends Well*' in Richard Dutton and Jean E. Howard (eds), *A Companion to Shakespeare's Works*, 4 vols. Oxford: Blackwell, vol. 4, 343; and Bicks, Caroline (2006), 'Planned parenthood: Minding the quick woman in *All's Well*', *Modern Philology*, 103, 304, 322–31.

49 Freud (1953–74), '"A child is being beaten": A Contribution to the Study of the Origin of Sexual Perversions' in *Complete Psychological Works*, vol. 17, 188.

50 Freud (1953–74) 'Some Psychical Consequences of the Anatomical Distinction Between the Sexes,' in *Complete Psychological* Works, vol. 19, 256.

51 See Shakespeare (1967), Hunter (ed.), 124.

Chapter 7

1 Porter, Joseph A. (1988), *Shakespeare's Mercutio: His History and Drama*. Chapel Hill and London: University of North Carolina Press; Goldberg, Jonathan (1994), 'Romeo and Juliet's open Rs' in *Queering the Renaissance*, Jonathan Goldberg (ed.). Durham and London: Duke University Press, 218–35; and Armstrong, Philip (2001), *Shakespeare in Psychoanalysis*. London and New York: Routledge, 195–224.

2 Hall, Calvin S. (1983), *A Primer of Freudian Psychology*. New York: Octagon Books, 91–3, explains Freud's conception of reaction formation.

3 Shakespeare, William (2012), *Romeo and Juliet*, René Weis (ed.). London and New York: Bloomsbury, 1.1.20–2. All further references in this chapter will be to this edition and will be noted in the text by act, scene and line numbers.

4 Henke, James T. (1974), *Renaissance Dramatic Bawdy (Exclusive of Shakespeare): An Annotated Glossary and Critical Essays*, 2 vols. Salzburg: Institut für Englische Sprache und Literatur, Universität Salzburg, vol. 2, 86, provides a gloss of 'backward' that is illuminating for Shakespeare's use of 'back'. Partridge, Eric (1990) *Shakespeare's Bawdy*. London and New York: Routledge, 215, clarifies that 'weapon', 'instrument', 'tool' and 'sword' can all designate the penis.

5 Partridge (1990), 96–7, 193, 190. Henke (1974), vol. 2, 229, 156, provides the bawdy designations for 'piece' and 'flesh'; and Rubinstein, Frankie (1989), *A Dictionary of Shakespeare's Sexual Puns and their Significance*, 2nd edn. London: Macmillan, 165, the designation for 'move'.

6 Partridge (1990), 197, elucidates the lewd meaning of 'take', and Rubinstein (1989), 298, of 'wall'.

7 Armstrong (2001), 196.

8 Hall (1983), 92.

9 Shakespeare, William (1980), *Romeo and Juliet*, Brian Gibbons (ed.). London and New York: Methuen, 108.

10 See, for example, Bray, Alan (1982), *Homosexuality in Renaissance England*. New York: Gay Men's Press; Sedgwick,

Eve Kosofsky (1985), *Between Men: English Literature and Male Homosexual Desire*. New York: Columbia University Press; Smith, Bruce R. (1991), *Homosexual Desire in Shakespeare's England: A Cultural Poetics*. Chicago: University of Chicago Press; and Goldberg, Jonathan (1992), *Sodometries: Renaissance Texts, Modern Sexualities*. Stanford: Stanford University Press.

11 Quoted in Smith (1991), 74.

12 Traub, Valerie (1992), *Desire and Anxiety: Circulations of Sexuality in Shakespearean Drama*. London: Routledge, 139.

13 Rubinstein (1989), 110, defines 'giddy' as 'lecherous, deviating from accepted sexual norms'. Henke (1974), vol. 2, 86, 301, glosses 'backward' as an 'innuendo of sodomy' and 'turn' of copulation.

14 Porter (1988), 155, 158, 159.

15 Porter, Joseph A. (1984), 'Mercutio's brother', *South Atlantic Review*, vol. 49, no. 4, 37.

16 Shakespeare, William (1984), *Romeo and Juliet*, G. Blakemore Evans (ed.). Cambridge: Cambridge University Press, 80. Blakemore Evans believes the lines 'may comment obliquely on the relations between Romeo, Rosaline, and Juliet'. I believe they comment on the relationship between Romeo and Mercutio.

17 Shakespeare (2012), Weis (ed.), 184.

18 Rubinstein (1989), 246.

19 Shakespeare, William (2000), *Romeo and Juliet*, Jill L. Levenson (ed.). Oxford: Oxford University Press, 231, clarifies that '*counterfeit* and *slip* both refer to false coins'.

20 Rubinstein (1989), 195, looks specifically at this passage and clarifies the bawdy implications. Shakespeare (2012), Weis (ed.), 213, concurs that there may be a bawdy meaning intended '(as in modern slang "to pump")'.

21 Rubinstein (1989), 306, glosses 'wit', 'whit' and 'white' as 'puns on each other and on genitals'. She (137, 248), also sees a reference to 'the rear, behind' in 'jest' and in 'sole', which can refer to 'the bottom of a thing'.

22 Shakespeare (2012), Weis (ed.), 215.

23 Rubinstein (1989), 25, 85, sees references to buggery in 'bite' and claims the 'ear' can refer to the 'arse'.
24 Shakespeare (2012), Weis (ed.), 215.
25 Shakespeare (2000), Levenson (ed.), 232. The sodomitic undertone to the dialogue makes me wonder if the repeated references to 'goose' are related to the slang meaning of 'to goose' that the *OED*, *v* 5 defines as 'to poke, tickle, etc., (a person) in a sensitive part, esp. the genital or anal regions; sometimes, more specifically, = fuck *v* 1'. I also wonder if the reason it has not been noted as such is the tendency to read the play from a heteronormative perspective and to downplay the sexually charged relationship between the men. Although the first reference the *OED* cites is from 1879–80, Kiernan, Pauline (2008), *Filthy Shakespeare: Shakespeare's Most Outrageous Sexual Puns*. New York: Gotham Books, 39, notes, 'very often words were only officially recorded in the *Oxford English Dictionary* long after they had already been in use for some time. The first record of the word "cock" meaning "penis," for example, is dated 1730 in the *OED*, when, in fact, it had been in use for more like two hundred years.' This may be the case with 'goose' as well.
26 Freud (1953–74), 'Mourning and Melancholia' in *Complete Psychological Works*, vol. 14, 244, 246.
27 Ibid., 245.
28 Ibid., 246, 245.
29 Ibid., 251.
30 Traub (1992), 134.
31 Shakespeare (2012), Weis (ed.), 209.
32 Henke (1974), vol. 2, 183, 189.
33 Ibid., 94.
34 Shakespeare (2012), Weis (ed.), 235, notes that the *OED* first records the second meaning in 1600 in a quote from *Timon of Athens*, but concedes, 'Mercutio's stung response suggests that the meaning may have been around earlier.'
35 Rubinstein (1989), 55.
36 Ibid.

37 Freud (1953–74), 'Some Neurotic Mechanisms in Jealousy, Paranoia and Homosexuality' in *Complete Psychological Works*, vol. 18, 225.
38 Porter (1984), 37–8.
39 Rubinstein (1989), 154.
40 Ibid., 32. She cites Dover, K. J. (1980), *Greek Homosexuality*. New York: Vintage, who claims, '"In many contexts and almost invariably in poetry, the passive partner is called *pais*, "boy".'
41 For example, see Shakespeare (2012), Weis (ed.), 237.
42 Freud, 'Mourning and Melancholia', in *Complete Psychological Works*, vol. 14, 248–9.
43 Ibid., 246.
44 Smith, Bruce R. (1992), 'Making a Difference: Male/male "desire" in Tragedy, Comedy, and Tragi-comedy' in *Erotic Politics: Desire on the Renaissance Stage*, Susan Zimmerman (ed.). New York and London: Routledge, 136, concurs: 'Whatever the circumstances, one law of tragedy remains sacrosanct: the ending of homoerotic desire is death.'

Epilogue

1 Bloom, Harold (1994), *The Western Canon: The Books and School of the Ages*. New York: Harcourt Brace, 390.

BIBLIOGRAPHY

Adelman, Janet (1982), '"Anger's my meat": Feeding, Dependency, and Aggression in *Coriolanus*' in Murray M. Schwarz and Coppélia Kahn (eds), *Representing Shakespeare: New Psychoanalytic Essays*. Baltimore and London: Johns Hopkins University Press, 129–49.

Adelman, Janet (1989), 'Bed Tricks: On Marriage as the end of Comedy in *All's Well That Ends Well* and *Measure for Measure*' in Norman N. Holland, Sidney J. Homan and Bernard J. Paris (eds), *Shakespeare's Personality*. Berkeley: University of California Press, 151–74.

Adelman, Janet (1992), *Suffocating Mothers: Fantasies of Maternal Origin in Shakespeare's Plays, 'Hamlet' to 'The Tempest'*. New York: Routledge.

Alizade, Mariam (2005), 'Incest: The Damaged Psychic Flesh' in Giovanna Ambrosio (ed.), *On Incest: Psychoanalytic Perspectives*. London and New York: Karnac, 101–14.

Altman, Joel, B. (1993), 'Review of *Disowning Knowledge of Six Plays of Shakespeare* by Stanley Cavell', *Medieval and Renaissance Drama in England*, 6, 225–34.

Ambrosio, Giovanna (ed.) (2005), *On Incest: Psychoanalytic Perspectives*. London and New York: Karnac.

Argentieri, Simona (2005), 'Incest Yesterday and Today: From Conflict to Ambiguity' in Giovanna Ambrosio (ed.), *On Incest: Psychoanalytic Perspectives*. London and New York: Karnac, 17–50.

Armstrong, Philip (2000), *Shakespeare's Visual Regime: Tragedy, Psychoanalysis, and the Gaze*. New York: Palgrave.

Armstrong, Philip (2001), *Shakespeare in Psychoanalysis*. London and New York: Routledge.

Aronson, Alex (1972), *Psyche and Symbol in Shakespeare*. Bloomington: Indiana University Press.

Auden, W. H. (1948), *The Dyer's Hand and Other Essays*. New York: Random House.

Barber, C. L. (1959), *Shakespeare's Festive Comedy: A Study of Dramatic Form and Its Relation to Social Custom*. Princeton: Princeton University Press.

Barber, C. L. (1982), 'The Family in Shakespeare's Development: Tragedy and Sacredness' in Murray M. Schwartz and Coppélia Kahn (eds), *Representing Shakespeare: New Psychoanalytic Essays*. Baltimore and London: Johns Hopkins University Press, 188–202.

Barber, C. L. (1989), 'Shakespeare in the Rising Middle Class' in Norman N. Holland, Sidney J. Homan and Bernard J. Paris (eds), *Shakespeare's Personality*. Berkeley: University of California Press, 17–40.

Barber, C. L. and Richard P. Wheeler (1986), *The Whole Journey: Shakespeare's Power of Development*. Berkeley: University of California Press.

Berger, Harry Jr (1979), '*King Lear*: The Lear family romance', *Centennial Review*, 23, 348–76.

Berger, Harry Jr (1985a), 'Psychoanalyzing the Shakespeare Text: The First Three Scenes of the *Henriad*' in Patricia Parker and Geoffrey H. Hartman (eds), *Shakespeare and the Question of Theory*. New York and London: Methuen, 210–29.

Berger, Harry Jr (1985b), 'Text Against Performance: The Gloucester Family Romance' in Peter Erickson and Coppélia Kahn (eds), *Shakespeare's 'Rough Magic': Renaissance Essays in Honor of C. L. Barber*. Newark: University of Delaware Press, 210–29.

Berger, Harry Jr (1997), *Making Trifles of Terrors: Redistributing Complicities in Shakespeare*, Peter Erickson (ed.). Stanford: Stanford University Press.

Berger, Harry Jr (2004), 'What Did the King Know and When Did He Know It? Shakespearean Discourses and Psychoanalysis' in Russ McDonald (ed.), *Shakespeare: An Anthology of Criticism and Theory, 1945–2000*. Oxford: Blackwell, 365–98.

Bergeron, David M. (2007), '"The credit of your father": Absent Fathers in *All's Well, That Ends Well*' in Gary Waller (ed.), *'All's Well, That Ends Well': New Critical Essays*. New York and London: Routledge, 169–82.

Bicks, Caroline (2006), 'Planned parenthood: Minding the quick woman in *All's Well*', *Modern Philology*, 103, 299–331.

Bloom, Harold (1994), *The Western Canon: The Books and School of the Ages*. New York: Harcourt Brace.

Bloom, Harold (1999), *Shakespeare: The Invention of the Human*. London: Fourth Estate.
Bock, Philip K. (1993), '"Neither two nor one:" Dual Unity in *The Phoenix and the Turtle*' in B. J. Sokol (ed.), *The Undiscover'd Country: New Essays on Psychoanalysis and Shakespeare*. London: Free Association Books, 39–56.
Bodkin, Maud (1934), *Archetypal Patterns in Poetry: Psychological Studies of Imagination*. London: Oxford University Press, H. Milford.
Bray, Alan (1982), *Homosexuality in Renaissance England*. New York: Gay Men's Press.
Cavell, Stanley (1987), *Disowning Knowledge in Six Plays of Shakespeare*. Cambridge: Cambridge University Press.
Coleridge, Samuel Taylor (1904), *Lectures and Notes on Shakspere and Other English Poets*. London: G. Bell and Sons.
Coleridge, Samuel Taylor (1987), *Lectures 1808–1819: On Literature*, R. A. Foakes (ed.), 2 vols. Princeton: Princeton University Press.
Colman, E. A. M. (1976), *The Dramatic Use of Bawdy in Shakespeare*. London: Longman.
Coursen, Herbert R. (1986), *The Compensatory Psyche: A Jungian Approach to Shakespeare*. Lanham, MD: University Press of America.
Coursen, Herbert R. (1992), *Shakespearean Performance as Interpretation*. Newark: University of Delaware Press.
Crews, Frederick C. (1986), *Skeptical Engagements*. New York: Oxford University Press.
Dover, Kenneth J. (1980), *Greek Homosexuality*. New York: Vintage.
Dryden, John (1821), *An Essay of Dramatic Poesy* in Sir Walter Scott (ed.), *The Works of John Dryden*, 18 vols, 2nd edn. Edinburgh: Constable, vol. 15, 283–382.
Eissler, Kurt R. (1971), *Discourse on Hamlet and 'Hamlet': A Psychoanalytic Inquiry*. New York: International Universities Press.
Ellerbeck, Erin (2011), 'Adoption and the language of horticulture in *All's Well That Ends Well*', *SEL: Studies in English Literature*, 51, 305–26.
Erikson, Erik (1968), *Identity: Youth and Crisis*. New York: W. W. Norton.

Erlich, Avi (1977), *Hamlet's Absent Father*. Princeton: Princeton University Press.
Evans, Bertrand (1960), *Shakespeare's Comedies*. Oxford: Clarendon Press.
Evans, Dylan (1966), *An Introductory Dictionary of Lacanian Psychoanalysis*. London and New York: Routledge.
Faber, M. D. (1970), *The Design Within: Psychoanalytic Approaches to Shakespeare*. New York: Science House.
Faber, M. D. (1993), 'Hamlet and the Inner World of Objects' in B. J. Sokol (ed.), *The Undiscover'd Country: New Essays on Psychoanalysis and Shakespeare*. London: Free Association Books, 57–90.
Farrell, Kirby (1989), 'Love, Death, and Patriarchy in *Romeo and Juliet*' in Norman N. Holland, Sidney J. Homan and Bernard J. Paris (eds), *Shakespeare's Personality*. Berkeley: University of California Press, 86–102.
Field, Catherine (2007), '"Sweet practicer, thy physic I will try": Helena and her "good receipt" in *All's Well, That Ends Well*' in Gary Waller (ed.) *'All's Well, That Ends Well': New Critical Essays*. New York and London: Routledge, 194–208.
Fineman, Joel (1982), 'Fratricide and Cuckoldry: Shakespeare's Doubles' in Murray M. Schwarz and Coppélia Kahn (eds), *Representing Shakespeare: New Psychoanalytic Essays*. Baltimore and London: Johns Hopkins University Press, 70–109.
Fineman, Joel (1986), *Shakespeare's Perjured Eye: The Invention of Poetic Subjectivity in the Sonnets*. Berkeley: University of California Press.
Forker, Charles R. (1989), '"A little more than kin, and less than kind": Incest, intimacy, narcissism, and identity in Elizabethan and Stuart drama', *Medieval and Renaissance Drama in England*, 4, 13–51.
Freedman, Barbara (1989), 'Misrecognizing Shakespeare' in Norman N. Holland, Sidney J. Homan and Bernard J. Paris (eds), *Shakespeare's Personality*. Berkeley: University of California Press, 244–60.
Freedman, Barbara (1991), *Staging the Gaze: Postmodernism, Psychoanalysis and Shakespearian Comedy*. Ithaca: Cornell University Press.
Freud, Anna (1946), *The Ego and the Mechanisms of Defense*. New York: International Universities Press.

Freud, Sigmund (1953–74), *The Standard Edition of the Complete Psychological Works of Sigmund Freud*, James Strachey (trans. and ed.), 24 vols. London: Hogarth Press and the Institute of Psycho-Analysis.

Freud, Sigmund (1953–74), '"A child is being beaten": A Contribution to the Study of the Origin of Sexual Perversions' in *The Standard Edition of the Complete Psychological Works of Sigmund Freud*, vol. 17, 175–204.

Freud, Sigmund (1953–74), 'An Outline of Psycho-analysis' in *The Standard Edition of the Complete Psychological Works of Sigmund Freud*, vol. 23, 138–207.

Freud, Sigmund (1953–74), 'Creative Writers and Day-Dreaming' in *The Standard Edition of the Complete Psychological Works of Sigmund Freud*, vol. 9, 141–54.

Freud, Sigmund (1953–74), 'Delusions and Dream in Jensen's *Gradiva*' in *The Standard Edition of the Complete Psychological Works of Sigmund Freud*, vol. 9, 7–93.

Freud, Sigmund (1953–74), 'The Dissolution of the Oedipus Complex' in *The Standard Edition of the Complete Psychological Works of Sigmund Freud*, vol. 19, 173–82.

Freud, Sigmund (1953–74), 'The Ego and the Id' in *The Standard Edition of the Complete Psychological Works of Sigmund Freud*, vol. 19, 1–59.

Freud, Sigmund (1953–74), 'Mourning and Melancholia' in *The Standard Edition of the Complete Psychological Works of Sigmund Freud*, vol. 14, 238–60.

Freud, Sigmund (1953–74), *New Introductory Lectures on Psycho-Analysis*, '33, Femininity' in *The Standard Edition of the Complete Psychological Works of Sigmund Freud*, vol. 22, 112–35.

Freud, Sigmund (1953–74), 'Obsessions and Phobias: Their Psychical Mechanism and their Aetiology' in *The Standard Edition of the Complete Psychological Works of Sigmund Freud*, vol. 3, 69–84.

Freud, Sigmund (1953–74), 'On Psychotherapy' in *The Standard Edition of the Complete Psychological Works of Sigmund Freud*, vol. 7, 255–68.

Freud, Sigmund (1953–74), 'Repression' in *The Standard Edition of the Complete Psychological Works of Sigmund Freud*, vol. 14, 141–58.

Freud, Sigmund (1953–74), 'Some Character-types met with in Psycho-analytic Work' in *The Standard Edition of the Complete Psychological Works of Sigmund Freud*, vol. 14, 309–33.

Freud, Sigmund (1953–74), 'Some Neurotic Mechanisms in Jealousy, Paranoia and Homosexuality' in *The Standard Edition of the Complete Psychological Works of Sigmund Freud*, vol. 18, 223–32.

Freud, Sigmund (1953–74), 'Some Psychical Consequences of the Anatomical Distinction Between the Sexes' in *The Standard Edition of the Complete Psychological Works of Sigmund Freud*, vol. 19, 241–60.

Freud, Sigmund (1953–74), 'Splitting of the Ego in the Process of Defence' in *The Standard Edition of the Complete Psychological Works of Sigmund Freud*, vol. 23, 271–8.

Freud, Sigmund (1953–74), *The Interpretation of Dreams* in *The Standard Edition of the Complete Psychological Works of Sigmund Freud*, vols 4 and 5.

Freud, Sigmund (1953–74), 'The Theme of the Three Caskets' in *The Standard Edition of the Complete Psychological Works of Sigmund Freud*, vol. 12, 291–301.

Freud, Sigmund (1953–74), 'The Unconscious' in *The Standard Edition of the Complete Psychological Works of Sigmund Freud*, vol. 14, 159–204.

Freud, Sigmund (1953–74), *Three Essays on the Theory of Sexuality*, 'III The Transformations of Puberty' in *The Standard Edition of the Complete Psychological Works of Sigmund Freud*, vol. 7, 207–45.

Freud, Sigmund (1953–74), *Totem and Taboo* in *The Standard Edition of the Complete Psychological Works of Sigmund Freud*, vol. 13, 1–162.

Frye, Northrop (1965), *A Natural Perspective: The Development of Shakespearean Comedy and Romance*. New York: Columbia University Press.

Frye, Northrop (2006), *Anatomy of Criticism: Four Essays*, Robert Denham (ed.). Toronto: University of Toronto Press.

Garber, Marjorie (2000), 'Second-best Bed' in Carla Mazzio and Douglas Trevor (eds), *Historicism, Psychoanalysis and Early Modern Culture*. New York: Routledge, 376–96.

Garner, Shirley Nelson (1989), 'Male Bonding and the Myth of Women's Deception in Shakespeare's Plays' in Norman

N. Holland, Sidney J. Homan and Bernard J. Paris (eds), *Shakespeare's Personality*. Berkeley: University of California Press, 135–50.

Girard, René (1991) *A Theater of Envy: William Shakespeare*. New York: Oxford University Press.

Glass, James M. (1993), *Shattered Selves: Multiple Personality in a Postmodern World*. Ithaca and London: Cornell University Press.

Goethe, Johann Wolfgang von (1998), *Conversations of Goethe with Johann Peter Eckermann*, J. K. Moorhead (ed.), John Oxenford (trans.). New York: Da Capo Press.

Gohkle, Madelon (1980), '"I wooed thee with my sword": Shakespeare's Tragic Paradigms' in Murray M. Schwarz and Coppélia Kahn (eds), *Representing Shakespeare: New Psychoanalytic Essays*. Baltimore and London: Johns Hopkins University Press, 170–87.

Goldberg, Jonathan (1992), *Sodometries: Renaissance Texts, Modern Sexualities*. Stanford: Stanford University Press.

Goldberg, Jonathan (1994), '*Romeo and Juliet*'s open Rs' in *Queering the Renaissance*, Jonathan Goldberg (ed.). Durham and London: Duke University Press, 218–35.

Goldberg, Jonathan (2000) 'The Anus in *Coriolanus*' in Carla Mazzio and Douglas Trevor (eds), *Historicism, Psychoanalysis and Early Modern Culture*. New York and London: Routledge, 260–71.

Greenblatt, Stephen (1986), 'Psychoanalysis and Renaissance Culture' in Patricia Parker and David Quint (eds), *Literary Theory/Renaissance Texts*. Baltimore: Johns Hopkins University Press, 210–24.

Greenblatt, Stephen (2005), *Renaissance Self-Fashioning*. Chicago and London: University of Chicago Press.

Guillory, John (2000), '"To please the wiser sort": Violence and Philosophy in *Hamlet*' in Carla Mazzio and Douglas Trevor (eds), *Historicism, Psychoanalysis, and Early Modern Culture*. New York and London: Routledge, 82–109.

Hall, Calvin S. (1973), *A Primer of Jungian Psychology*. New York: New American Library, 1973.

Hall, Calvin S. (1983), *A Primer of Freudian Psychology*. New York: Octagon Books.

Hawkins, Sherman (1989), 'Aggression and the Project of the Histories' in Norman N. Holland, Sidney J. Homan and Bernard

J. Paris (eds), *Shakespeare's Personality*. Berkeley: University of California Press, 41–65.

Henke, James T. (1974), *Renaissance Dramatic Bawdy (Exclusive of Shakespeare): An Annotated Glossary and Critical Essays*, 2 vols. Salzburg: Institut für Englische Sprache und Literatur, Universität Salzburg.

Hillman, David (2000), 'The Inside Story' in Carla Mazzio and Douglas Trevor (eds), *Historicism, Psychoanalysis, and Early Modern Culture*: New York: Routledge, 299–324.

Hodgdon, Barbara (1987), 'The making of virgins and mothers: Sexual signs, substitute scenes and doubled presences' in *All's Well That Ends Well*', *Philological Quarterly* 66, 47–71.

Holland, Norman N. (1960), 'Freud on Shakespeare', *PMLA: Publications of the Modern Language Association of America*, 75, 163–73.

Holland, Norman N. (1966), *Psychoanalysis and Shakespeare*. New York: McGraw-Hill.

Holland, Norman N. (1980), 'Hermia's Dream' in Murray M. Schwarz and Coppélia Kahn (eds), *Representing Shakespeare: New Psychoanalytic Essays*. Baltimore and London: Johns Hopkins University Press, 1–20.

Holland, Norman N. (1989a), *Shakespeare's Personality*. Sidney J. Homan and Bernard J. Paris (eds). Berkeley: University of California Press.

Holland, Norman N. (1989b), 'Sons and Substitutions: Shakespeare's Phallic Fantasy' in Norman N. Holland, Sidney J. Homan and Bernard J. Paris (eds), *Shakespeare's Personality*. Berkeley: University of California Press, 66–85.

Horney, Karen (1950), *Neurosis and Human Growth: The Struggle Toward Self-Realization*. New York: Norton.

Hunter, Robert Grams (1965), *Shakespeare and the Comedy of Forgiveness*. New York: Columbia University Press.

Jekels, Ludwig (1970), 'The Riddle of Shakespeare's *Macbeth*' in M. D. Faber (ed.), *The Design Within: A Psychoanalytic Approach to Shakespeare*. New York: Science House, 235–49.

Johnson, Samuel (1952), 'Preface to Shakespeare' in Walter Raleigh (ed.), *Johnson on Shakespeare*. London: H. Frowde, 9–63.

Jones, Ann Rosalind and Peter Stallybrass (2000), 'Fetishisms and Renaissances' in Carla Mazzio and Douglas Trevor (eds),

Historicism, Psychoanalysis and Early Modern Culture. New York: Routledge, 20–35.
Jones, Ernest (1910), 'The Oedipus-complex as an explanation of Hamlet's mystery: A study in motive', *The American Journal of Psychology*, 21, 72–113.
Jones, Ernest (1953–7), *The Life and Works of Sigmund Freud*, 3 vols. New York: Basic Books.
Jones, Ernest (1976), *Hamlet and Oedipus*. New York and London: Norton.
Jung, Carl G. (1959), *The Archetypes and the Collective Unconscious*, R. F. C. Hull (trans.). London: Pantheon Books.
Kahn, Coppélia (1981), *Man's Estate: Masculine Identity in Shakespeare*. Berkeley: University of California Press.
Kahn, Coppélia (1986), 'The Absent Mother in *King Lear*' in Margaret W. Ferguson, Maureen Quilligan and Nancy J. Vickers (eds), *Rewriting the Renaissance: The Discourse of Sexual Difference in Early Modern Europe*. Chicago and London: University of Chicago Press, 33–49.
Kerrigan, William (1989), 'The Personal Shakespeare: Three Clues' in Norman N. Holland, Sidney J. Homan and Bernard J. Paris (eds), *Shakespeare's Personality*. Berkeley: University of California Press, 175–90.
Kerrigan, William (1994), *Hamlet's Perfection*. Baltimore: Johns Hopkins University Press.
Kiernan, Pauline (2008), *Filthy Shakespeare: Shakespeare's Most Outrageous Sexual Puns*. New York: Gotham Books.
Kirsch, Arthur (1981), *Shakespeare and the Experience of Love*. Cambridge: Cambridge University Press.
Klein, Melanie (1975), *Envy and Gratitude and Other Works 1946–63*. New York: Free Press.
Kohut, Heinz (1971), *The Analysis of Self: A Systematic Approach to the Psychoanalytic Treatment of Narcissistic Personality Disorders*. Madison: International Universities Press.
Krier, Theresa (2001), *Birth Passages: Maternity and Nostalgia, Antiquity to Shakespeare*. Ithaca: Cornell University Press.
Krims, Marvin Bennett (2006), *The Mind According to Shakespeare: Psychoanalysis in the Bard's Writing*. London: Praeger.
Kris, Ernst (1970), 'Prince Hal's Conflict' in M. D. Faber (ed.), *The Design Within: Psychoanalytic Approaches to Shakespeare*. New York: Science House, 389–407.

Lacan, Jacques (1977), *Ecrits*, Alan Sheridan (trans.). New York: Norton.

Lacan, Jacques (1982), 'Desire and the Interpretation of Desire in *Hamlet*' in Shoshana Felman (ed.), *Literature and Psychoanalysis: The Question of Reading, Otherwise*. Baltimore: Johns Hopkins University Press, 11–52.

Lehnhof, Kent R. (2007), 'Performing Woman: Female Theatricality in *All's Well, That Ends Well*' in Gary Waller (ed.), *'All's Well, That Ends Well': New Critical Essays*. New York and London: Routledge, 111–24.

Lenz, Carolyn Ruth Swift, Gayle Greene and Carol Thomas Neely (eds) (1983), *The Woman's Part: Feminist Criticism of Shakespeare*. Urbana: University of Illinois Press.

Leverenz, David (1982), 'The Woman in Hamlet: An Interpersonal View' in Murray M. Schwarz and Coppélia Kahn (eds), *Representing Shakespeare: New Psychoanalytic Essays*. Baltimore and London: Johns Hopkins University Press, 110–28.

Levin, Gerald (1975), *Sigmund Freud*. Boston: Twayne.

Levin, Richard A. (1980), '*All's Well That Ends Well*, and "All seems well"', *Shakespeare Studies*, 13, 131–44.

Lupton, Julia Reinhard and Kenneth Reinhard (1993), *After Oedipus: Shakespeare in Psychoanalysis*. Ithaca and London: Cornell University Press.

Magee, William H. (1971), 'Helena, a female Hamlet', *English Miscellany*, 22, 31–46.

Mahler, Margaret (1969), *On Human Symbiosis and the Vicissitudes of Individuation*. London: International Universities Press.

Mahler, Margaret (1975), *The Psychological Birth of the Human Infant*. New York: Basic Books.

Mannoni, Octave (1956), *Prospero and Caliban: The Psychology of Colonization*, Pamela Powesland (trans.), 2nd edn. New York: Praeger.

Marshall, Cynthia (2002), *The Shattering of the Self: Violence, Subjectivity, and Early Modern Texts*. Baltimore: Johns Hopkins University Press.

Marshall, Cynthia (2003), 'Review of *Shakespeare's Visual Regime: Tragedy, Psychoanalysis and the Gaze* by Philip Armstrong', *Shakespeare Quarterly*, 54, 235–8.

Maus, Katharine Eisaman (2000), 'Sorcery and Subjectivity in Early Modern Discourses of Witchcraft' in Carla Mazzio and Douglas

Trevor (eds), *Historicism, Psychoanalysis, and Early Modern Culture*. New York and London: Routledge, 325–48.

Maver, Igor (1994), 'Review of *Character as a Subversive Force in Shakespeare: The History and Roman Plays* by Bernard J. Paris', *The Review of English Studies*, 45, 564–6.

Mazzio, Carla (2000), 'The Melancholy of Print: *Love's Labour's Lost*' in Carla Mazzio and Douglas Trevor (eds), *Historicism, Psychoanalysis, and Early Modern Culture*. New York and London: Routledge, 186–227.

Mazzio, Carla and Douglas Trevor (eds) (2000), *Historicism, Psychoanalysis, and Early Modern Culture*. New York and London: Routledge.

McCandless, David (1994), 'Helena's bed-trick: Gender and performance in *All's Well That Ends Well*', *Shakespeare Quarterly*, 45, 449–68.

Miller, David Lee (2003), *Dreams of the Burning Child: Sacrificial Sons and the Father's Witness*. Ithaca: Cornell University Press.

Mukherji, Subha (1996), '"Lawful deed": Consummation, custom, and law in *All's Well That Ends Well*', *Shakespeare Survey*, 49, 181–200.

Neely, Carol Thomas (1989), 'Shakespeare's Women: Historical Facts and Dramatic Representations' in Norman N. Holland, Sidney J. Homan and Bernard J. Paris (eds), *Shakespeare's Personality*. Berkeley: University of California Press, 116–34.

Neely, Carol Thomas (2004), *Distracted Subjects: Madness and Gender in Shakespeare and Early Modern Culture*. Ithaca and London: Cornell University Press.

Nevo, Ruth (1987a), 'Motive and Meaning in *All's Well That Ends Well*' in John W. Mahon and Thomas A. Pendleton (eds), *'Fanned and Winnowed Opinions': Shakespearean Essays Presented to Harold Jenkins*. London and New York: Methuen, 26–51.

Nevo, Ruth (1987b) *Shakespeare's Other Language*. New York: Methuen.

Novy, Marianne (1989), 'Shakespeare and the Bonds of Brotherhood' in Norman N. Holland, Sidney Homan and Bernard J. Paris (eds), *Shakespeare's Personality*. Berkeley: University of California Press, 103–15.

Paris, Bernard J. (1989), '*The Tempest*: Shakespeare's Ideal Solution' in Norman N. Holland, Sidney Homan and Bernard

J. Paris (eds), *Shakespeare's Personality*. Berkeley: University of California Press, 206–25.

Paris, Bernard J. (1991a), *Bargains with Fate: Psychological Crises and Conflict in Shakespeare and His Plays*. New York: Plenum Press.

Paris, Bernard J. (1991b), *Character as a Subversive Force in Shakespeare: The History and Roman Plays*. London: Associated University Presses.

Partridge, Eric (1990), *Shakespeare's Bawdy*. London and New York: Routledge.

Plasse, Maria A. (1992), 'Review of *Staging the Gaze: Postmodernism, Psychoanalysis, and Shakespearean Comedy* by Barbara Freedman', *College Literature*, 19, 144–7.

Pope, Alexander (1958), 'Preface to Shakespeare' in D. Nichol Smith (ed.), *Shakespeare Criticism: A Selection (1623–1840)*. London: Oxford University Press, 42–50.

Porter, Joseph A. (1984), 'Mercutio's brother', *South Atlantic Review*, vol. 49, no. 4, 31–41.

Porter, Joseph A. (1988), *Shakespeare's Mercutio: His History and Drama*. Chapel Hill and London: University of North Carolina Press.

Rank, Otto (1971), *The Double: A Psychoanalytic Study*, Harry Tucker Jr. (trans.). Chapel Hill: University of North Carolina Press.

Rank, Otto (1992), *The Incest Theme in Literature and Legend: Fundamentals of a Psychology of Literary Creation*, Gregory C. Richter (trans.). Baltimore and London: Johns Hopkins University Press.

Reid, Stephen (1968), 'Othello's jealousy', *American Imago*, 25, 274–93.

Reid, Stephen (1969), '"I am Misanthropos" – A psychoanalytic reading of Shakespeare's *Timon of Athens*', *Psychoanalytic Review*, 56, 442–52.

Reid, Stephen (1970a), 'A psychoanalytic reading of *Troilus and Cressida* and *Measure for Measure*', *Psychoanalytic Review*, 57, 263–82.

Reid, Stephen (1970b), 'Desdemona's guilt', *American Imago*, 27, 245–62.

Reid, Stephen (1970c), 'In defense of Goneril and Regan', *American Imago*, 27, 226–44.

Reid, Stephen (1970d), 'The Winter's Tale', American Imago, 27, 263–78.

Reid, Stephen (1974), 'Hamlet's melancholia', American Imago, 31, 378–400.

Reid, Stephen (1976), 'Othello's occupation: Beyond the pleasure principle', The Psychoanalytic Review, 63, 555–70.

Reik, Theodor (1970), 'Jessica, My Child' in M. D. Faber (ed.), The Design Within: Psychoanalytic Approaches to Shakespeare. New York: Science House, 441–62.

Roberts, Jeanne Addison (1993), 'Review of Shakespeare's Other Language by Ruth Nevo', Shakespeare Studies, 21, 287–90.

Rogers, Robert (1991), Self and Other: Object Relations in Psychoanalysis and Literature. New York: New York University Press.

Rubinstein, Frankie (1989), A Dictionary of Shakespeare's Sexual Puns and their Significance, 2nd edn. London: Macmillan.

Sachs, Hanns (1970), 'The Measure in Measure for Measure' in M. D. Faber (ed.), The Design Within: Psychoanalytic Approaches to Shakespeare. New York: Science House, 479–97.

Sachs, Wulf (1957a), Black Anger. New York: Grove Press.

Sachs, Wulf (1957b), Black Hamlet. New York: Grove Press.

Sanderson, Richard K. (1992), 'Review of A Theater of Envy: William Shakespeare by Rene Girard', Rocky Mountain Review of Language and Literature, 46, 76–8.

Schiesari, Juliana (1992), The Gendering of Melancholia: Feminism, Psychoanalysis and the Symbolics of Loss in Renaissance Literature. Ithaca: Cornell University Press.

Schwartz, Murray M. (1970), 'Between Fantasy and Imagination: A Psychological Exploration of Cymbeline' in Frederick C. Crews (ed.), Psychoanalysis and Literary Process. Cambridge, MA: Winthrop Publishers, 219–83.

Schwartz, Murray M. (1973), 'Leontes' jealousy in The Winter's Tale', American Imago, 30, 250–73.

Schwartz, Murray M. (1975), 'The Winter's Tale: Loss and transformation', American Imago, 32, 145–99.

Schwartz, Murray M. (1980), 'Shakespeare through Contemporary Psychoanalysis' in Murray M. Schwartz and Coppélia Kahn (eds), Representing Shakespeare: New Psychoanalytic Essays. Baltimore and London: Johns Hopkins University Press, 21–32.

Schwartz, Murray M. and Coppélia Kahn (eds) (1980), *Representing Shakespeare: New Psychoanalytic Essays*. Baltimore and London: Johns Hopkins University Press.

Sedgwick, Eve Kosofsky (1985), *Between Men: English Literature and Male Homosexual Desire*. New York: Columbia University Press.

Shakespeare, William (1967), *All's Well That Ends Well*, G. K. Hunter (ed.). London: Methuen.

Shakespeare, William (1980), *Romeo and Juliet*, Brian Gibbons (ed.). London and New York: Methuen.

Shakespeare, William (1984), *Romeo and Juliet*, G. Blakemore Evans (ed.). Cambridge: Cambridge University Press.

Shakespeare, William (2000), *Romeo and Juliet*, Jill L. Levenson (ed.). Oxford: Oxford University Press.

Shakespeare, William (2006), *Measure for Measure, All's Well That Ends Well, and Troilus and Cressida*, David Bevington and David Scott Kastan (eds). New York: Bantam Dell.

Shakespeare, William (2012), *Romeo and Juliet*, René Weis (ed.). London and New York: Bloomsbury.

Sheppard, Angela (1993), '"Soiled mother or soul of woman?" A Response to *Troilus and Cressida*' in B. J. Sokol (ed.), *The Undiscover'd Country: New Essays on Psychoanalysis and Shakespeare*. London: Free Association Press, 130–49.

Simpson, John and Edmund Weiner (eds) (2011), *Oxford English Dictionary*. Oxford: Oxford University Press.

Skura, Meredith Anne (1980), 'Interpreting Posthumus' Dream from Above and Below: Families, Psychoanalysts, and Literary Critics' in Murray M. Schwartz, and Coppélia Kahn (eds), *Representing Shakespeare: New Psychoanalytic Essays*. Baltimore and London: Johns Hopkins University Press, 203–16.

Skura, Meredith Anne (1981), *The Literary Use of the Psychoanalytic Process*. New Haven: Yale University Press.

Skura, Meredith Anne (1989), 'Discourse and the individual: The case of colonialism in *The Tempest*', *Shakespeare Quarterly*, 40, 42–69.

Smith, Bruce R. (1991), *Homosexual Desire in Shakespeare's England: A Cultural Poetics*. Chicago: University of Chicago Press.

Smith, Bruce R. (1992), 'Making a Difference: Male/male "Desire" in Tragedy, Comedy, and Tragi-comedy' in Susan Zimmerman (ed.), *Erotic Politics: Desire on the Renaissance Stage*. New York and London: Routledge, 127–49.

Snyder, Susan (1988), '*All's Well That Ends Well* and Shakespeare's Helens: Text and subtext, subject and object', *English Literary Renaissance*, 18, 66–77.

Sokol, B. J. (1993), '*The Tempest*, "All torment, trouble, wonder and amazement": A Kleinian reading' in B. J. Sokol (ed.), *The Undiscover'd Country: New Essays on Psychoanalysis and Shakespeare*. London: Free Asociation Books, 179–216.

Sokol, B. J. (ed.) (1993), *The Undiscover'd Country: New Essays on Psychoanalysis and Shakespeare*. London: Free Association Books.

Sprengnether, Madelon (née Gohlke) (1989), 'The Boy Actor and Femininity in *Antony and Cleopatra*' in Norman N. Holland, Sidney J. Homan and Bernard J. Paris (eds), *Shakespeare's Personality*. Berkeley: University of California Press, 191–205.

Stephens, Lyn (1993), '"A wilderness of monkeys": A Psychodynamic Study of *The Merchant of Venice*' in B. J. Sokol (ed.), *The Undiscover'd Country: New Essays on Psychoanalysis and Shakespeare*. London: Free Association Books, 91–129.

Stewart, J. I. M. (1949), *Character and Motive in Shakespeare: Some Recent Appraisals Examined*. London and New York: Longmans, Green and Co.

Stockholder, Kay (1987), *Dream Works: Lovers and Families in Shakespeare's Plays*. Toronto: University of Toronto.

Stone, James W. (2010), *Crossing Gender in Shakespeare: Feminist Psychoanalysis and the Difference Within*. New York: Routledge.

Sulloway, Frank J. (1991), 'Reassessing Freud's case histories: The social construction of psychoanalysis', *Isis*, 82, 245–75.

Sundelson, David (1983), *Shakespeare's Restorations of the Father*. New Brunswick: Rutgers University Press.

Tesone, Juan Eduardo (2005), 'Incest(s) and the Negation of Otherness' in Giovanna Ambrosio (ed.), *On Incest: Psychoanalytic Perspectives*. London and New York: Karnac, 51–64.

Traister, Barbara Howard (2003), '"Doctor She": Healing and Sex in *All's Well That Ends Well*' in Richard Dutton and Jean E. Howard (eds), *A Companion to Shakespeare's Works*, 4 vols. Oxford: Blackwell, vol. 4, 333–47.

Traub, Valerie (1992), *Desire and Anxiety: Circulations of Sexuality in Shakespearean Drama*. London: Routledge.

Trevor, Douglas (2000), 'George Herbert and the Scene of Writing' in Carla Mazzio and Douglas Trevor (eds), *Historicism, Psychoanalysis, and Early Modern Culture*. New York and London: Routledge, 228–58.

Vickers, Brian (1993), *Appropriating Shakespeare: Contemporary Critical Quarrels*. New Haven and London: Yale University Press.

Waller, Gary (ed.) (2007), *'All's Well, That Ends Well': New Critical Essays*. New York and London: Routledge.

Waller, Gary (ed.) (2009), 'Shakespeare's Reformed Virgin' in Konrad Eisenbichler (ed.), *Renaissance Medievalisms*. Toronto: Centre for Reformation and Renaissance Studies, 107–19.

Wangh, Martin (1970), '*Othello*: The tragedy of Iago' in M. D. Faber (ed.), *The Design Within: Psychoanalytic Approaches to Shakespeare*. New York: Science House, 157–68.

Welldon, Estela V. (2005), 'Incest: A Therapeutic Challenge' in Giovanna Ambrosio (ed.), *On Incest: Psychoanalytic Perspectives*. London and New York: Karnac, 81–100.

Westlund, Joseph (1984), *Shakespeare's Reparative Comedies: A Psychoanalytic View of the Middle Plays*. Chicago: University of Chicago Press.

Wheeler, Richard P. (1981), *Shakespeare's Development and the Problem Comedies: Turn and Counter-Turn*. Berkeley: University of California Press.

Wheeler, Richard P. (1987), 'Psychoanalytic criticism and teaching Shakespeare', *ADE Bulletin*, 87, 19–23.

Willbern, David (1989), 'What is Shakespeare?' in Norman N. Holland, Sidney J. Homan and Bernard J. Paris (eds), *Shakespeare's Personality*. Berkeley: University of California Press, 225–43.

Winnicott, D. W. (1971), *Playing and Reality*. London: Basic Books.

INDEX

abuse, sexual 119
Acts and Monuments 104
Adelman, Janet 63, 64, 71–3, 74
  Suffocating Mothers 71–2
adolescence 7, 10, 65, 66, 67, 96
Adonis 66
After Oedipus 81
All's Well That Ends Well 9, 43, 44, 52, 54, 73, 107–31, 168
American Imago 35
analytical psychology 26, 27
androgyny 94
Angelo 24, 53, 73
anima 27, 28, 46, 47
animus 27, 28
Antigonus 60
Antipholus of Syracuse 68
Antonio 28, 42, 51, 78, 141
Antony *see* Mark Antony
Antony and Cleopatra 54, 73–4, 87
anxiety 13
archetypal criticism 30
archetypes 6, 28, 39
Ariel 79
Armstrong, Philip 95, 96, 97, 98, 133
  Shakespeare in Psychoanalysis 95
  Shakespeare's Visual Regime 97
Aronson, Alex 39
As You Like It 52, 53, 75–6
assertion 56
Auden, W. H. 28
Aufidius 21
autonomy 27

Banquo 21, 26, 98
Barber, C. L. 54, 56
  Whole Journey, The 54, 62
Bargains with Fate 86
Bassanio 16
Beatrice 44
being 1
beliefs 55
Benedick 44
Benjamin, Walter 76
Benvolio 136, 137, 138, 140, 141, 143, 144, 147, 149, 150, 151, 154, 156, 157, 159, 160
Berger, Harry, Jr 57–9
Bertram 9, 53, 73, 108, 109, 110, 111, 114, 115, 116, 117, 118, 119, 120, 121, 122, 123, 124, 125, 126, 127, 128, 129, 130
Bethlem Hospital 103
Beyond the Pleasure Principle 36

Birth Passage 92
Black Anger 96
Black Hamlet 96
Bloom, Harold 2, 165
Blos, Peter 65
Boccaccio, Giovanni 126
Bock, Philip K. 78
Bodkin, Maud 27, 28
body, female 75, 102
body parts 7
Bolingbroke 26, 29, 58
Bottom 82
Bradley, A. C. 95
Broken Heart, The 104
Brutus 21, 39, 87

Caliban 47, 51, 79
Capulet 154
Cassio 25
Cassius 21, 39, 87, 89
castration 75, 82, 125
castration fears 14, 34, 42, 49, 53, 65, 165
catharsis 16
Cavell, Stanley 44, 45, 46
  Disowning Knowledge in Six Plays of Shakespeare 44
Cesario 89
Character as a Subversive Force in Shakespeare 87
Chodorow, Nancy 65
Christian theology 43
Christianity 44
Civilization and Its Discontents 44
Cixous, Hélène 94
Claudio 39, 44, 89
Claudius 4, 15, 18, 19, 20, 26, 27, 31, 34, 35, 45, 67, 72, 78, 83, 97, 98, 121

Cleopatra 38, 87, 94
Cloten 37
coitus 114
Coleridge, Samuel Taylor 2
Comedy of Errors, The 68, 84, 103
Compensatory Psyche, The 46
condensation 13
conscience 14
consciousness 12, 16, 27, 60, 83, 118, 126, 127
Cordelia 16–17, 27, 35, 39, 58, 68, 73, 81, 82, 86, 98, 104
Coriolanus 21, 44, 54, 67, 100
Coriolanus (character) 46, 72
Cornwall 45
Countess of Rousillon 9, 108, 109, 110, 111, 112, 117, 119, 120, 121, 122, 123, 124, 129, 130, 131, 168
Coursen, H. R. 46, 47, 82
  Compensatory Psyche, The 46
  Shakespearean Performance as Interpretation 82
Cressida 79
cross-dressing 93
Crossing Gender in Shakespeare 93
cruelty 24
cultural materialism 71
Cymbeline 37, 43, 44, 50, 60, 74
Cymbeline (character) 60

dark lady 56–7, 87
death wish 124
decomposing 13, 18, 21
deconstructivism 71

defence mechanisms 5, 10, 13, 37, 126, 135, 142, 163
defence strategies 86, 88
delusional jealousy 29, 157
Demetrius 89
depression 37
Desdemona 25, 28, 35, 36, 39, 43, 46, 47, 73, 80, 94, 98
Design Within, The 23
Desire and Anxiety 74
developmental psychology 10
Devil 28
Diana 126, 127, 129
Dinnerstein, Dorothy 65
Disowning Knowledge in Six Plays of Shakespeare 44
displacement 13
Distracted Subjects 100
Don Pedro 52, 89
dream interpretation 16
dream structure 60
Dream Works 60
dreams 15, 16, 25
Dreams of the Burning Child 105
Dryden, John 1
Duke Senior 51, 61
Duncan 26

Edgar 45, 58, 81, 86
Edmund 35, 45
ego 4, 7, 29, 39, 12, 13, 88, 161
  infantile 37
Ego and the Id, The 76
ego psychologists 65, 70, 95
Eissler, K. R. 33, 34
Emde Boas, Conrad van 63
envy 89

Erikson, Erik 48, 53, 65, 95
Erlich, Avi 33, 34
extraversion 46, 47

Faber, M. D. 23–4, 25, 78
Falstaff 26, 28, 29, 51, 75
family 55
fantasies, sexual 129
Farrell, Kirby 62
father figures 41–2
female characters 63, 64, 65, 168
female sexuality 37
femininity 65
feminism 8, 49, 81, 91, 95, 168
feminist criticism 50, 71
feminist readings 80, 95
feminist scholarship 65, 92
feminist studies 7, 9
feminist theory 76
feminists 3, 10, 14, 32, 37, 40, 41, 64, 166
Ferdinand 39, 43
fetishism 99
Fineman, Joel 56–7
  Shakespeare's Perjured Eye 56
Fletcher 102
  Two Noble Kinsmen, The 102
Fliess, Wilhelm 15
Fool 81, 98
Ford, John 104
  Broken Heart, The 104
Fortinbras 34
Foxe, John 104
  Acts and Monuments 104
Frazier, George 30
  Golden Bough, The 30
Freedman, Barbara 63, 83–5

Staging the Gaze 83
Freud, Anna 13
Freud, Sigmund 1, 3, 5, 7, 9,
 11–21, 23, 24, 25, 27, 31,
 33, 34, 35, 37, 41, 43, 44,
 45, 46, 48, 53, 61, 71, 75,
 76, 78, 81, 82, 84, 85, 92,
 94, 95, 99, 105, 106, 107,
 109, 110, 119, 120, 121,
 123, 124, 125, 126, 129,
 130, 148, 149, 150, 157,
 159, 161, 165, 167
 *Beyond the Pleasure
  Principle* 36
 *Civilization and Its
  Discontents* 44
 constructs 42
 death wish 124
 dream theory 4
 Ego and the Id, The 76
 *Interpretation of Dreams,
  The* 12, 13, 15, 44, 105
 Mourning and Melancholia 19
 overboarding 134
 phallocentricism 3, 14, 17, 64
 reputation 2
 theories 6, 10, 23, 25, 29,
  32, 33, 36, 38, 39, 46,
  65, 71, 76, 79, 81, 88,
  96, 104
 Totem and Taboo 109, 110, 119
Friar Laurence 138, 140, 141,
 145, 151, 161, 162
Frye, Northrop 30

Gammer Gurton's Needle 102
Garber, Marjorie 99
Garner, Shirley Nelson 63–4
Gaunt 58
gaze 83, 97
gender 8, 14, 32, 65, 75, 93
gender studies 8
gendering 76
Gendering of Melancholia, The 76
Gertrude 19, 31, 32, 34, 46,
 67, 72, 77, 78, 83, 94,
 106, 107, 134
Girard, René 88, 89
 Theatre of Envy, A 88
Gloucester 35, 45, 58, 81, 98, 104
Goethe, Johann Wolfgang von 2
Goldberg, Jonathan 100, 133, 139
Golden Bough, The 30
Goneril 17, 27, 35, 36
Greenblatt, Stephen 3, 9, 69,
 84, 91, 100, 103, 106
 Renaissance Self-Fashioning 69, 103
Gregory 135, 138
Guillory, John 100
guilt 14, 17, 35, 43

Hal *see* Prince Hal
Hamlet 6, 12, 15, 16, 18, 20,
 21, 27, 31, 32, 33, 34,
 35, 44–5, 49, 53, 54, 55,
 56, 61, 67, 72, 74, 76,
 77, 81, 95, 99, 102, 105,
 107, 116, 130, 134, 165, 167
 dumb show 44–5, 97
 Murder of Gonzago 44, 83
Hamlet (character) 2, 4, 15, 18,
 19, 20, 26, 27, 31, 32,

34, 35, 42, 45, 46, 49,
55, 67, 72, 74, 76, 78,
80, 83, 86, 95, 98, 99,
100, 104, 106, 107, 116
melancholia 76–7
Hawkins, Sherman 62
Helena 9, 44, 52, 73, 89, 108,
109, 110, 111, 113, 114,
115, 116, 118, 119, 117,
120, 121, 122, 123, 124,
125, 126, 127, 129, 130,
168
Henriad 58, 75
Henry IV, Part 1 59, 74
Henry IV, Part 2 74
Henry IV (character) 42, 59
Henry V 74
Henry V (character) 42, 63
Hermia 48, 82, 83, 89
Hermione 35, 37, 38, 39, 60,
89, 92, 93, 106
Hero 39, 44
Hillman, David 99
historicism 9, 71, 76, 91, 93,
99, 100, 105, 166
*Historicism, Psychoanalysis,
and Early Modern
Culture* 99
Holland, Norman 32–3, 48,
61, 62, 63, 69, 77
*Psychoanalysis and
Shakespeare* 32–3
Shakespeare's Personality
61, 69
Homan, Sidney J. 61
Shakespeare's Personality 61
homoeroticism 75, 76, 100,
103, 133–63, 166
homosexuality 25, 29, 61, 96,
100, 134, 139, 141, 142

Horney, Karen 70, 71, 88
theories 85
Hotspur 26
humanism 92

Iachimo 37
Iago 3, 25, 28, 29, 39, 89, 166
id 12, 13, 14, 122
idealization 52
identity 48, 66–7
male 49, 65, 72
Imaginary 6, 31, 32, 56, 82, 97
Imogen 37, 44, 93
incest 20, 61, 107, 108, 109,
110, 111, 116, 117, 118,
119, 120, 121, 123, 126,
128, 129, 130
individuation 27, 47, 66
infancy 14
infanticide 105
infantile development theories
53
interiority 4
Interpretation of Dreams, The
12, 13, 15, 44, 105
introversion 46, 47
Irigaray, Luce 92, 94
Isabella 24, 53

Jacobson, Edith 65
Jacques 51
Jay, Nancy 105
jealousy, delusional 157
Jekels, Ludwig 23, 25, 26, 27
Jesus Christ 28, 46
Johnson, Samuel 2
jokes 15
Jones, Ann Rosalind 99
Jones, Ernest 6, 18, 19, 21, 31,
33, 34, 61, 78, 95

jouissance 104
Juliet 62, 137, 140, 141, 151, 152, 153, 161, 162, 163
Julius Caesar 21, 87
Jung, Carl 5, 6, 16, 23, 26, 27, 28, 78, 83
  personality types 46
  terminology 30
  theories 29, 46

Kahn, Coppélia 47, 64, 66, 67, 68, 96
  Man's Estate 65
  Representing Shakespeare 47
Katherine 67
Kent 81
Kernberg, Otto 52
Kerrigan, William 63
King Lear 16–17, 21, 27, 45, 54, 68, 73, 81, 86, 98, 102, 167
King of France 53, 112, 113, 114, 117, 118, 125, 127, 129, 130, 131
Kirsch, Arthur 43, 44
  Shakespeare and the Experience of Love 43
Klein, Melanie 7, 23, 36, 37, 39, 44, 45, 48, 71, 78, 79, 80
  theories 52, 79, 80, 88
Knights, L. C. 77
Kohut, Heinz 52
Krier, Theresa 92, 93, 95
  Birth Passage 92
Kris, Ernst 23, 25, 75
Kyd, Thomas 102
  Spanish Tragedy 102

Lacan, Jacques 5, 6–7, 8, 23, 31, 32, 41, 45, 59–60, 63, 70, 71, 76, 81, 82, 83, 84, 85, 92, 95, 97, 99, 104, 105, 107, 165, 166
  Law of the Father 75
  méconnaissance 63
  theories 56, 57, 59, 60, 75, 76, 91, 104
Lady Macbeth 17, 26, 38, 47, 67, 81
Laertes 7, 32, 74
Lafew 113, 130
Laing, R. D. 48
language 31, 57, 58, 60, 93, 102, 104, 105, 133, 135, 144, 145, 147, 152
Lavatch 108, 123, 125, 127, 130
Lavinia 104
Law of the Father 31
Lear 16–17, 36, 39, 45, 46, 58, 68, 73, 81, 86, 98, 107
Legendre, Pierre 111
Lehnhof, Kent R. 111
Leontes 29, 35, 38, 46, 60, 68, 74, 89, 92, 105, 166
Literary Use of the Psychoanalytic Process 50
Love's Labour's Lost 42, 92, 99
Lucio 51
Lupton, Julia Reinhard 81
  After Oedipus 81
Lysander 48, 89

Macbeth 17, 21, 25, 27, 53, 54, 67, 98, 102, 105

Macbeth (character) 17, 26, 27, 29, 72, 81, 98
Macduff 21, 26
machismo 135, 139
madness 101, 102, 103
Mahler, Margaret 7, 48, 53, 54, 65
male characters 64, 65, 66, 72, 168
male identity 65
Malvolio 61, 85, 93
Mamillius 60
Man's Estate 65
Mannoni, Octave 96
  Prospero and Caliban 96
Marina 69
Mark Antony 21, 38–9, 72, 87, 94
Marshall, Cynthia 103, 104
  Shattering of the Self, The 103
Mary Tudor 106
matricide 33
Maus, Katharine Eisaman 99
Mazzio, Carla 99
  Historicism, Psychoanalysis, and Early Modern Culture 99
Measure for Measure 24, 36, 42, 43, 44, 50, 52, 53, 54, 73
méconnaissance 63, 84
melancholia 76–7, 99, 102, 148, 149, 150, 159, 160, 161
Menenius 21
mental illness 101, 103
Merchant of Venice, The 16, 28, 42, 52, 53, 78, 81, 141, 167

Mercutio 10, 133, 134, 137, 138, 139, 140, 141, 142, 143–4, 145, 146, 147, 148, 149, 150, 151, 153, 155, 156, 157, 158, 159, 160, 161, 162
Merry Wives of Windsor, The 67, 103
Midsummer Night's Dream, A 48, 82
Miller, David Lee 105, 106
  Dreams of the Burning Child 105
mind 12
Miranda 39, 43, 69, 79
misogyny 34, 42, 49, 63, 65, 77, 93
misrecognition 63, 84
Montague 138, 140, 149
Montaigne, Michel de 43, 73
mother imago 38
motivation 12, 59
mourning 21, 45, 76, 80, 116, 121, 161
Mourning and Melancholia 19
Much Ado About Nothing 43
myth 16, 27, 30
mythoi 6, 30

narcissism 52
Neely, Carol Thomas 63, 100–3
  Distracted Subjects 100
neurosis 14
Nevo, Ruth 59–61
Novy, Marianne 63
Nurse 161

Oberon 61, 84
object relations psychology 36

object relations readings 82
object relations theory/theorists 7, 8, 41, 49, 53, 65, 70, 72, 77, 96
objet petit a 32, 85
Octavius 87
Oedipus complex 1, 4, 6, 9, 14, 15, 18, 19–20, 25, 26, 34, 36, 37, 46, 55, 81, 96, 165
  feminine 107–31
Oedipus myth 84
Oedipus Rex 6, 16, 107
Olivia 68, 85, 102
Ophelia 7, 19, 77, 80, 83, 106
orgasm 113, 115
Original Sin 25, 43
Orsino 85
Othello 27, 36, 43, 53, 54, 56, 61, 67, 73, 74, 80, 98
Othello (character) 3, 25, 28, 29, 35, 36, 43, 46, 72, 73, 74, 80, 89, 94, 98, 166
Other 31, 32, 51, 97, 98
otherness 96
overboarding 134
oxymorons 137

Pandarus 89
Paris, Bernard J. 61, 63, 85, 86, 87, 88
  Bargains with Fate 86,
  Character as a Subversive Force in Shakespeare 87
  Shakespeare's Personality 61
Parolles 115, 127
patriarchy 42
Paul, Saint 43
Paulina 38, 93

penis 112, 135, 141, 145, 147, 148, 156
penis envy 14
Perdita 38, 69
performance criticism 82
Pericles 60, 107
Persephone myth 30
persona 39
personality 12, 14
perversion, sexual 15
Petrarch 56–7, 92, 136, 137, 139, 141, 144, 145, 148, 150, 152, 161, 162
Petruchio 67
phallic images 49
phallus 31, 32, 75, 77, 110, 141, 153, 155, 159
Phantasiemensch 20
Phoenix and the Turtle, The 78
pleasure principle 12, 36
plot structures 30
Polixenes 29, 35, 38, 166
Polonius 18, 20, 86
Pope, Alexander 2
Porter, Joseph A. 133
Portia 42, 53, 78
post-colonial studies 166
post-colonialism 51
post-Freudians 48
Posthumus 37, 44, 50, 74
preconscious 12
Prince Hal 25–6, 46, 51
projection 13
Prospero 42, 47, 51, 56, 60, 63, 79, 80, 87, 107
Prospero and Caliban 96
prostitution 116
Proteus 89
Psychoanalysis and Shakespeare 32–3

Psychoanalytic Review 35
psychobiography 3, 7, 17, 20, 33, 62, 63, 87
psychoneurosis 19
psychosexual development 13, 19, 31
psychosis 31
pudendum 113, 118
puns 133, 140, 141, 143, 145, 148, 162

queer critics 133, 134
queer studies 163, 166
queer theory 9–10
queerness 167

Rank, Otto 6, 20, 21, 24, 25, 95
Rape of Lucrece, The 88
reaction formation 20
Real 6, 31, 82
reality principle 12, 13
Reformation 55
Regan 17, 27, 35, 36
Reid, Stephen 35, 36, 37, 43
Reik, Theodor 28
Reinhard, Kenneth 81
  After Oedipus 81
Renaissance Self-Fashioning 69, 103
Representing Shakespeare 47
repression 4, 12, 13, 14, 15, 16, 19, 86
Richard II 94
Richard II (character) 42, 58, 94
ritual 30, 55, 105
Riviere, Joan 98
Rogers, Robert 80
  Self and Other 80

Romeo 10, 62, 67, 133, 134, 135, 136, 137, 138, 139, 140, 141, 142, 143, 144, 145, 147, 146, 148, 149, 150, 151, 152, 153, 154, 155, 156, 157, 158, 159, 161, 162, 163
Romeo and Juliet 9, 67, 96, 133–63, 166–7
Rosalind 53, 76, 102
Rosaline 137, 138, 141, 142, 145, 149, 150, 151
Rubinstein, Frankie 112

Sachs, Hanns 23, 24
Sachs, Wulf 96
  Black Anger 96
  Black Hamlet 96
sacrifice 105
sadomasochism 104
same-sex eroticism 10
Samson 134, 135, 136, 138, 139, 153, 155
Schiesari, Juliana 76–7
  Gendering of Melancholia, The 76
Schwartz, Murray M. 35, 37, 38, 47
  Representing Shakespeare 47
self 6, 38, 39, 51, 126
Self and Other 80
semantics 31
sexual abuse, childhood 119
sexual fantasies 50, 129
sexual perversion 15
sexuality 44, 48, 63, 72, 74, 75, 100
  female 37, 74, 75
Shadow 39

Shakespeare and the Experience of Love 43
Shakespeare in Psychoanalysis 95
Shakespeare's Development and the Problem Comedies 53
Shakespeare's Perjured Eye 56
Shakespeare's Personality 61, 65, 69
Shakespeare's Reparative Comedies 52
Shakespeare's Restorations of the Father 41
Shakespeare's Visual Regime 97
Shakespearean Performance as Interpretation 82
Shattering of the Self, The 103
Sheppard, Angela 79
Shylock 28, 42, 51, 78
sickness 130
signification 7
Skura, Meredith Anne 50–51
   Literary Use of the Psychoanalytic Process 50
slips of the tongue 15, 20
Sokol, B. J. 79
sonnets 4, 56–7, 87, 88, 133, 167
   sonnet 135 57
   sonnet 136 57
Sophocles 6, 107
   Oedipus Rex 6, 107
South Africa 96
Spanish Tragedy 102
splitting 13, 18, 21, 37, 79, 80, 105, 126, 127
Sprengnether, Madelon 64
Staging the Gaze 83

Stallybrass, Peter 99
Stephens, Lyn 78
Stewart, J. I. M. 29
Stockholder, Kay 60, 61
   Dream Works 60
Stone, James W. 93, 94, 95
   Crossing Gender in Shakespeare 93
stress reparation 52
structuralism 31
subjectivity 11, 12, 56, 72, 76, 83
sublimation 24
submission 56
Suffocating Mothers 71–2
Sullivan, Harry Stack 48
Sundelson, David 41, 42, 43
   Shakespeare's Restorations of the Father 41
superego 4, 13, 14, 76, 125, 126
Symbolic 6, 31, 56, 82, 84, 85, 97
symbolism 48
symbolization 13
syphilis 75, 113, 130

taboo 5, 111, 121
tabula rasa 27
Taming of the Shrew, The 67, 84
Tempest, The 42, 51, 74, 87
terminology 5, 11, 30, 49
Theatre of Envy, A 88
theology, Christian 43
Timon 36, 37
Timon of Athens 54
Titania 82, 84
Titus Andronicus 21, 104
Totem and Taboo 109, 119
transvestism 93

Traub, Valerie 64, 74–5
  Desire and Anxiety 74
Trevor, Douglas 99
  Historicism, Psychoanalysis, and Early Modern Culture 99
Troilus 72, 79
Troilus and Cressida 36, 54, 73, 74, 75, 88, 89
Twelfth Night 52, 68, 84, 85, 93, 103
Two Gentlemen of Verona, The 88
Two Noble Kinsmen, The 102
Tybalt 10, 134, 140, 153–4, 155, 156, 157, 158, 159, 160, 161, 162

Ulysses 88
unconscious 1, 4, 6, 12, 16, 24, 27, 30, 31, 50, 57, 59, 61, 124, 130
  collective 6
Undiscover'd Country, The 77

Valentine 89
Venus 66

Venus and Adonis 66
vicarious pleasure 20
Vincentio 24, 44, 50, 51, 52, 53
Viola 52, 68, 85, 93, 102
Violence and the Sacred 88
Volumnia 49, 67

Wangh, Martin 23, 25
Westlund, Joseph 52
  Shakespeare's Reparative Comedies 52
Wheeler, Richard P. 53, 54, 62
  Whole Journey, The 54, 62
  Shakespeare's Development and the Problem Comedies 53
Willbern, David 63
Winnicott, D. W. 7, 8, 23, 38, 39, 48, 53, 54, 65, 71, 72, 81, 85, 92
  theories 93
Winter's Tale, The 29, 30, 35, 37, 39, 46, 60, 61, 74, 89, 92, 105
witchcraft 99, 101
witches (*Macbeth*) 26